IMAGES
*of America*

# HARRISBURG AND THE SUSQUEHANNA RIVER

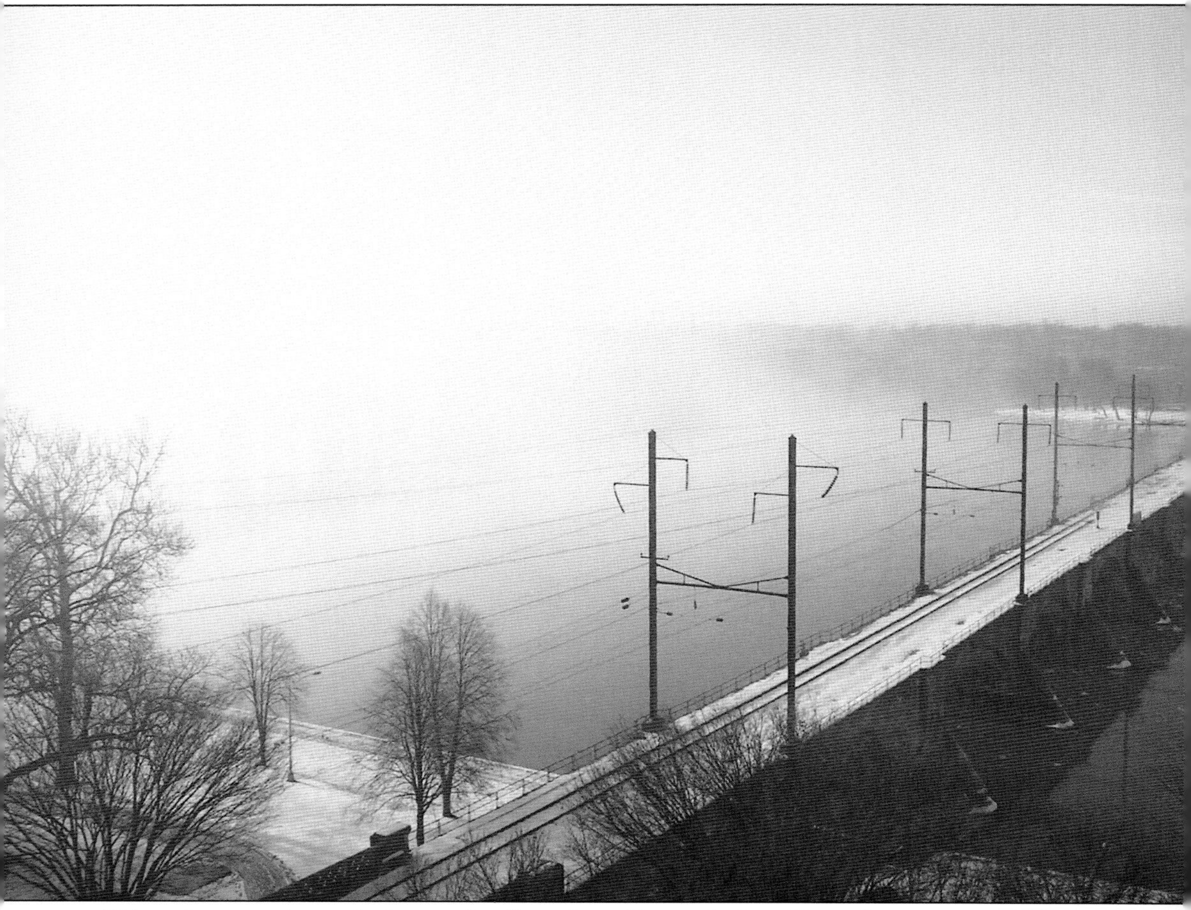

Taken from an elevated view at the Harrisburg Hospital along Front Street on a cold January morning, this image captures a shroud of fog draped over the Philadelphia & Reading (left) and Cumberland Valley Railroad Bridges. (Courtesy of the author.)

**On the Cover:** Bathers at the Municipal Beach on the northern end of City Island pause to have their photograph taken by City Beautiful advocate J. Horace McFarland around 1920. (Courtesy of the Historical Society of Dauphin County.)

IMAGES
*of America*

# Harrisburg and the Susquehanna River

Erik V. Fasick

ARCADIA
PUBLISHING

ISBN 978-1-4671-2298-6

Published by Arcadia Publishing
Charleston, South Carolina

Printed in the United States of America

Library of Congress Control Number: 2014947951

For all general information, please contact Arcadia Publishing:
Telephone 843-853-2070
Fax 843-853-0044
E-mail sales@arcadiapublishing.com
For customer service and orders:
Toll-Free 1-888-313-2665

Visit us on the Internet at www.arcadiapublishing.com

*To Danielle, Jack, and Julia, without whose patience and understanding I would not have been able to ford this river*

# Contents

# ACKNOWLEDGMENTS

As always, I owe many thanks and much gratitude to the numerous individuals who contributed in a multitude of ways to this work by providing suggestions, perspective, and quite often a patient ear for the endless questions, rants, and ravings that I presented on a daily basis throughout the formative process of this work. I am greatly indebted to the Historical Society of Dauphin County, the Board of Trustees of the Historical Society of Dauphin County, and staff. Without access to the society's vast and wonderful archives, such a project would never have been fully realized, as all images contained within this volume are derived from its collections unless indicated otherwise. The volume was rounded out by the gracious offerings of Keith Ward, Carol Schleig, Ken Frew, Greg Sloan, Annalisa Young, Historic Harrisburg Association, the Library of Congress, and the congregation of Zion Lutheran Church of Harrisburg, who provided me with images from their own collections.

However, photographs alone did not make this volume possible. It was also shaped from the rich ideas, stories, suggestions, and sometimes just a helping hand lent to me by Michelle Fox, Rick Hartman, Calobe Jackson, Rev. David D. Biser, Howard Parker, Cindy Essig, Daniel J. Tomaso, Nicole McMullen, Janet Mulligan Bowen, the staff of the Pennsylvania State Library, and my acquisitions editor, Abby Walker.

I would be remiss if I did not also acknowledge my debt to the scholarly and artistic works of J. Horace McFarland, Luther R. Kelker, William A. Kelker, Adam B. Hamilton, Richard H. Steimetz Sr., Robert D. Hoffsommer, Dan Cupper, C.L. Siebert Jr., Herbert H. Harwood Jr., and Edgar L. Ward.

Thank you all.

# Introduction

The relationship between the Susquehanna River and the residents of the Harrisburg area began long before pioneer John Harris arrived in 1719. Native Americans relied heavily on the river and established settlements along it near the mouths of the Yellow Breeches and Conodoguinet Creeks. They also discovered a natural plateau in the riverbed that extended from present-day Paxton Street on the eastern shore to the Bottleneck on the western side, which permitted fording the river in water no more than one to two feet deep throughout much of the year. This ford would become useful enough to the Native Americans that trails extended out from it on both sides of the river. Harris would profit greatly from establishing a trading post and ferry at both ends of this ford. The trails would become major roads, bringing trappers, soldiers, and families to the growing settlement. The ford would later be referred to by local Harrisburg residents as "the Riffles."

While the ferry business remained profitable during the 18th century for the Harris family and the other ferry operators who plied their trade on the river, growing populations led to serious discussions in 1809 regarding the need for a more stable means of crossing the Susquehanna River that was not dictated by fickle river currents. This discussion resulted in the formation of the Harrisburg Bridge Company, and by 1817 a wooden covered bridge was opened that, for a fee, provided a dependable link to the west. This bridge also eased the way for Harrisburg's designation as the state capital, which it was granted in October 1812. The Harrisburg Bridge Company, and the men who comprised it, held a monopoly over the river for more than 60 years. In 1890, the Walnut Street Bridge, financed by the People's Bridge Company, was completed. This new bridge was marketed as an alternative to the monopoly held by the Harrisburg Bridge Company and the tolls it imposed. However, while the People's Bridge offered an option, the end result was still the same. Bridge tolls would remain in place for another 60 years until the completion of the M. Harvey Taylor Bridge in 1952.

The People's Bridge, however, did more than just add another avenue across the Susquehanna. It opened up opportunities on the large island opposite the city, which ultimately would be known as City Island. Up to that point, City Island was used largely for farming purposes, and it was anything but a destination for pleasure-seekers. That distinction was left to Independence Island, where picnics, band concerts, dances, and swimming abounded throughout the warm weather months. Its remote location in the middle of the river gave it the feel of a private resort much farther away from home. The opening of the People's Bridge changed all of that. In the years that followed, the City of Harrisburg acquired, or leased, portions of the privately owned Island Park and put in place a plan to pull Harrisburg's residents away from the privately held Independence Island and keep them and their money from fleeing the city to destinations such as Atlantic City. The result was construction of city-run bathing beaches, playgrounds, and athletic facilities on the newly reimagined City's Island. These activities were augmented by the presence of a baseball franchise formed by the Harrisburg Athletic Club. The Harrisburg Athletic Club set the stage for a long-standing tradition of baseball on City Island in the form of semiprofessional, Negro

League, company, church, and high school teams that shared time on the baseball diamonds there well into the 1950s. After the boys of summer left the fields, semiprofessional, college, and high school football games brought fans onto the island in the autumn months.

These civic improvements were not confined to the City's Island. In fact, they were the by-product of the City Beautiful movement, which began on December 20, 1900, when Mira Lloyd Dock stood before the Harrisburg Board of Trade, speaking out against the vast wasteland that the city had become from careless sanitation and industrial practices. Up to that point, raw sewage was being dumped directly into the river. This practice provided a breeding ground for typhoid, as the riverbanks were also heavily utilized by the children of the city who came to the water to escape the summer heat. Beginning in 1900 and culminating in 1915, the city put into motion a variety of civic projects that included an improved sewage system, a riverfront promenade and steps that led down to the water's edge, a retaining dam that kept the water at a higher level suitable for river activities, a water filtration plant, and a well-manicured and safe riverfront park.

This newfound civic pride was funneled into a water carnival in 1907 that showcased the aquatic prowess of Harrisburg's citizens and highlighted their affinity for the river. The water carnival would be rebranded as the Kipona Festival in 1916. *Kipona*, which the August 31, 1946, *Harrisburg Telegraph* says is derived from a Lenni-Lenape term meaning "sparkling waters," was an apropos moniker given the wholesale effort focused on improving the waterfront after years of neglect. Although good intentions abounded, Kipona failed to make an annual appearance on several occasions during its early years due to wars and financial difficulty. However, it would be revived after each hiatus and was greeted like an old friend by crowds of thousands lining the riverfront. And while the Kipona Festival continues to this day, its purpose has changed greatly from the early years. The early water carnivals and Kipona celebrated an interaction between the community and the river. Swimming, canoe-tilting, and boating events put people into the water, whereas the modern Kipona Festivals that followed World War II moved towards more spectator sports such as speedboat races.

After World War II, City Island and the riverfront fell out of favor with local residents as trips in the family car provided a broader range of destination choices away from the confines of the city. By 1952, the Senators were gone, and with them went the other sporting events. The island bathing beaches were passed over for large community pools that appeared in and around the city. Over the next 30 years, City Island would fall into disrepair and gradually gain a reputation as a destination to avoid.

This changed in the 1980s, as opportunity once again was seized by Mayor Stephen R. Reed, who possessed the foresight to envision City Island as an entertainment destination. A new baseball park, Riverfront Stadium, was built, and a minor league franchise was brought back as the Senators returned to the island after a 35-year absence. Football and soccer franchises would follow and gain their own fan followings. Rock concerts with major acts such as the Grateful Dead, Bob Dylan, Metallica, Kiss, and Willie Nelson were brought to City Island to perform. Concerted efforts were made to make the island a family-friendly destination, which included the building of a small-gauge rail line that encircled the island. The city realized that the island could be a great asset if it was given the proper attention and funding, and moving forward, it will be funding that will continue to dictate the relationship.

# *One*

# The Ford in the River

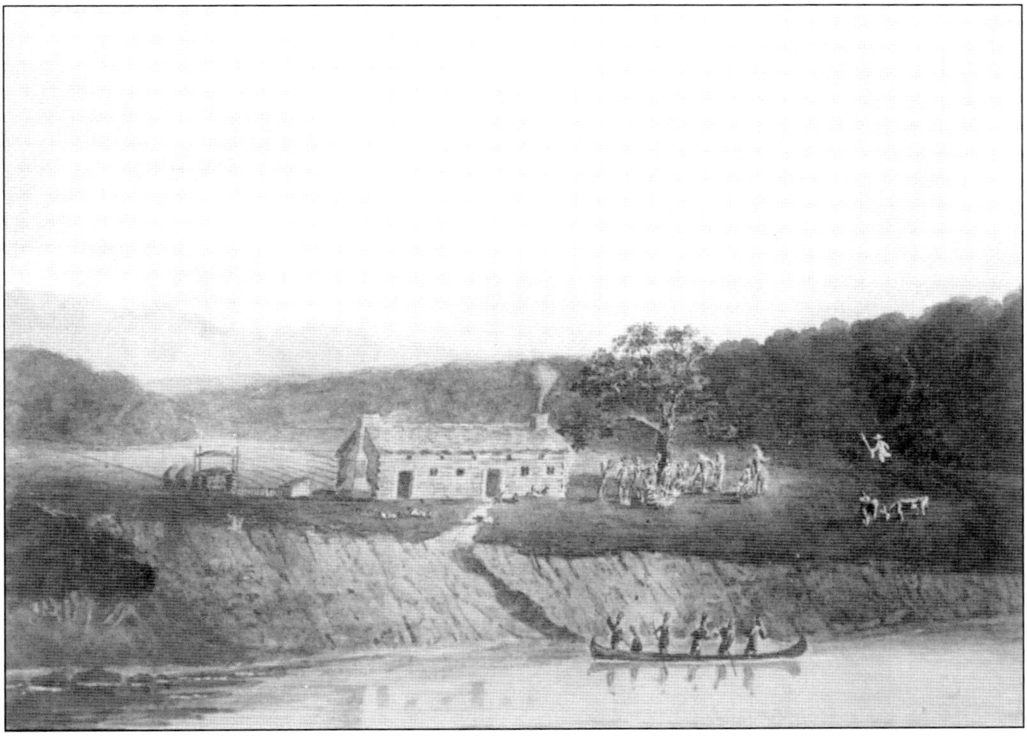

In 1719, the pioneer John Harris settled along the eastern bank of the Susquehanna River in a place where Native American trails met at a ford in the river. With land granted by the Penn family, he would provide an important, and lucrative, trading post, tavern, and ferry for the traders and settlers passing through the region.

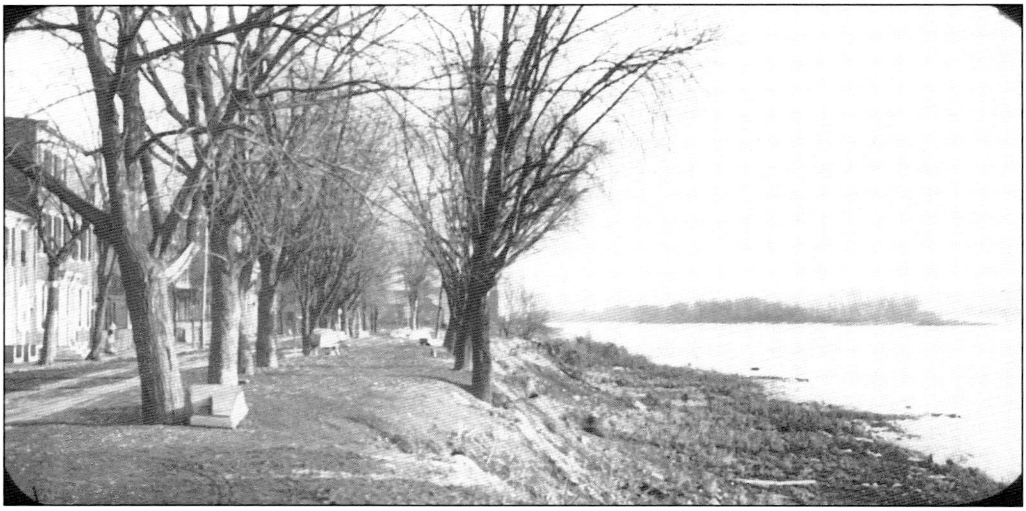

The exact location of Harris's ferry is no longer known, but it is believed to have been at the foot of Paxton Street. This image taken in 1900 (above), shows the gently sloping riverbank along the Susquehanna River in Shipoke, just south of the Philadelphia & Reading Railroad Bridge. It was at this location where a physical feature in the river known locally as the Riffles provided a natural raised walkway across the river during times of low water. The Riffles (below) extended from Paxton Street on the eastern shore passing just south of Turkey (City) Island, towards the western shore. Livestock, wagons, and travelers on foot were thus afforded a crossing through relatively shallow water over the rocky causeway without the need for a ferry.

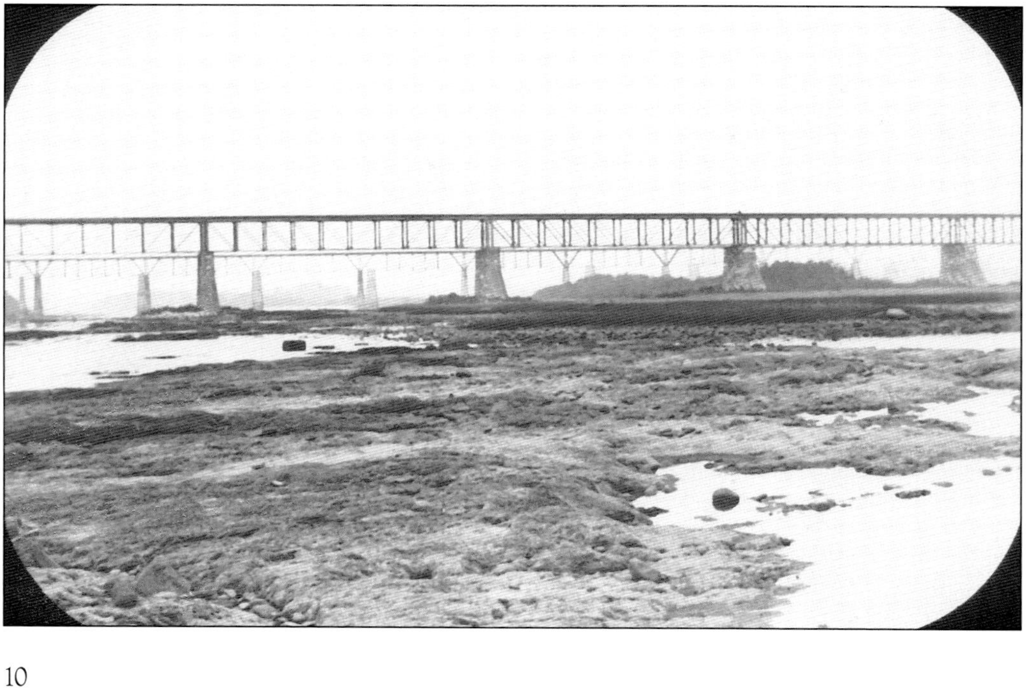

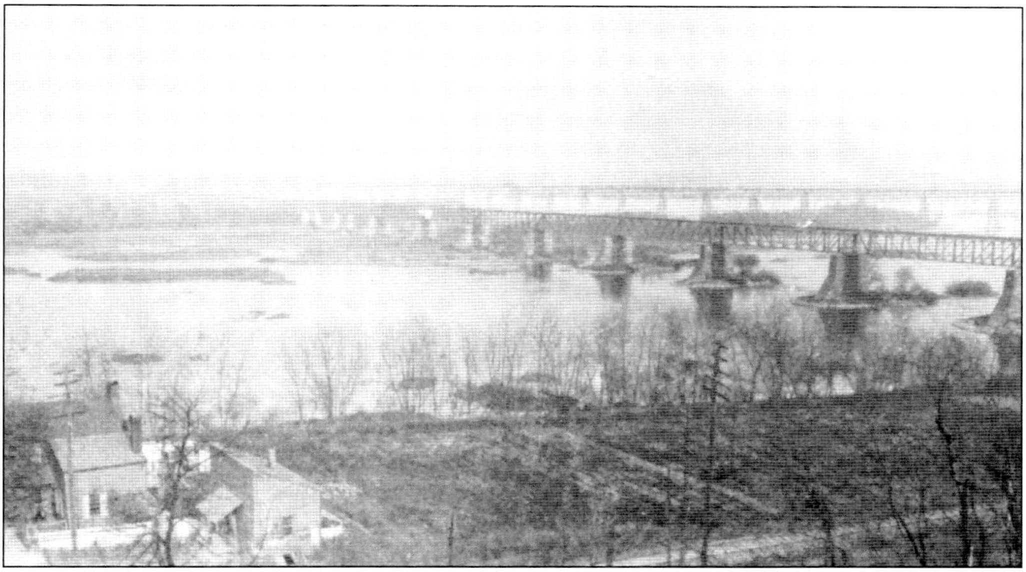

Shown here are two views, each taken around 1900, of the riverbank between the Camelback (later Market Street) and the Cumberland Valley Railroad Bridges on the West Shore of the Susquehanna River. Prior to reshaping the landscape to accommodate the railway lines, which included raising the embankments for the overhead bridge in the bottleneck, the riverbank gently sloped down to the river. One theory places the western landing point of the ferry at this location. The rights to the western portion of the ferry were purchased by William Kelso Sr. around 1759, and it included the ferry route from Turkey Island to the western shore.

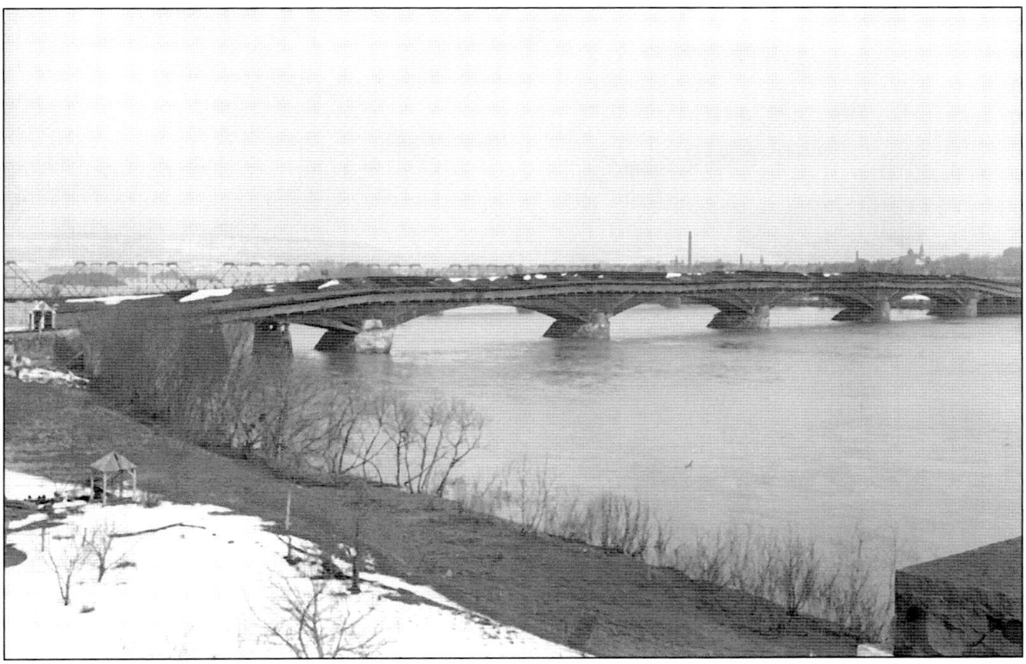

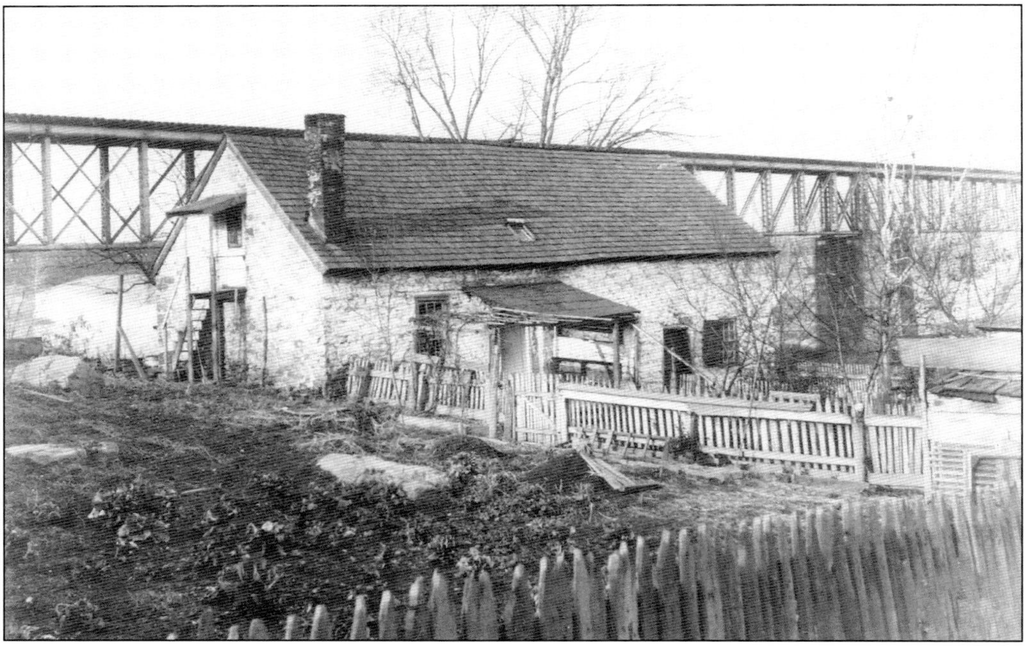

Built about 1734 by John Harris Sr., the Kelso Ferry House served as a shelter and tavern for travelers heading west. William Kelso Sr. obtained the structure from the Harris family when he purchased the rights to the western section of the ferry. The structure was located next to the Cumberland Valley Railroad Bridge and was the oldest edifice in the area until its demolition around 1905.

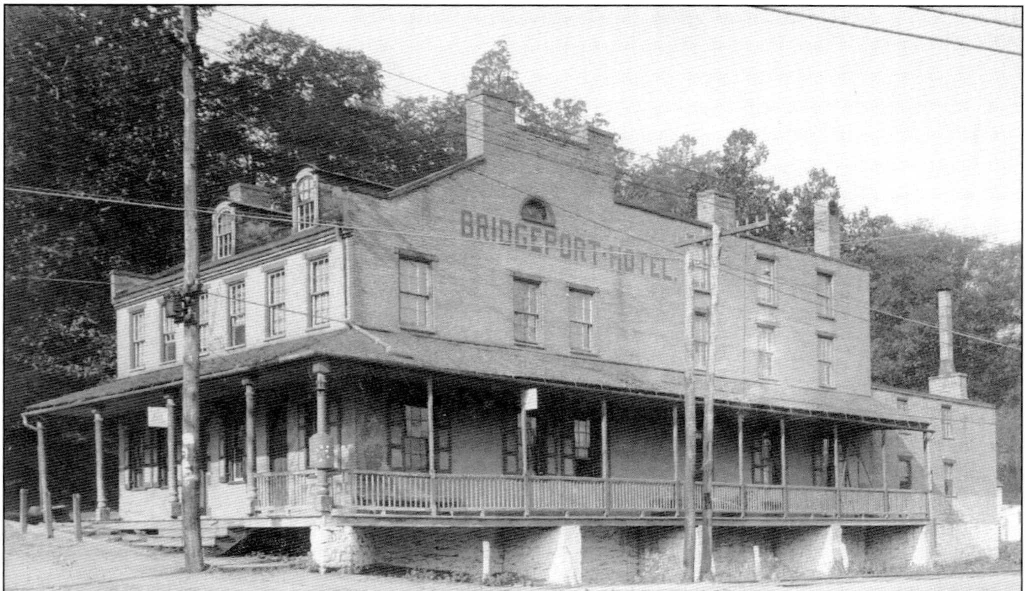


The Bridgeport Hotel, or Brick Hotel, was located on the West Shore, opposite the entrance to the Camelback Bridge. Built around 1830, it was torn down in 1905 to make way for the elevated railway bridge in the Bottleneck between Lemoyne and Wormleysburg. During the Civil War, the hotel served as a hospital. A Confederate soldier wounded at the skirmish at Oyster Point (in Camp Hill) was taken there and later died.

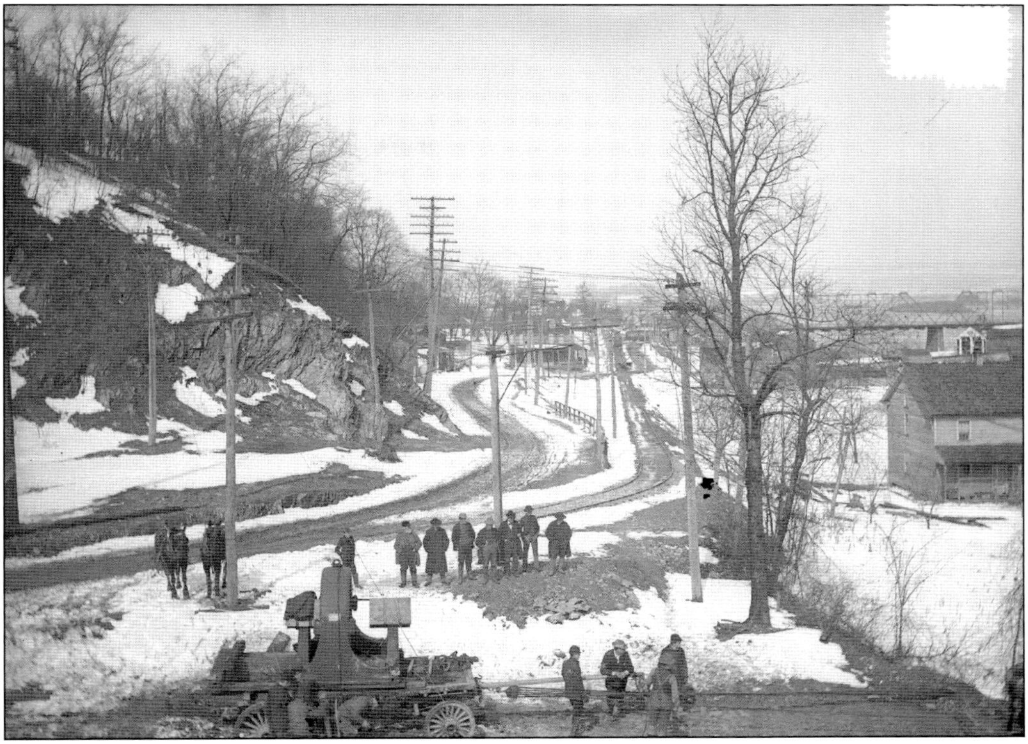

This image, with a view looking north into Wormleysburg as the trolleys from the Cumberland Valley Traction Company exit from the Walnut Street Bridge, shows the Bottleneck around the turn of the 20th century. The Bottleneck is believed to be a former streambed that emptied into the Susquehanna. This natural cut in the landscape served as a Native American pathway heading westward and later as a wagon trail road to Carlisle and points west.

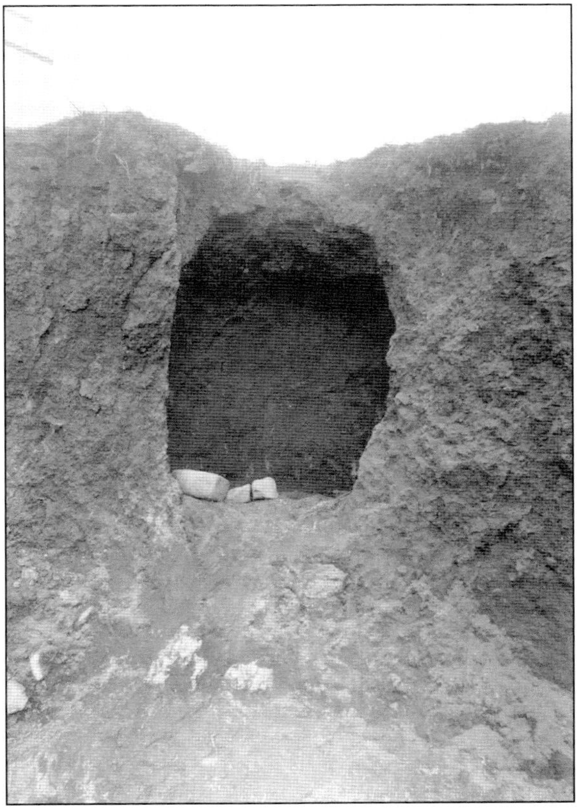

Long before the arrival of John Harris, or any other European settlers, Native Americans inhabited the region along the Susquehanna River. In August 1901, while grading for tracks of the Northern Central Railway was being done, 11 burial sites were unearthed along the bank of the river, just south of the Cumberland Valley Railroad Bridge. The graves contained skeletal remains, buried upright according to tradition, and various artifacts.

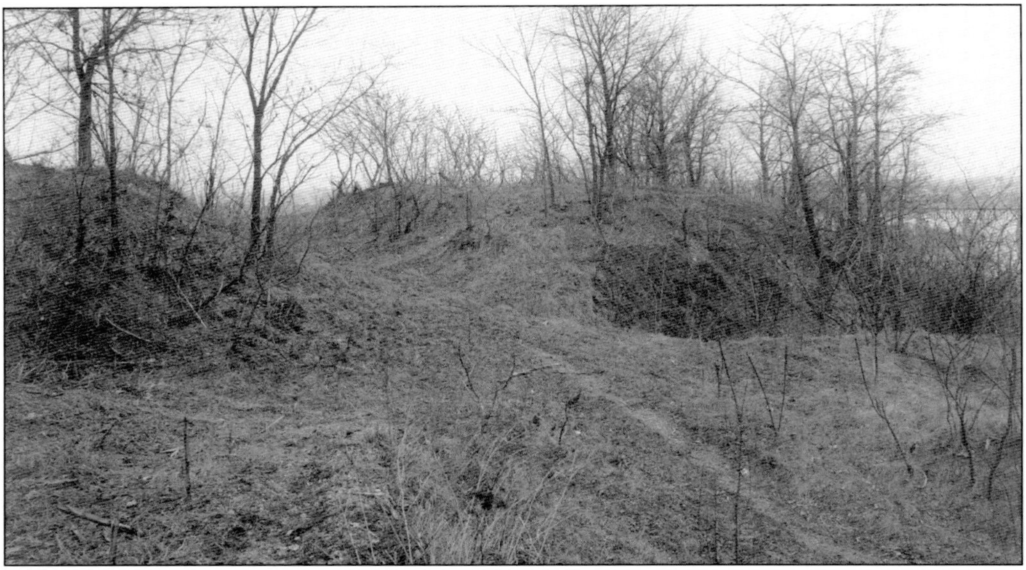

Above the Bottleneck is an elevated area known as Washington Heights. During the Civil War, an encampment known as Fort Washington was constructed to provide surveillance and defense from the threat of General Lee's army. A high-level target of the Confederates, Harrisburg held significance not only as the capital of Pennsylvania, but also as a railway hub and training center for troops at Camp Curtain.

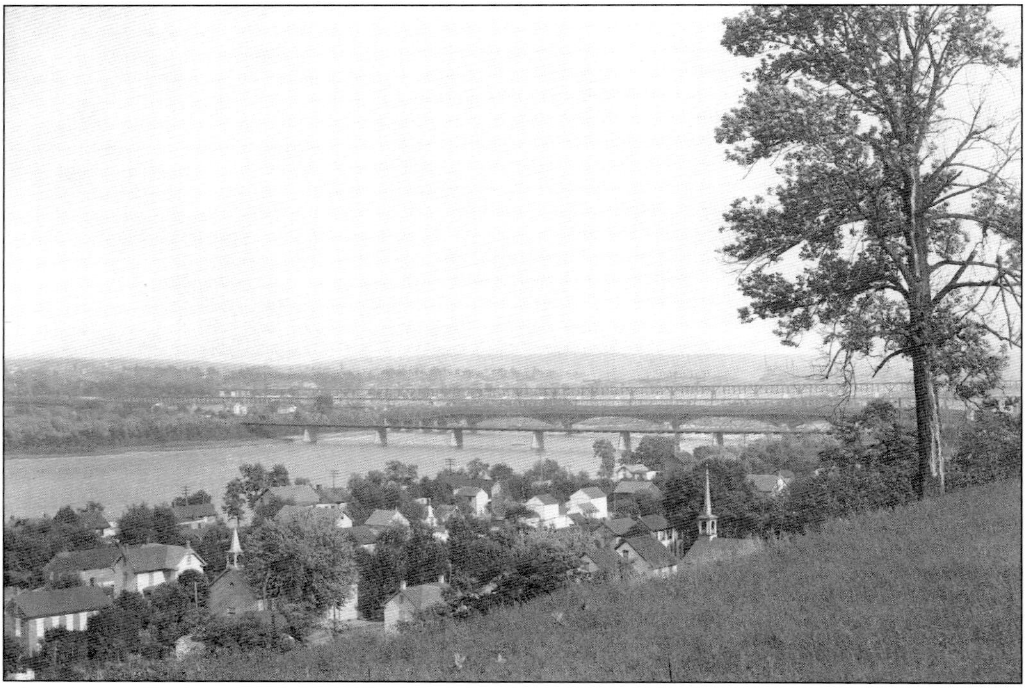

The village of Wormleysburg, seen here around 1900 from Washington Heights, had its beginnings in 1789 when founder John Wormley inherited a plot of land along the western shore of the Susquehanna from his father. He established a ferry separate from Harris's. In August 1815, as the Camelback Bridge was nearing completion, Wormley divided his family's land into individual plots, which effectively laid out the early settlement.

# *Two*

# SPANNING THE SUSQUEHANNA

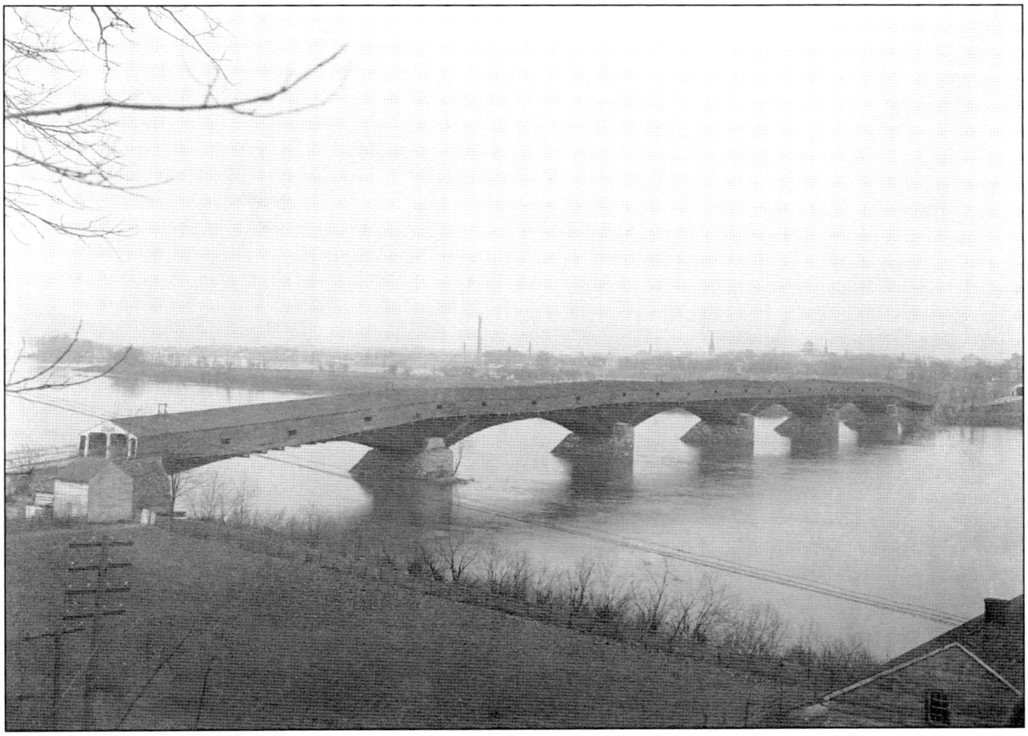

The Old Market Street Bridge was a covered wooden bridge that was the first to span the Susquehanna River at Harrisburg. Construction of the bridge was overseen by Theodore Burr and completed in 1817 at a cost of $192,000. The bridge consisted of two separate sections, with the arched western section seen here, about 1885, giving it the more common name of the Camelback Bridge.

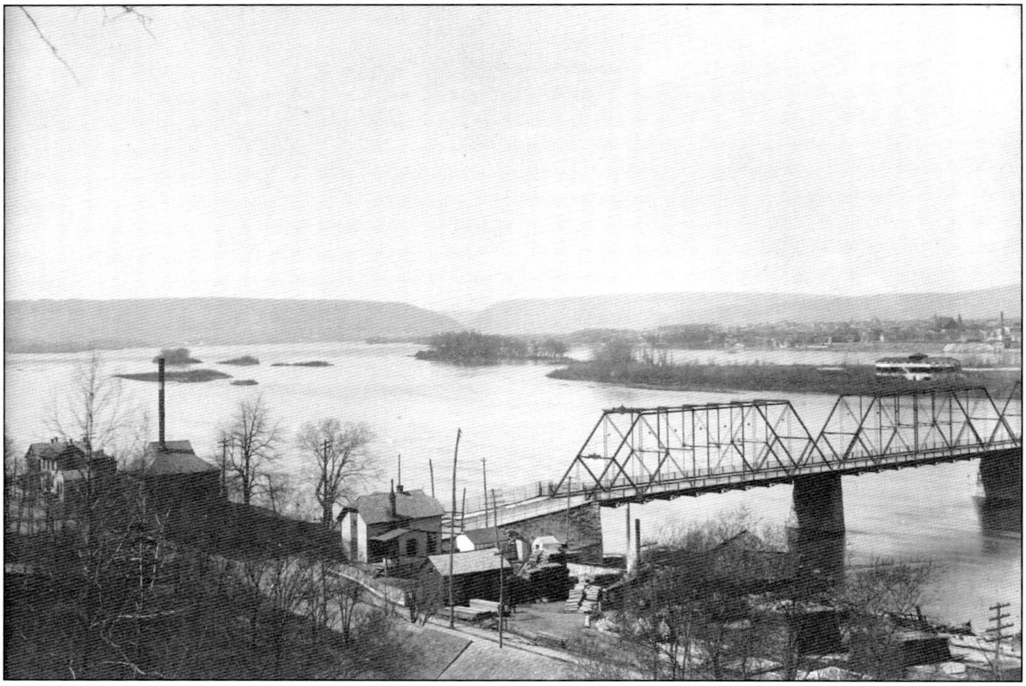

The c. 1894 images on these two pages show a panoramic view of the bridges crossing the Susquehanna River. Three of these bridges pass directly over City Island. The northernmost bridge, the Walnut Street Bridge, or the People's Bridge, is an iron truss structure completed in 1890, with materials supplied by the Phoenix Iron Company. The western portion was partially destroyed by ice floes in 1996.

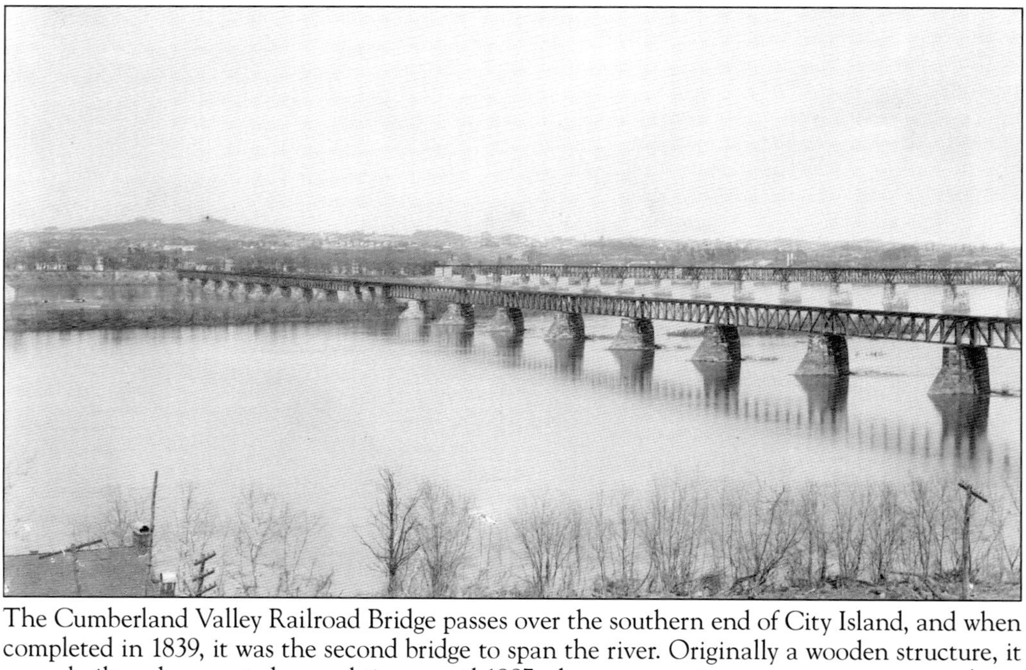

The Cumberland Valley Railroad Bridge passes over the southern end of City Island, and when completed in 1839, it was the second bridge to span the river. Originally a wooden structure, it was rebuilt and renovated several times until 1887 when an open iron truss structure, seen here, was completed. The iron bridge was rebuilt as a concrete structure that was completed in 1916.

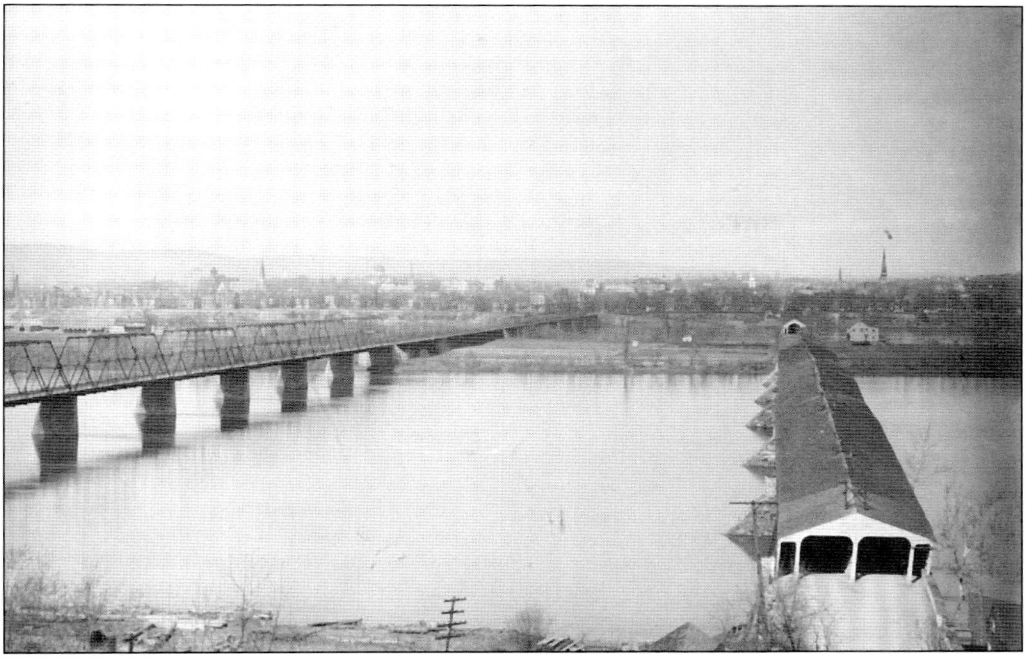

The Old Market Street Bridge was completed in 1817 and was the first bridge to span the Susquehanna at Harrisburg. The western half of the bridge had an arched, or humped appearance, and was better known as the Camelback Bridge. Battered and burned over the years, it was a fixture on the landscape of the capital city until 1902 when the eastern portion of the bridge was destroyed by ice floes.

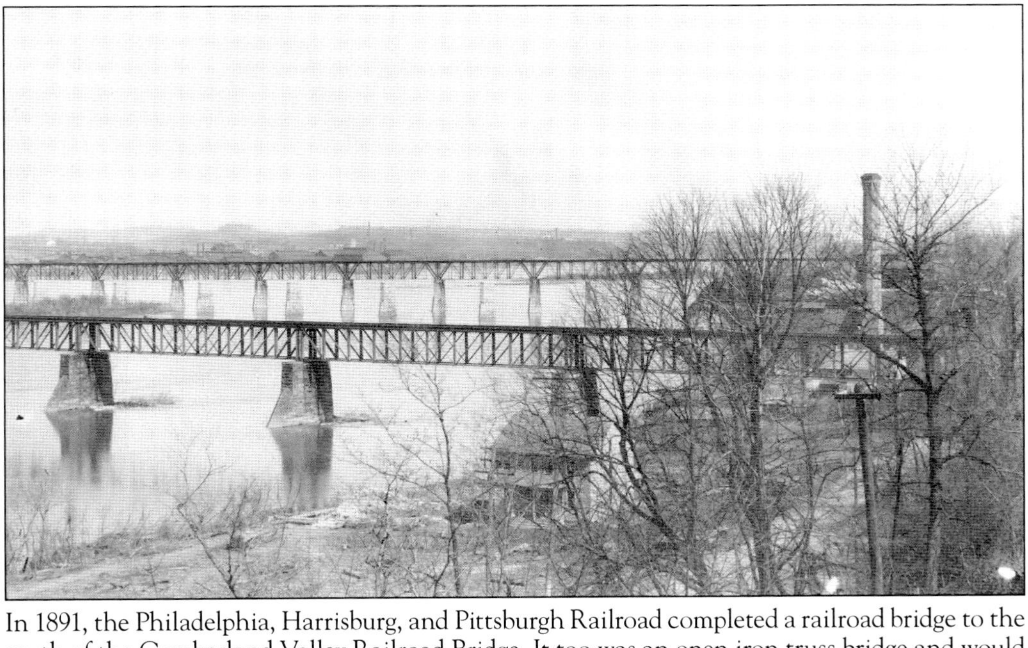

In 1891, the Philadelphia, Harrisburg, and Pittsburgh Railroad completed a railroad bridge to the south of the Cumberland Valley Railroad Bridge. It too was an open iron truss bridge and would ultimately be reconstructed as a concrete-arch bridge in 1924. Between these two bridges can be seen the piers of the South Pennsylvania Railroad that were finished in 1884. The completion of this bridge was abandoned when the railroad failed.

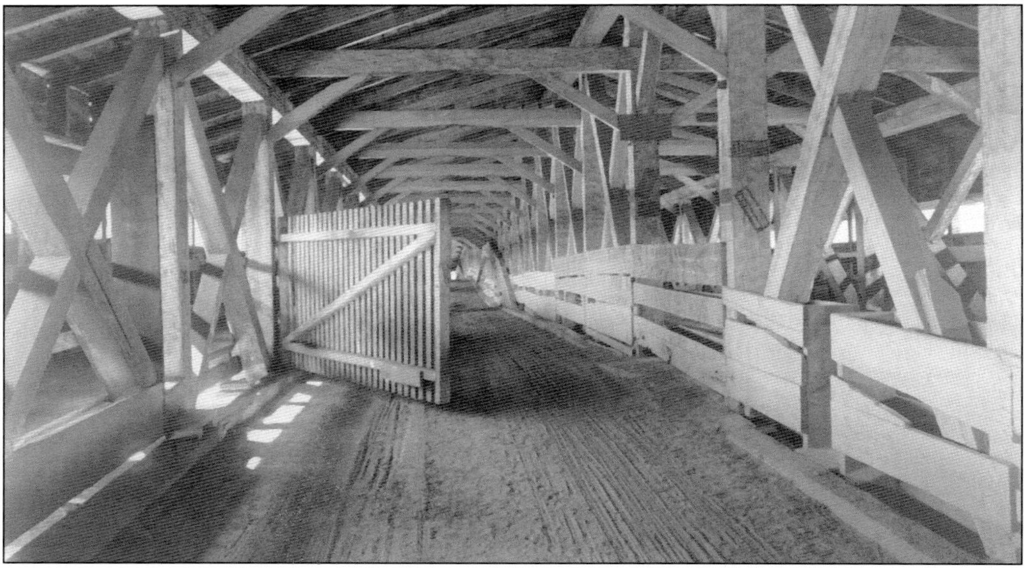

In 1842, Charles Dickens crossed over the Susquehanna River, passing through the Camelback Bridge and giving a detailed and darkly eloquent account of the crossing: "We crossed this river by a wooden bridge, roofed and covered in on all sides . . . It was profoundly dark; perplexed, with great beams, crossing and recrossing it at every possible angle; and through the broad chinks and crevices in the floor, the rapid river gleamed, far down below, like a legion of eyes. We had no lamps; and as the horses stumbled and floundered through this place . . . I really could not at first persuade myself as we rumbled heavily on, filling the bridge with hollow noises, and I held down my head to save it from the rafters above, but that I was in a painful dream; for I have often dreamed of toiling through such places."

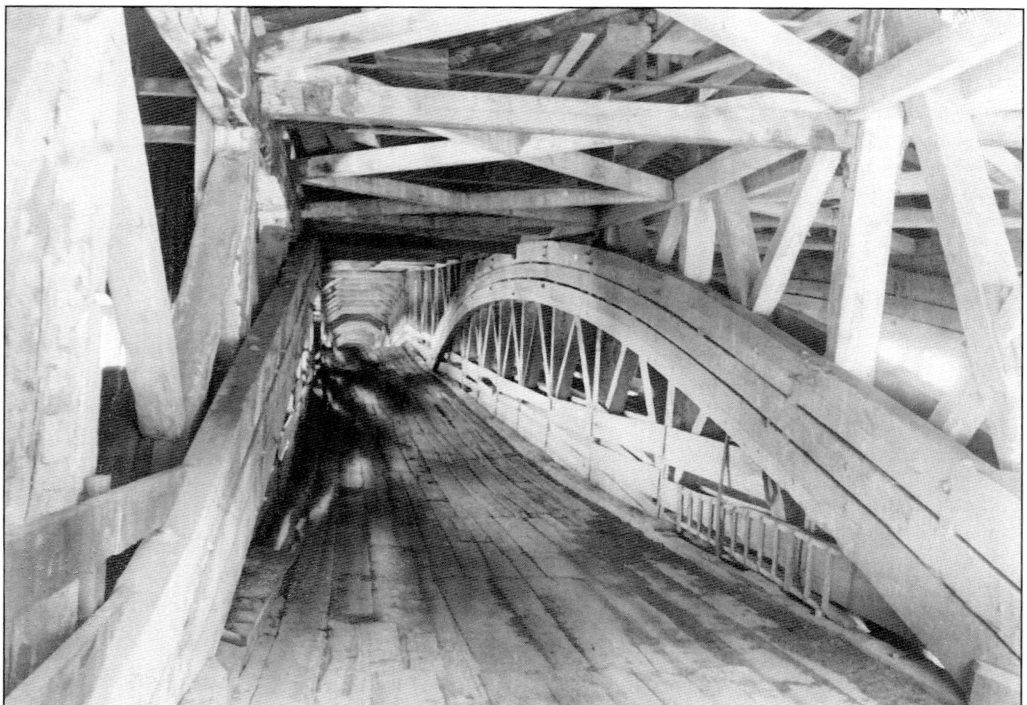

The Camelback Bridge was subjected to numerous natural disasters during its existence. However, nearly all of the destruction occurred on the eastern spans of the bridge. An ice floe in March 1846 destroyed the eastern side, and a fire resulting from an overturned lantern destroyed the eastern half of the bridge on May 25, 1866. Wind damage from storms occurring on June 26, 1877, (right) and again on October 8, 1884, tore portions of the roof and sides off of the bridge, again on the eastern side. Finally, on March 3, 1902, high water and ice combined to damage the second pier of the eastern side of the bridge, causing the second and third spans of the bridge to be carried away by the river's current (below). It was then decided the old bridge needed replacing.

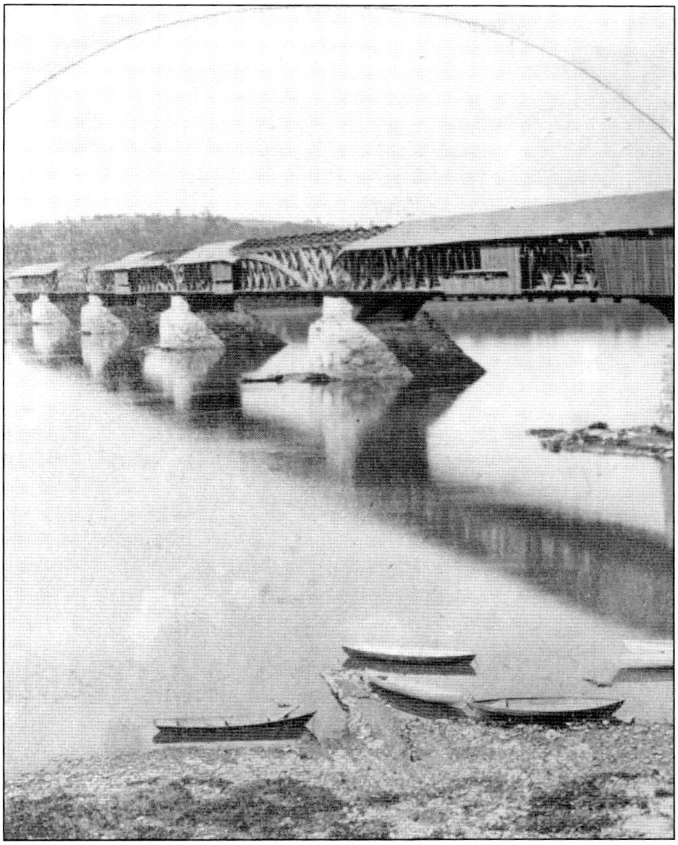

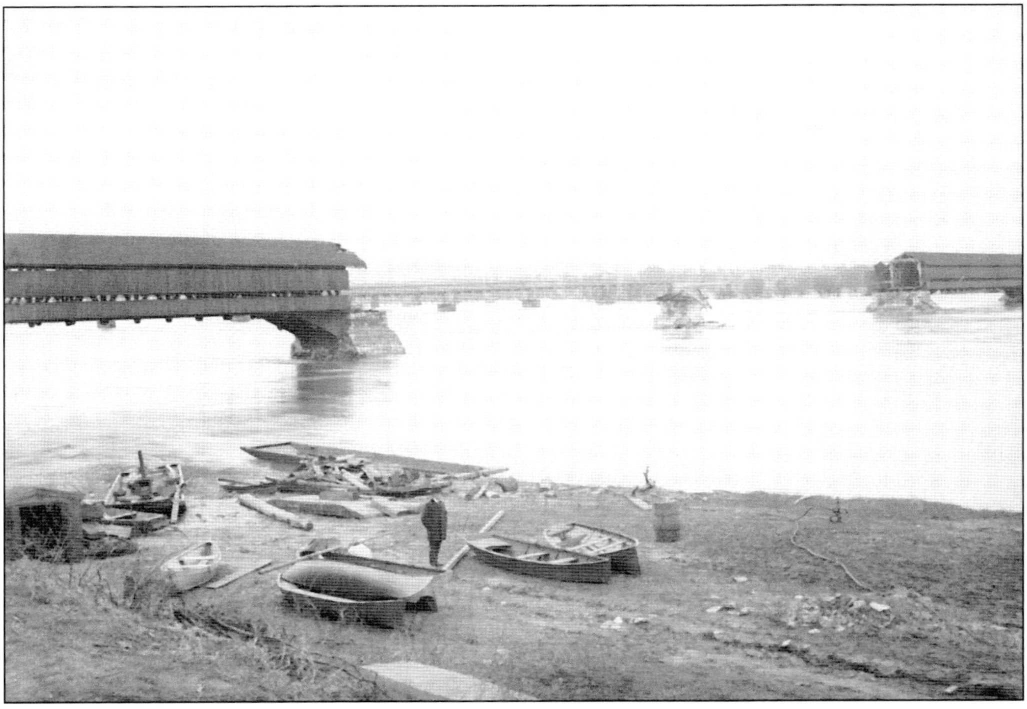

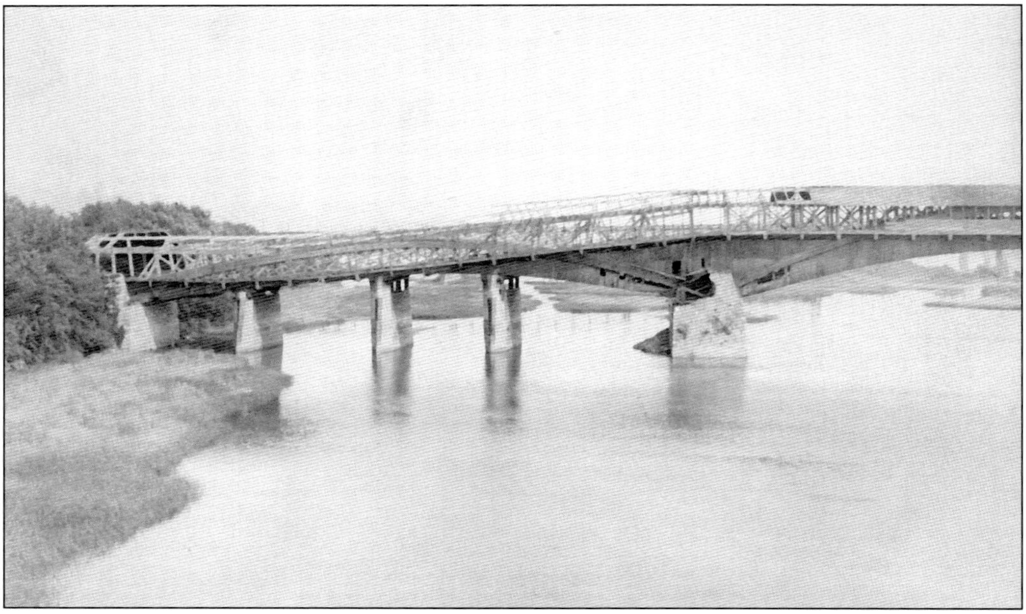

The panoramic view here shows the western section of the Camelback Bridge as it was being dismantled in the late summer of 1902. The bridge has been stripped of much of its exterior clapboard, leaving only a skeleton of the large timbers of the arched structure. In addition to stone piers, the bridge also utilized wooden piers at either end of the western section.

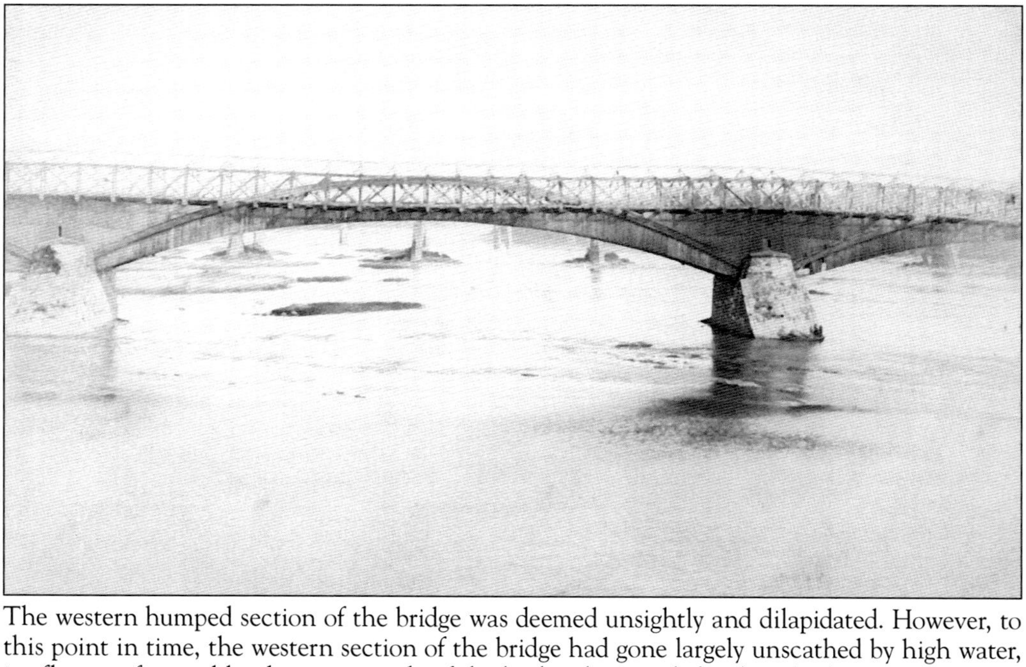

The western humped section of the bridge was deemed unsightly and dilapidated. However, to this point in time, the western section of the bridge had gone largely unscathed by high water, ice floes, or fire, unlike the eastern side of the bridge that needed to be rebuilt twice before the knockout blow inflicted by the flood of 1902.

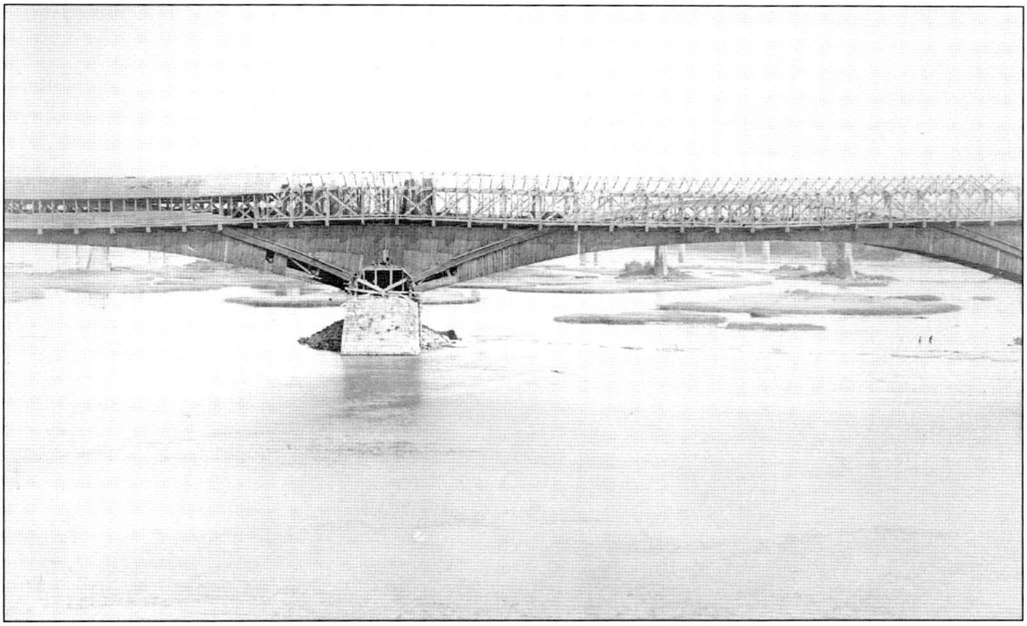

The demolition of the bridge was contracted out to J.S. Sible of the United Ice and Coal Company. Demolition began on the eastern half of the bridge in early August 1902, and by the end of September, the only portion of the bridge that remained was the stone piers.

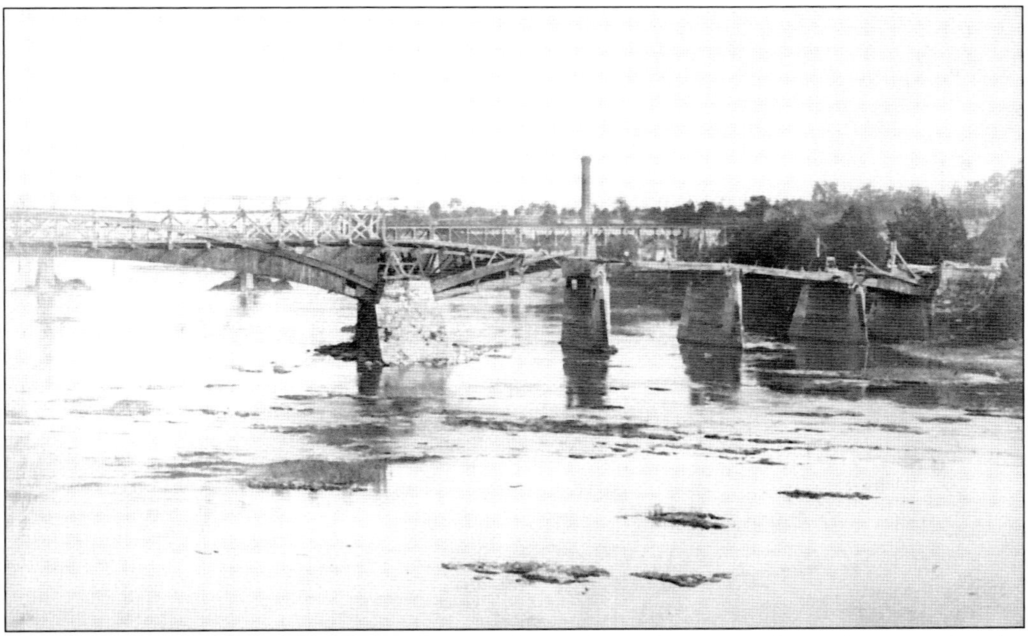

The timber, as it was cut from the structure, was dropped into the river and joined into crude rafts. It was then transported to a makeshift sawmill erected at Second and Muench Streets, where it was converted into various types of lumber suited for construction purposes. Some of it probably still exists in some city structures.

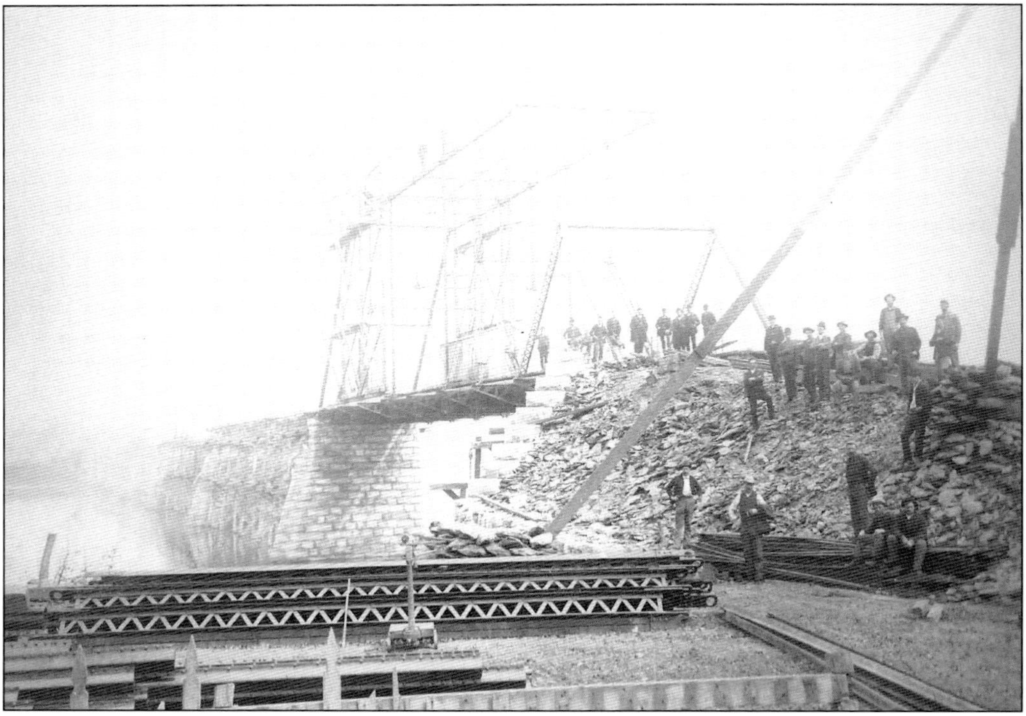

The People's Bridge, more commonly known today as the Walnut Street Bridge, opened for business on April 26, 1890, with the intent of breaking the monopoly and high tolls established by the Harrisburg Bridge Company and its Camelback Bridge. The image above shows the construction of the first span on the western side. The iconic iron bridgework was provided by the Phoenix Bridge Company of Phoenixville, Pennsylvania. The completed bridge included an elevated section that crossed over Hargest's (City) Island. This portion of the bridge was not held up by piers, but rather by a system of wooden trestles, as seen in the image below. This open design was filled in by December 1907, and the embankment hides the central portion of the bridge on the island. (Above, courtesy of the Historic Harrisburg Association.)

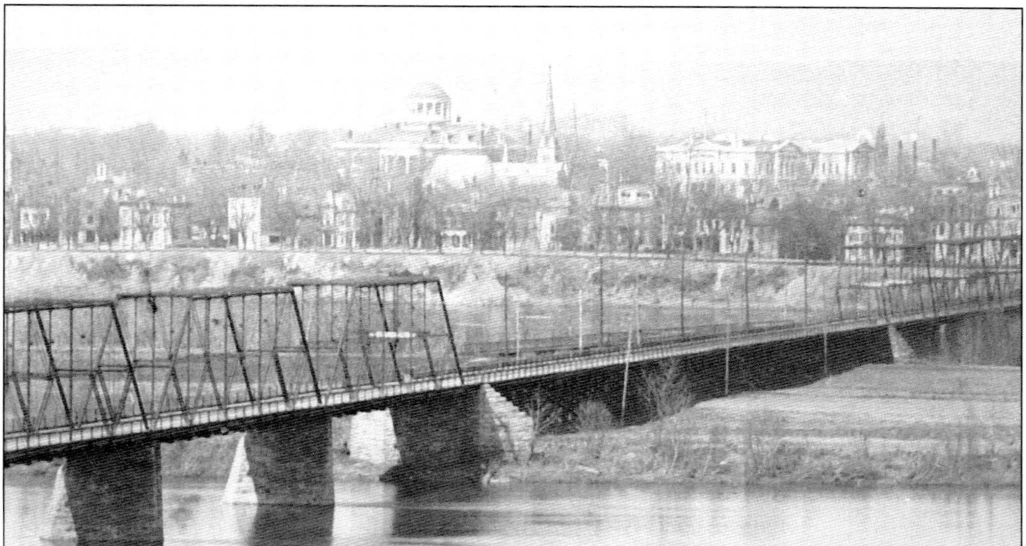

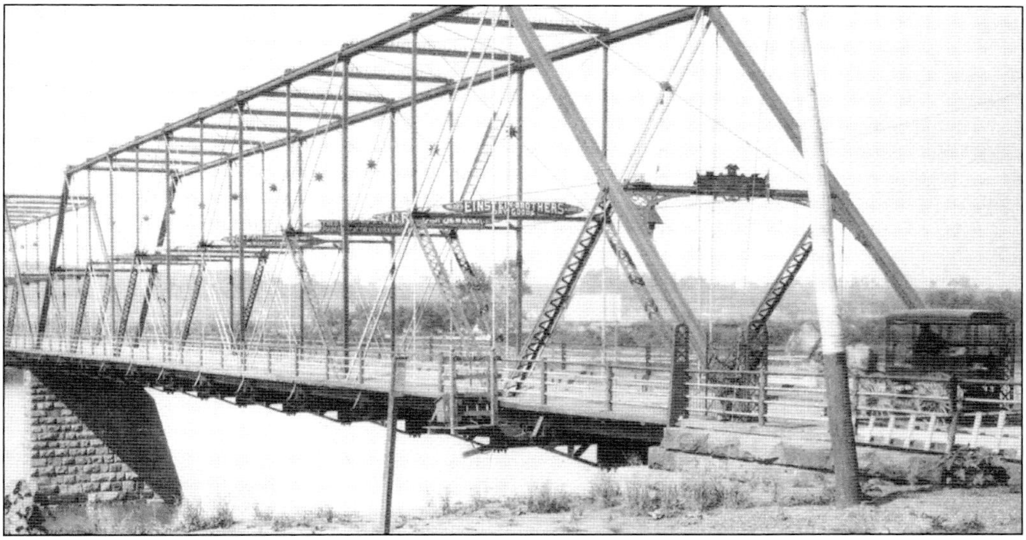

The first traffic to cross the bridge was subjected to a complex system of tolls. The cost to cross the bridge for an adult was 2¢; for a child, 1¢. A horse and four-wheeled vehicle, with driver, was 10¢, and a bicycle or tricycle was 5¢. The varied list continued based on the type of vehicle or livestock crossing the bridge. In 1894, the bridge was converted to allow the crossing of trolley cars, which continued until 1936 when a spring flood damaged the bridge. Afterwards, only pedestrian and vehicular traffic would cross the bridge until 1972. Flooding from Tropical Storm Agnes caused further damage, and all traffic thereafter was limited to pedestrians. An ice floe in January 1996 would destroy the western portion of the bridge, as it remains today.

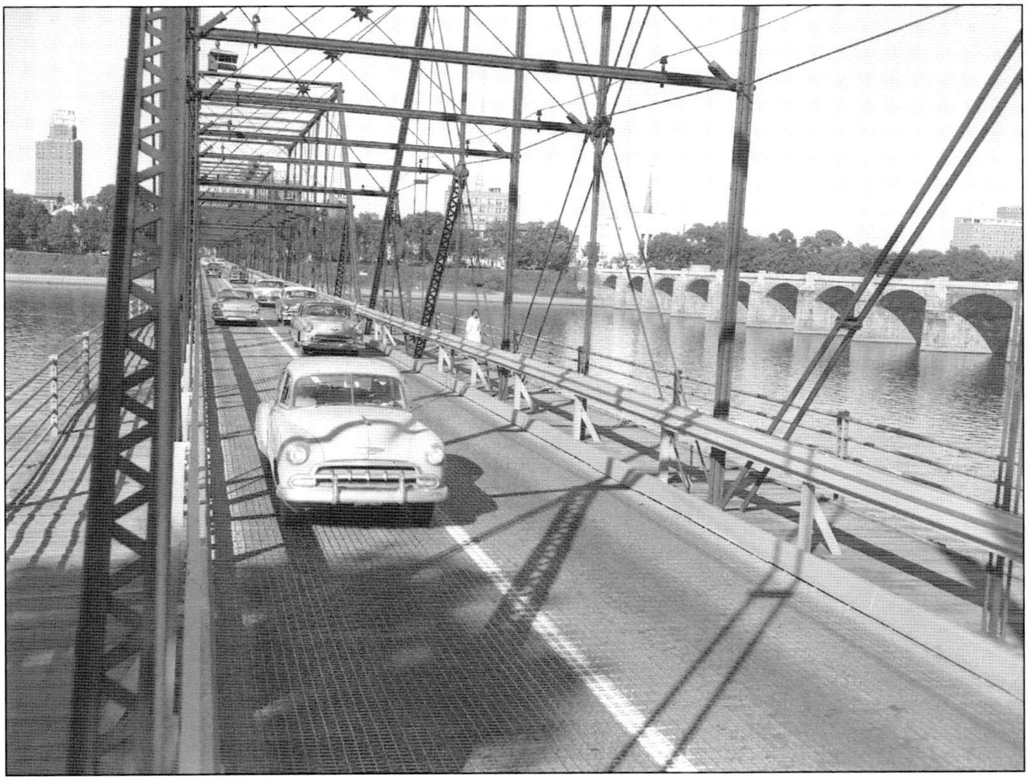

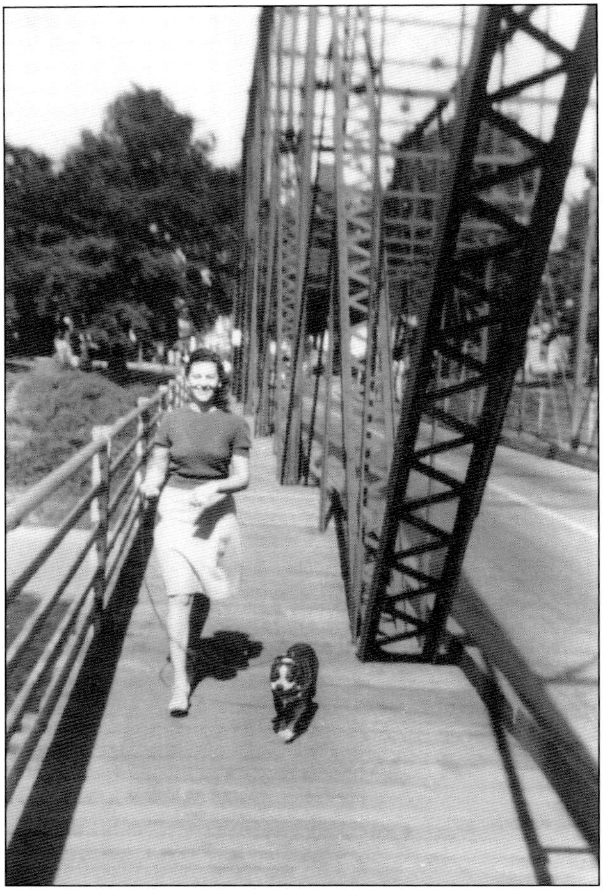

In the image at left, Jen Milesavic O'Brine runs across the northern walkway of the Walnut Street Bridge with her dog Peg in this view from 1940. The walkways afforded safe passage across the bridge when it was used as a toll bridge for motor vehicle traffic. In June 1972, Tropical Storm Agnes blew into the Susquehanna Valley, and the resulting record flooding brought raging waters and debris up to the level of the decking of the bridge. The bridge took the brunt of the abuse with only minimal damage to the structure, most of which was to the northern pedestrian walkway. The walkway was eventually removed, as it was no longer necessary when the bridge was closed to all but pedestrian traffic. (Left, courtesy of Carol Schleig.)

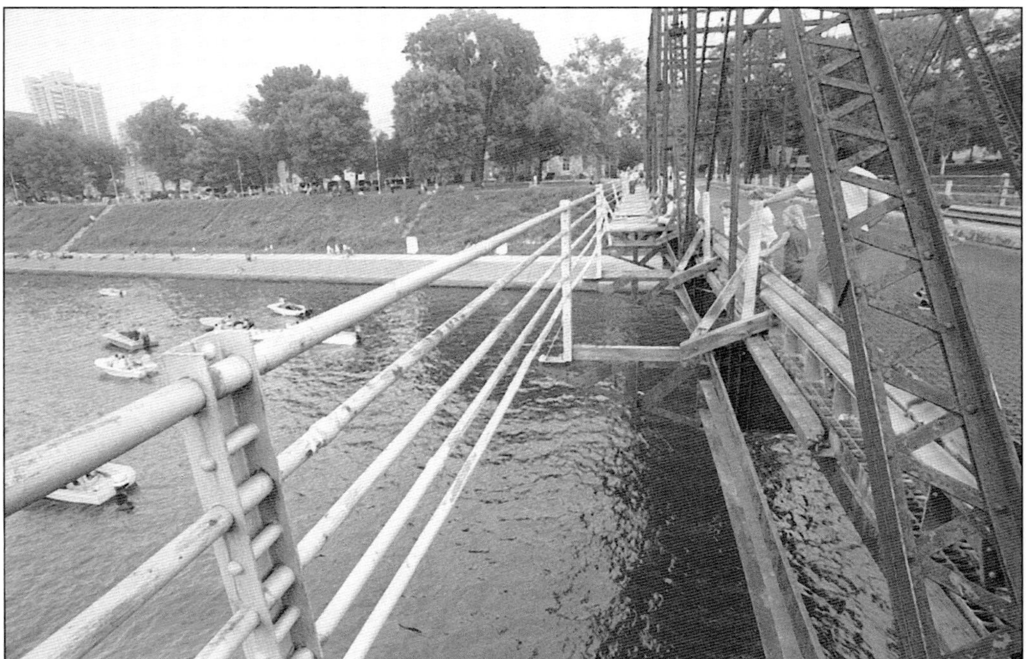

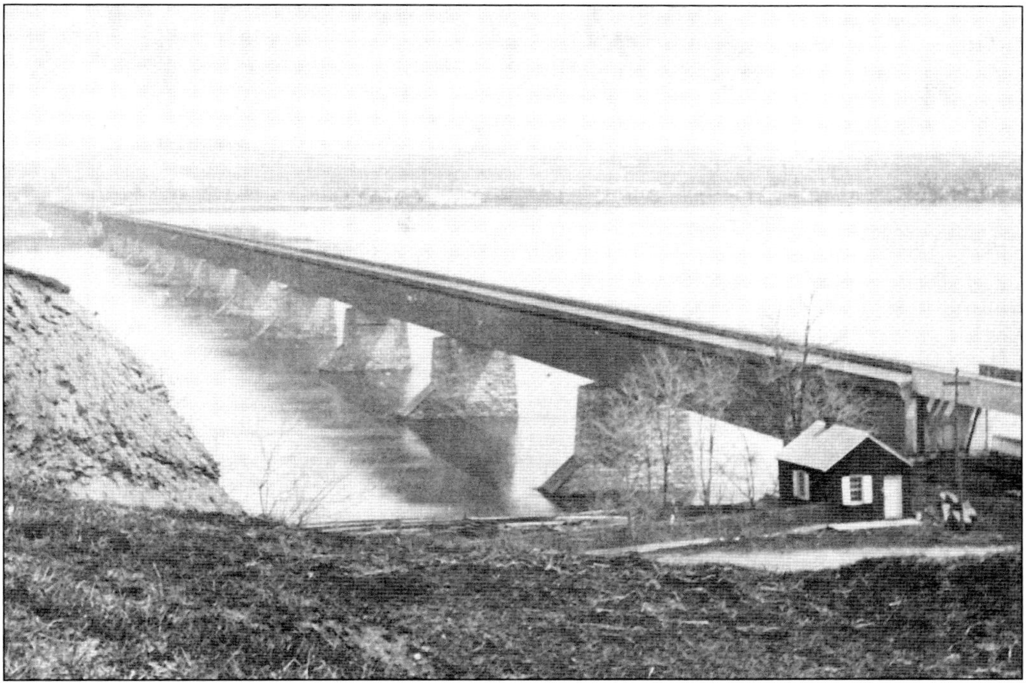

The Cumberland Valley Railroad Bridge officially opened on January 16, 1839, when a train of cars carrying several hundred passengers and with a locomotive on each end crossed the Susquehanna River. The bridge had a single track on the top deck, and served as a toll bridge from 1841 to 1855 as pedestrians and wagons crossed within the body of the bridge. The first version of the wooden bridge caught fire in 1844, and 20 of the 24 spans were destroyed in the blaze. The bridge was rebuilt and renovated several more times before it was replaced by an open iron truss bridge in 1887. The image above, taken around 1885, shows the western section of the bridge spanning the river, while the image below shows the bridge's western terminus entering the Riverton (Lemoyne) train yards, with the York Turnpike heading south.

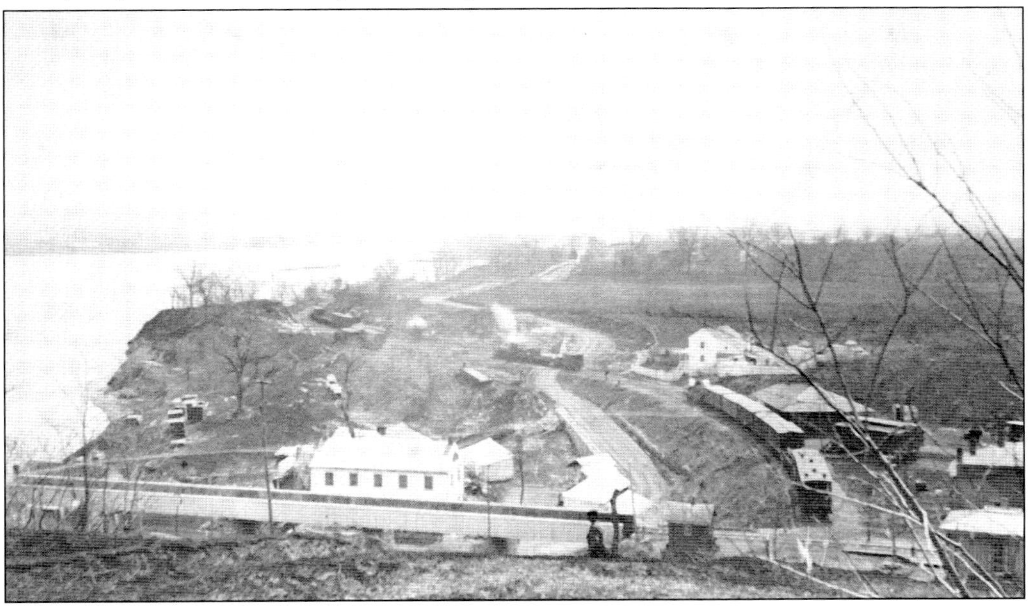

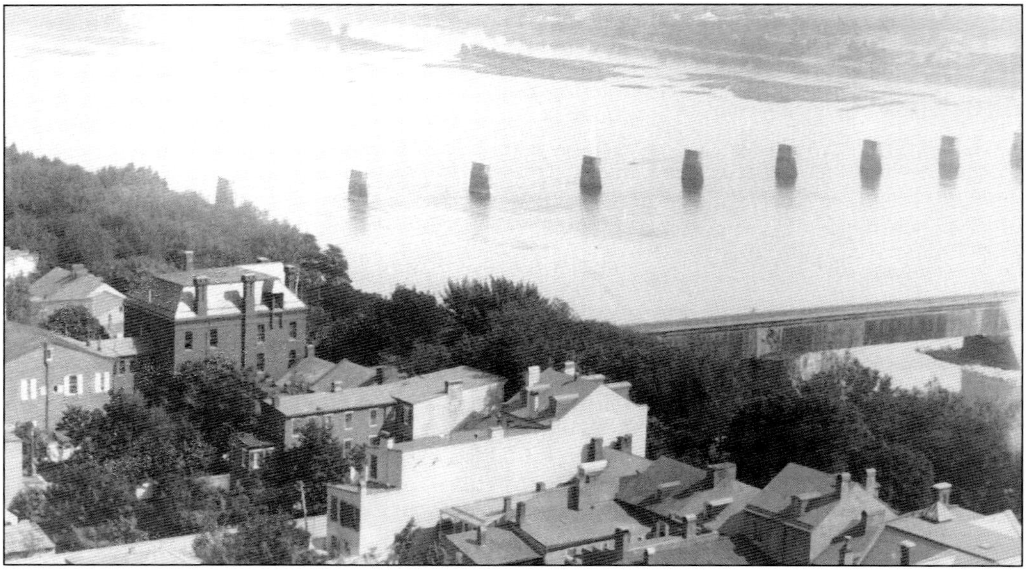

Vanderbilt's Piers (above) were completed in December 1884. The first block of black limestone, weighing 1,000 pounds, was placed into position on April 18, 1884, at the first pier located on Front and Paxton Streets. The stone for the piers was quarried from nearby York Haven. However, the remainder of the bridge was never completed, as the South Pennsylvania Railroad, financed by William H. Vanderbilt, never came to pass. In 1891, the open truss Philadelphia & Reading Railroad Bridge was completed, and it was situated next to Vanderbilt's Piers. Some believed that the proximity to the abandoned piers was deliberate, as they served as ice breakers for the new bridge. The Philadelphia & Reading Bridge was also taller than the neighboring Cumberland Valley Bridge, to stay above water during severe river flooding.

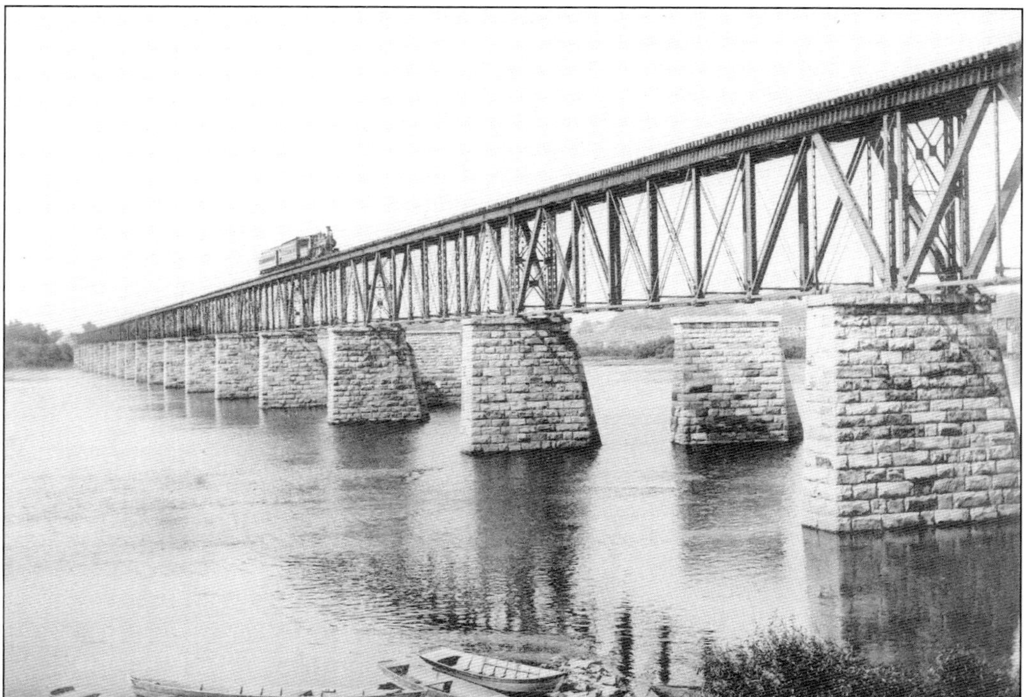

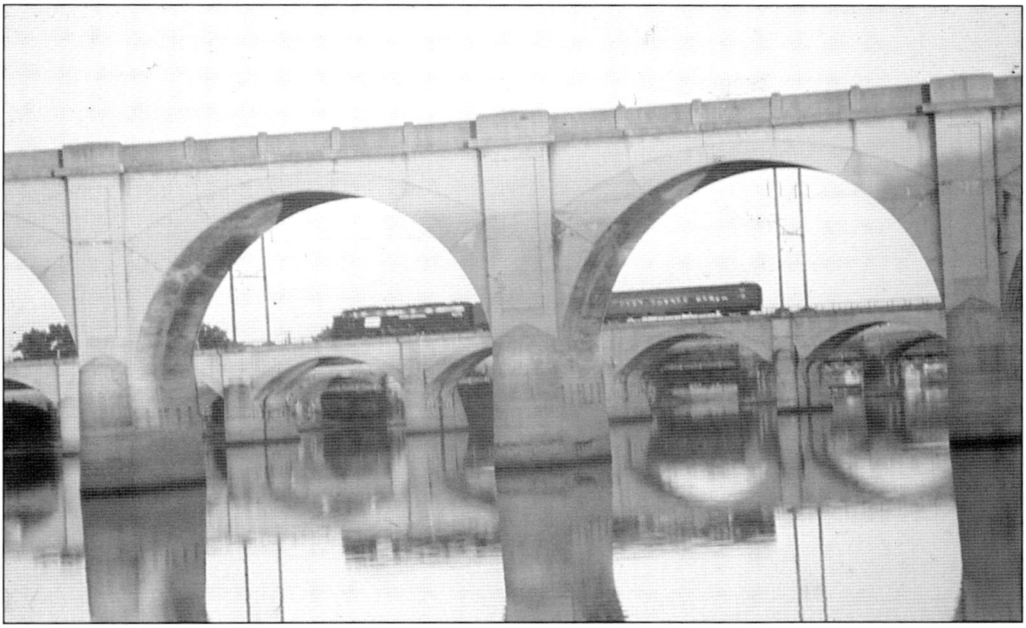

In 1916, the Cumberland Valley Railroad Bridge (background) was rebuilt as a concrete arch structure, updating the old iron truss bridge. The Philadelphia & Reading Railroad Bridge (foreground) would also be rebuilt as a concrete arch bridge, with construction completed in January 1924. The construction of the Philadelphia & Reading Bridge included the incorporation of Vanderbilt's Piers into the bridge's retaining walls that extend from Front to Second Streets.

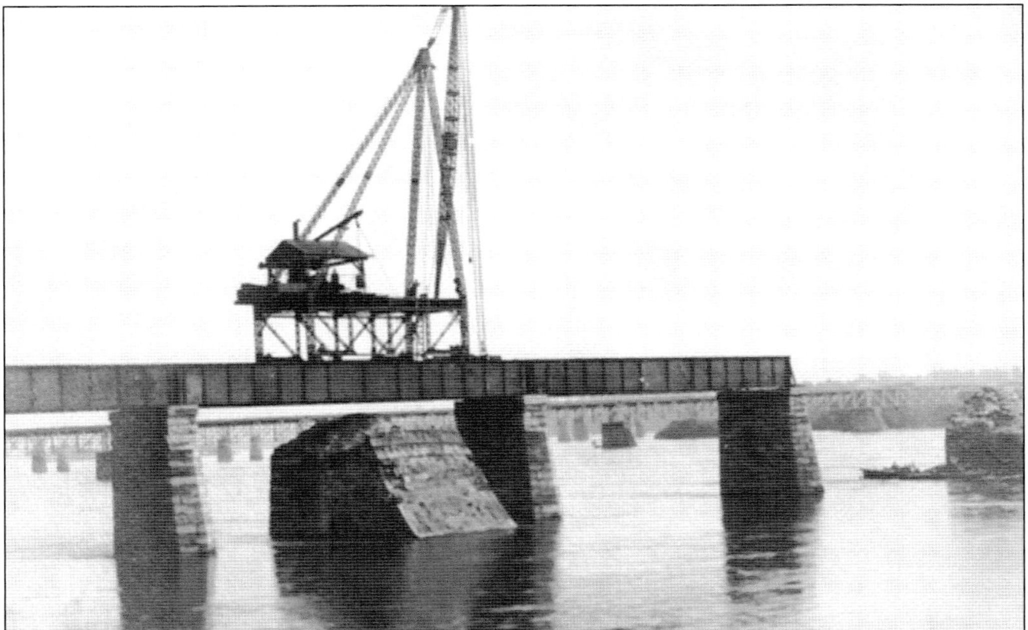

By October 1902, construction on the new Market Street Bridge piers had begun. The old bridge piers were left in place and the new bridge was built around them. By the following spring, much of the work on the piers was completed, and the steel girders of the new bridge were being set in place. (Courtesy of the family collection of Gregg Sloan.)

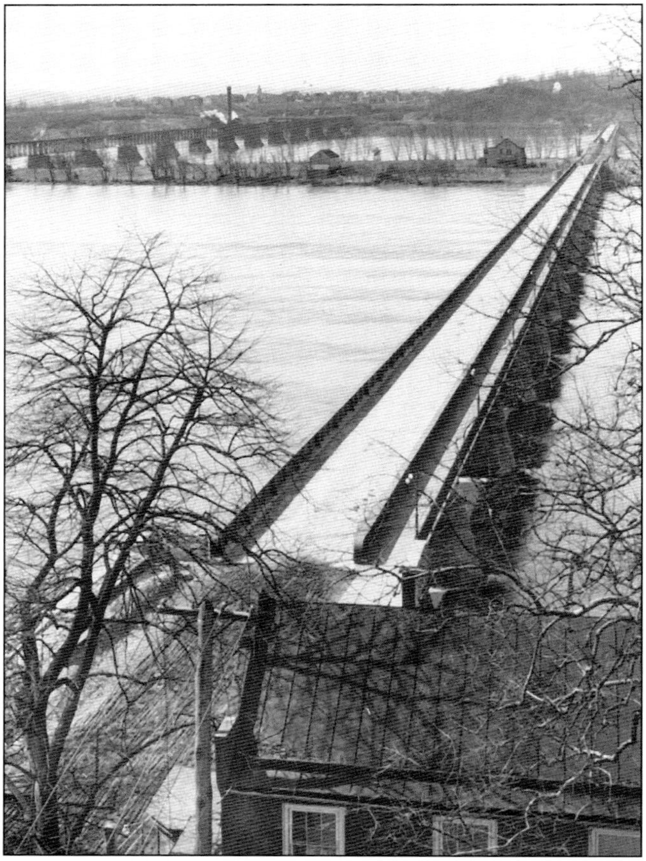

The new Market Street Bridge officially opened to the public at 6:45 a.m. on February 27, 1904, as William A. Kelker paid the first toll with pennies dating from 1812 to 1817. This new steel girder bridge accommodated two lanes of traffic and a separate walkway on the north side of the structure. The pillars from the old Department of Internal Affairs Building, which stood near the state capitol, were placed at the bridge's entrance in 1905. In the image below, taken soon after the bridge opened in 1904, horse-drawn vehicles pass over the island roadway between the two sections of the bridge. This depressed roadway would not be leveled until 1925, in preparation of a modernization project for the Market Street Bridge.

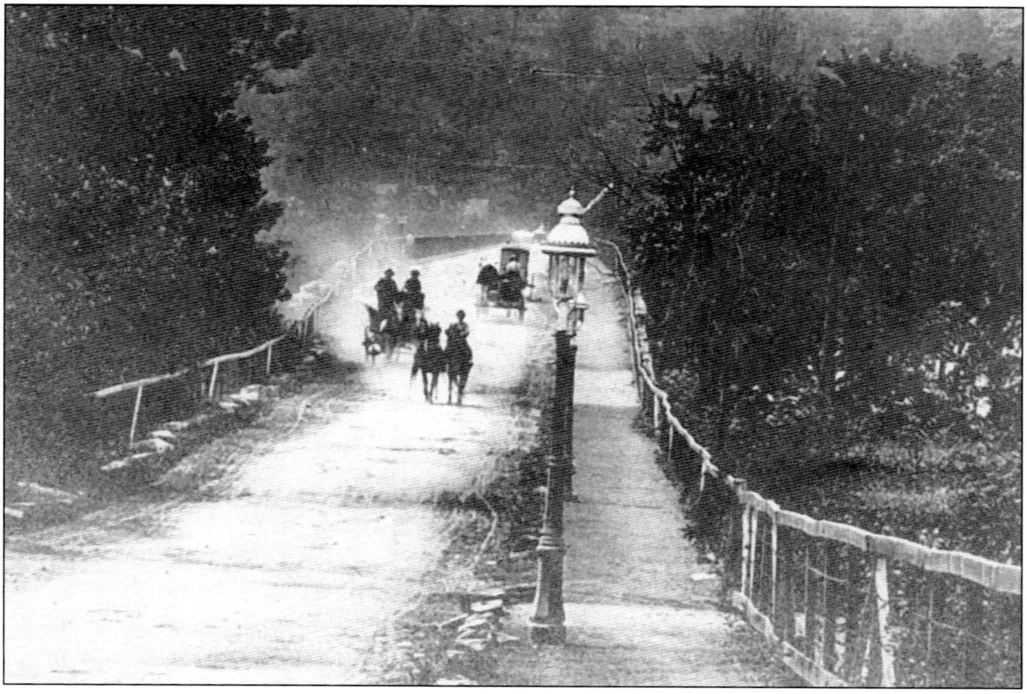

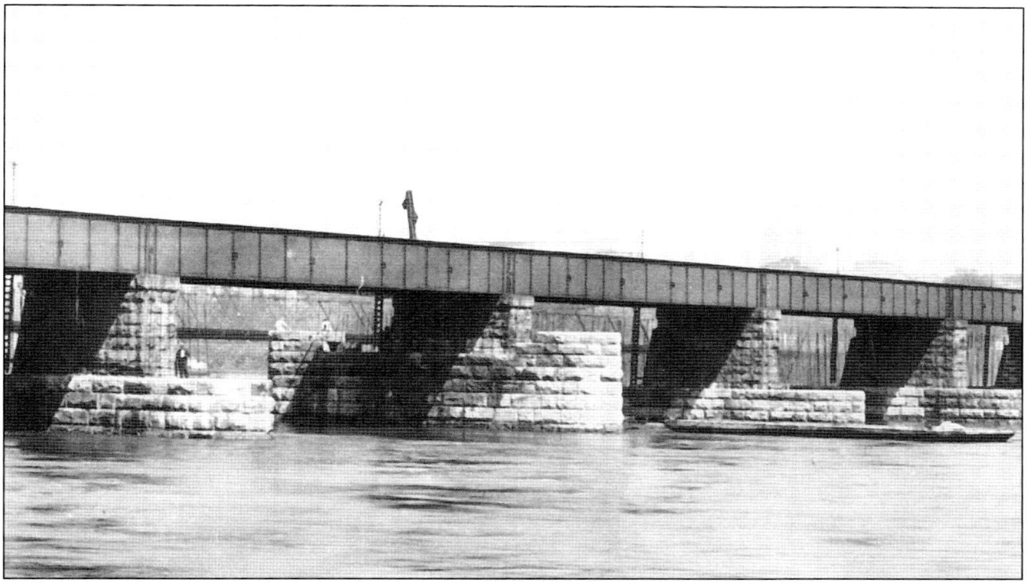

In the spring of 1926, under the direction of the James McGraw Construction Company, construction commenced on a project to widen the bridge from two to four lanes. The eastern section of the bridge would be rebuilt as a concrete structure. The existing two-lane girder structure on the eastern side would be dismantled. The steel girders would then be floated around the island to the western section of the bridge where they would be joined with the existing section on the western side, thus making it a four-lane divided bridge. The construction project culminated without fanfare on April 25, 1928, when it was opened for four lanes of traffic. This brought to a close a project that effectively started 26 years earlier, beginning with the removal of the damaged Camelback Bridge and the old tollhouses.

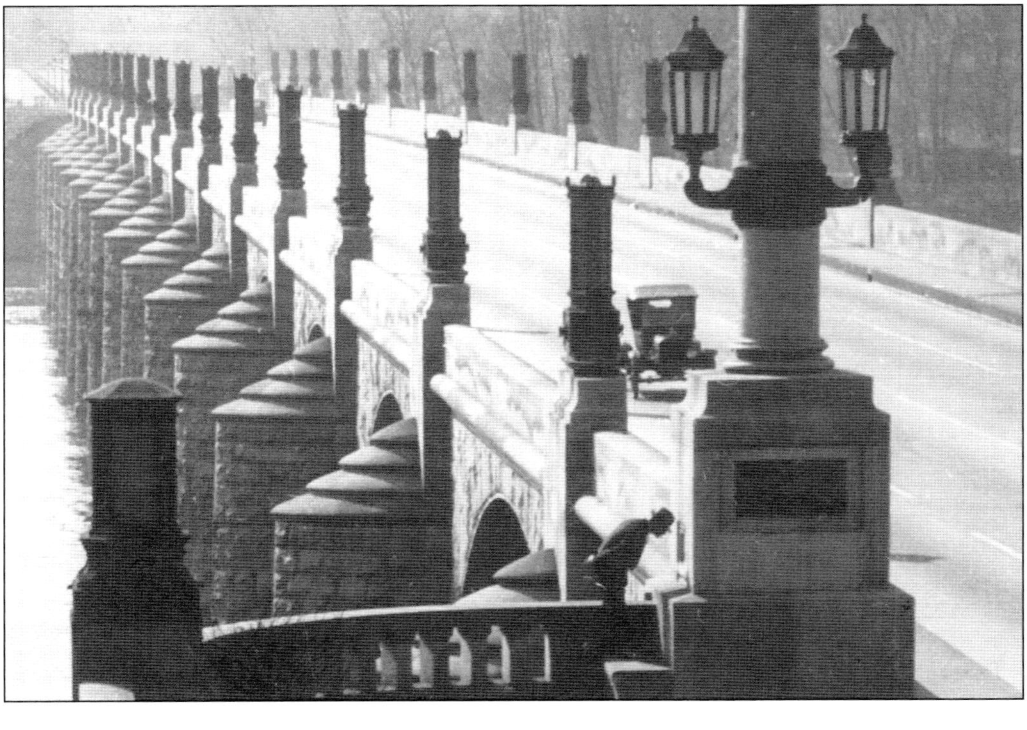

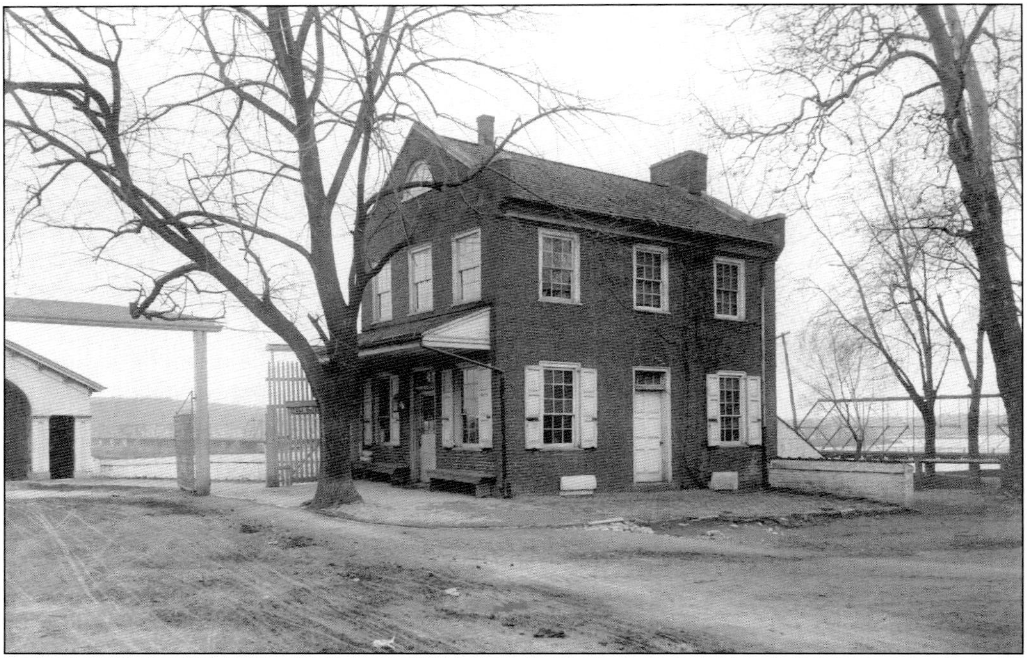

Collecting tolls at the Susquehanna River bridges in Harrisburg began in 1817, when the Camelback Bridge opened to the public. The image above shows the tollhouse along Front Street at the eastern entrance to the Camelback Bridge. The 2.5-story brick structure is referenced as early as 1844, when it hosted the annual meeting of the Harrisburg Bridge Company. The building was removed as part of the beautification process during the construction of the new Market Street Bridge. The tollhouse served as a farmers' market and gathering place for locals during the 19th century. The tollhouse at the western entrance to the Camelback Bridge is seen in the image below. It too was the site of a farmers' market; on Tuesdays and Fridays, local growers would bring their produce.

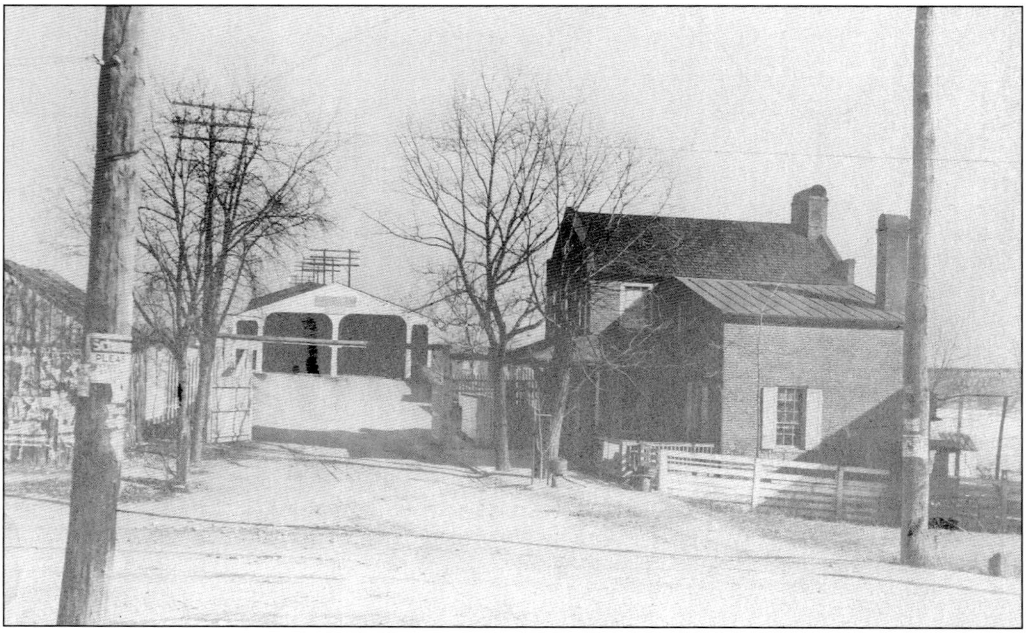

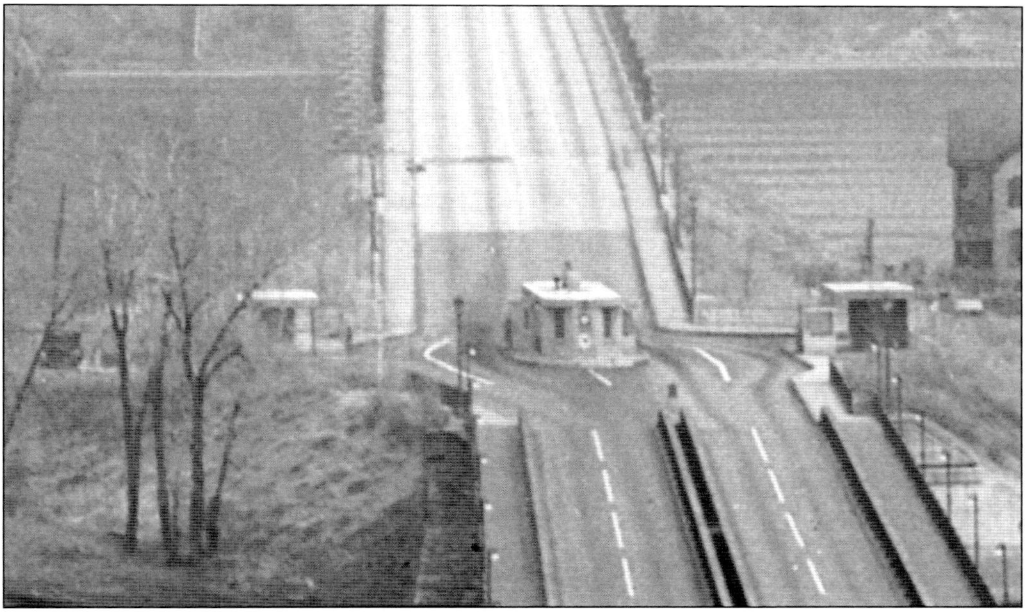

The image above shows the tollhouses on City Island for the Market Street Bridge, which were moved there in September 1925. In 1936, toll tickets could be purchased at the tollhouse for the price of $1 for 25 tickets. In March 1949, Sen. M. Harvey Taylor introduced a bill into the state legislature for a Susquehanna River bridge that would ultimately change the economic landscape of the region. It would be the first toll-free bridge in Harrisburg to cross the Susquehanna River. Construction for the M. Harvey Taylor Bridge broke ground on April 24, 1950, and the bridge was dedicated on January 24, 1952.

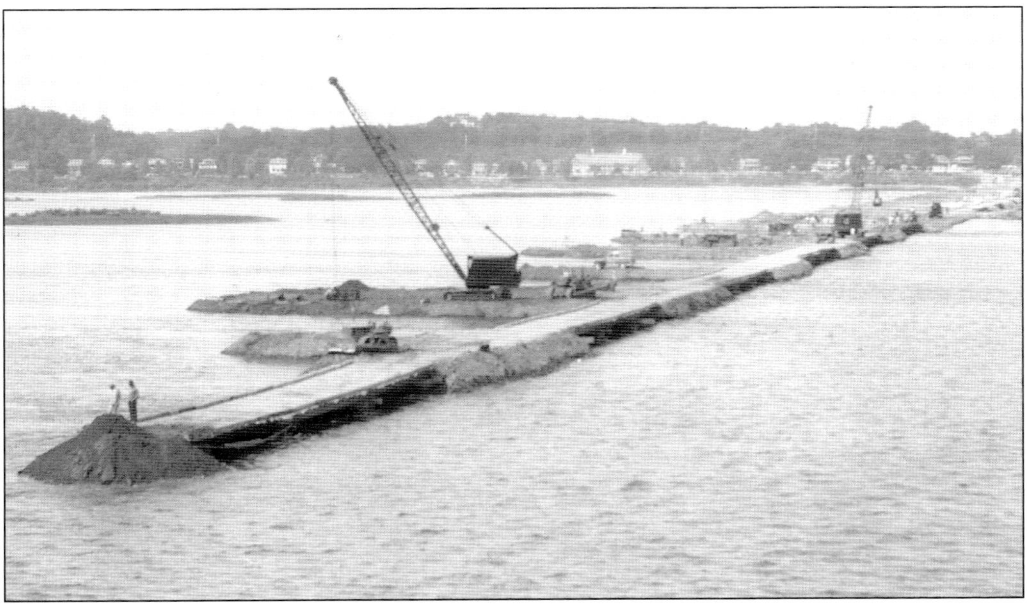

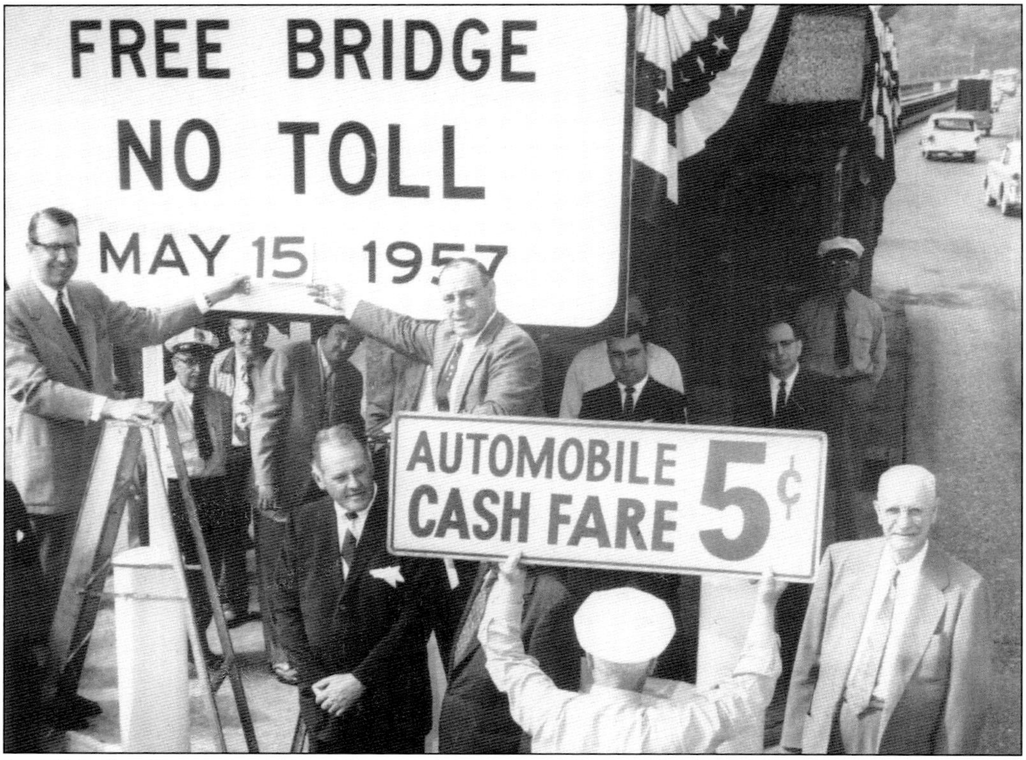


In 1950, the Commonwealth of Pennsylvania gained control of the 10 remaining toll bridges in the state, which included the Market Street and Walnut Street Bridges. The bridges were to continue collecting tolls until all of the debt related to the bridges was paid. On May 15, 1957, when the last 5¢ toll was collected and the bridge debt was satisfied, Gov. George Leader (above left) and Department of Highways secretary Joseph J. Lawler (to his right) revealed a sign declaring "Free Bridge, No Tolls," effectively ending an era that had lasted 140 years. The South Bridge was dedicated on January 22, 1960, with a small crowd in attendance. The $6 million project brought together a highway project linking Harrisburg with Baltimore, which is today Interstate 83.

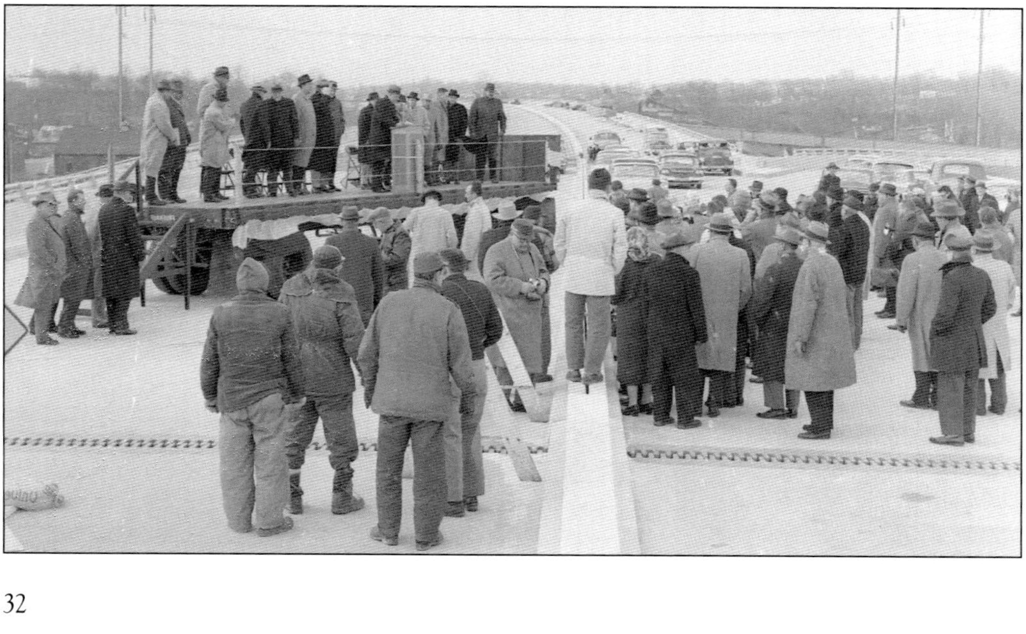

*Three*

# The Islands

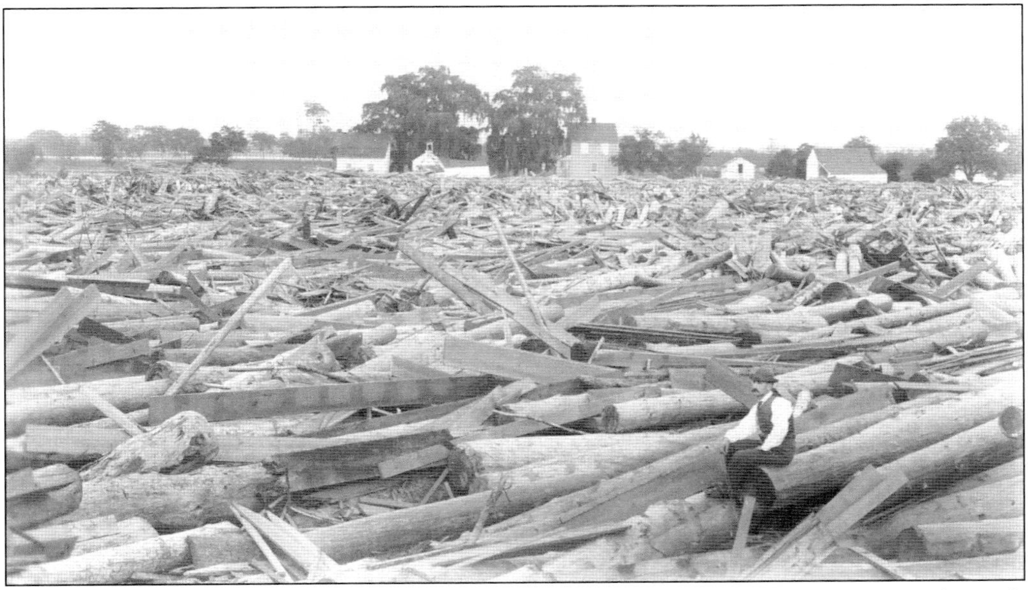

The Susquehanna River islands opposite Harrisburg were privately owned land up to the 20th century. They were utilized as farms, as seen here with McCormick's Island after the flood of 1889, and isolated places of leisure where residents could escape to a location that was near to home but seemed far away from harsh city life.

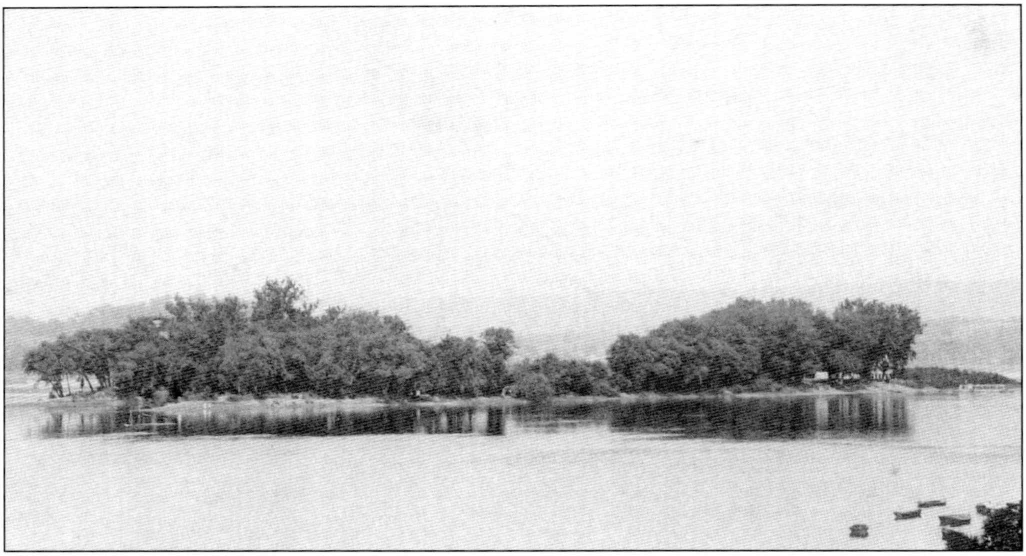

Independence Island, and its immediate neighbor, Bailey's Island, served as the recreational destination for the residents of Harrisburg for most of the 19th and early 20th centuries. Accessed by a cable ferry at the foot of Verbeke Street, the islands provided summer days of picnics, band concerts, dancing, swimming, and fishing. It is believed that the island was named after the popularity of such gatherings on the Fourth of July.

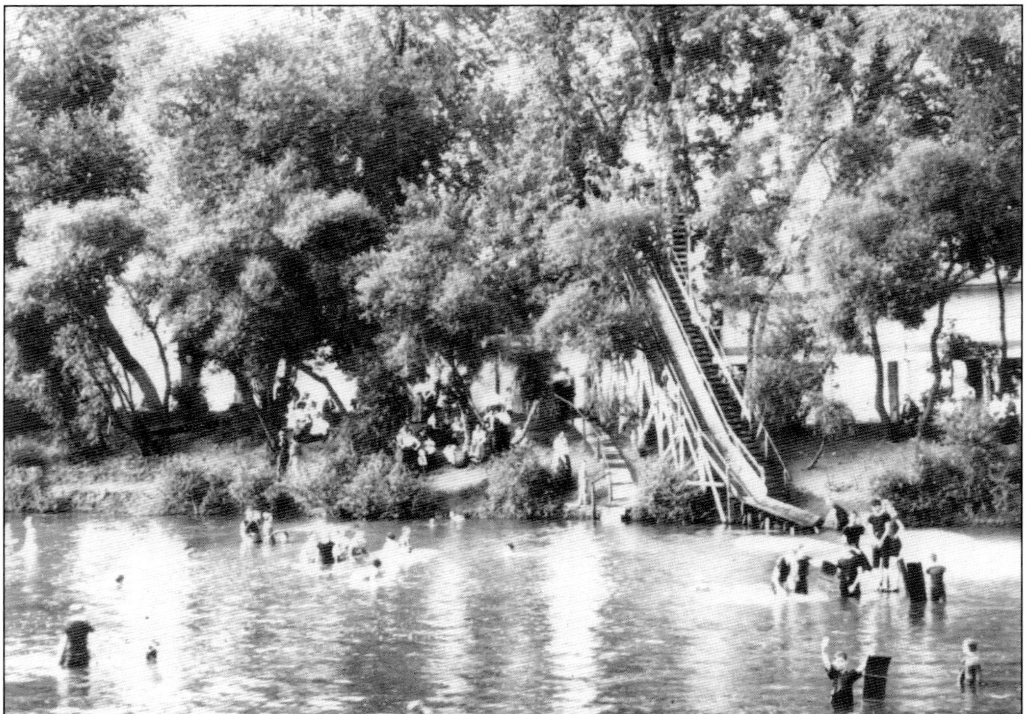

Located on the western side of Independence Island directly behind the dance hall was a favorite amusement known simply as "the Chute." Seen here in 1900, local children "Shoot the Chute" down the modified three-story coal chute and plunge into the channel between Independence and Bailey Islands.

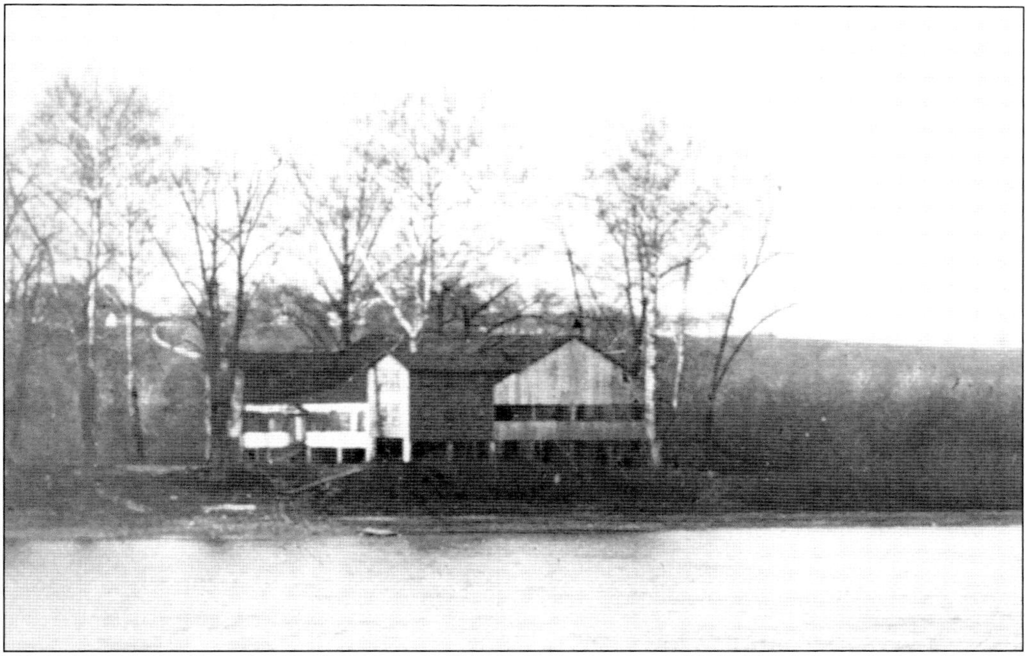

In the spring of 1886, the Grand Central roller-skating rink at Second and Cumberland Streets was moved to Independence Island. Seen here, the building became a popular dance hall, where residents could trip the light fantastic to the music played by local bands. The building was removed in 1924 when a private group made attempts to once again convert the island into an amusement center.

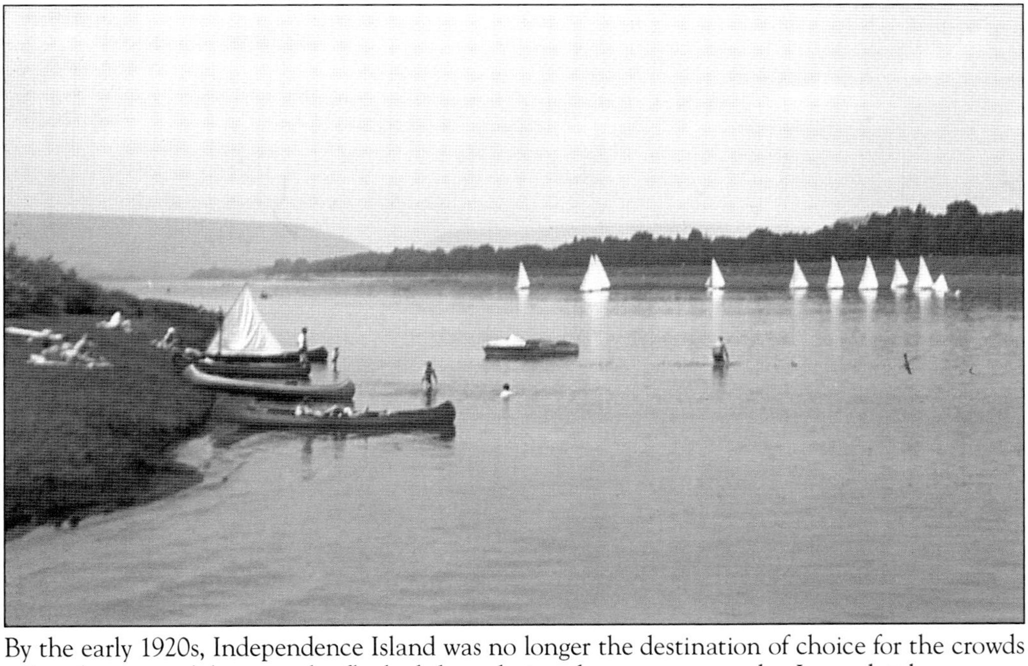

By the early 1920s, Independence Island was no longer the destination of choice for the crowds of beachgoers and dancers who flocked there during the summer months. Instead, it became an intimate destination for boaters who wished to be far from the maddening crowds. It has retained this distinction even to this day.

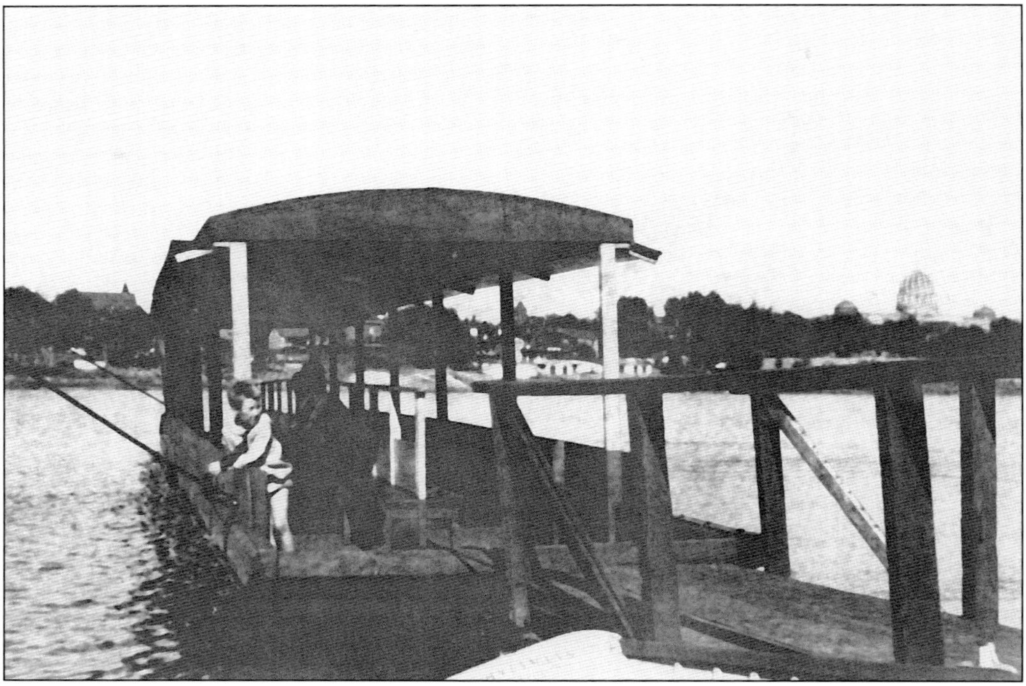

On August 9, 1913, the day before his seventh birthday, young William Henry German Jr. is taking a ride on the cable ferry as it sits docked at Independence Island. The cable ferry was the method of choice for accessing Independence Island during the late 18th and early 19th centuries, carrying thousands of passengers to the somewhat remote island destination

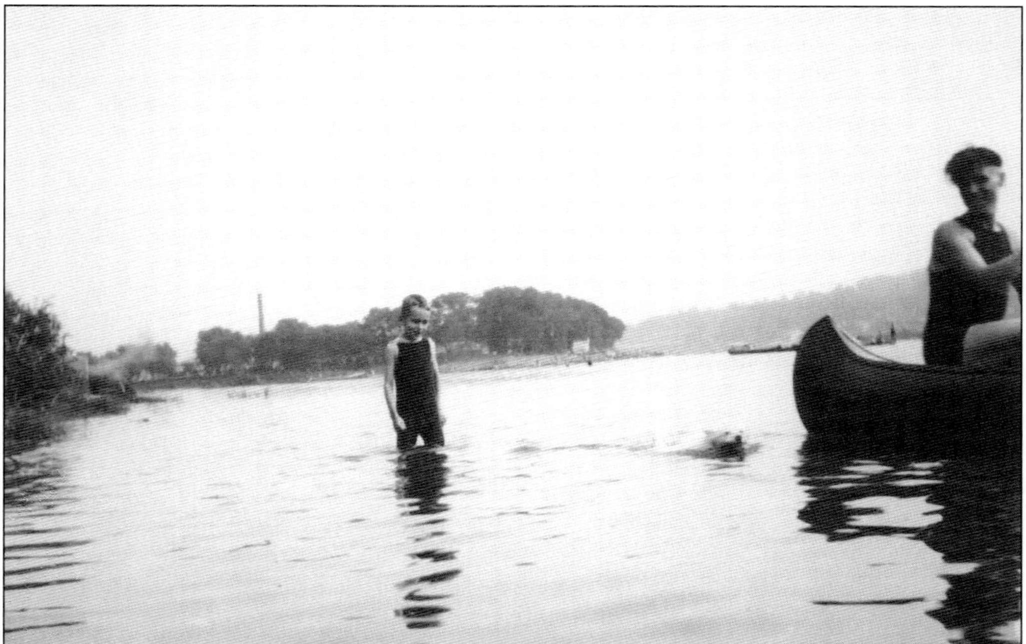

Enjoying the cool river on a warm summer day is the Cook family, along with their dog, in the calm lagoon that previously existed between Independence and Bailey Islands. In the background, the municipal beach at City Island can be seen in this view taken about 1920.

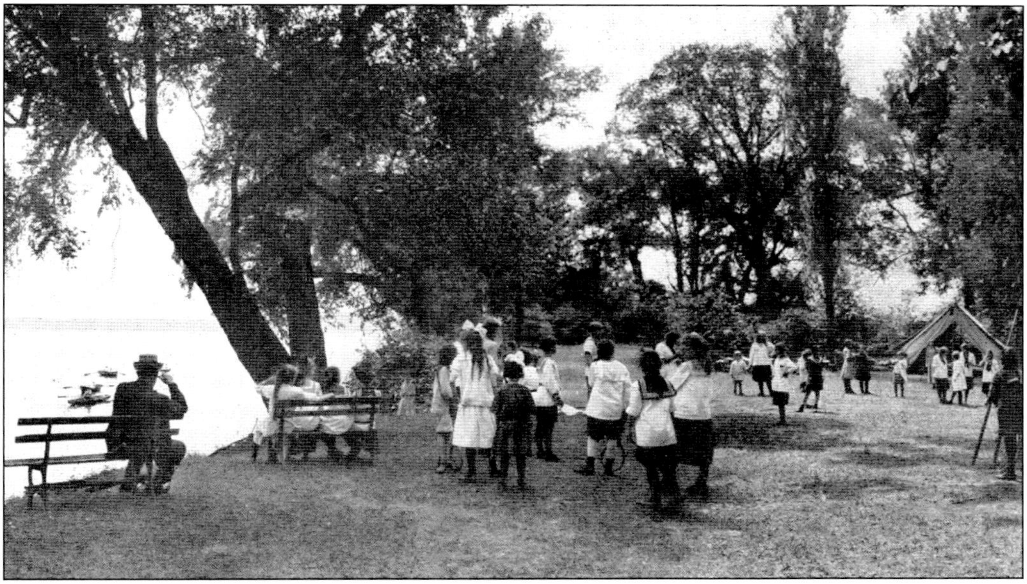

In May 1912, James McCormick gifted the 101-acre island bearing his family's name to the City of Harrisburg, to be used solely for park and recreational purposes. Situated in the northern portions of the city, the island was, up to that point, utilized primarily for farming purposes. By July of that year, a girls' summer camp with 42 girls attending was established on the island, as seen here, and given the name Kamp Kaughtinrein by the girls who spent the first night in a downpour. By August, the girls returned home and the boys arrived at the camp. The boys' and girls' days at camp were filled with swimming, boating, and vaudeville productions. By 1924, the McCormick Island summer camp fell out of favor due to general lack of interest and it was discontinued.

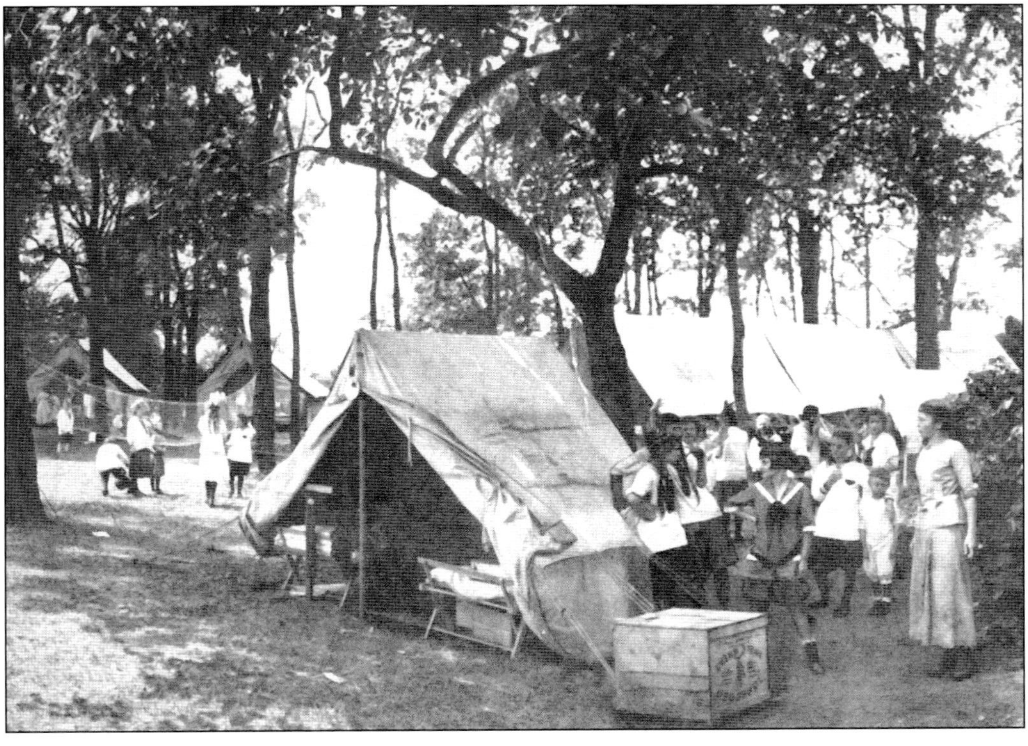

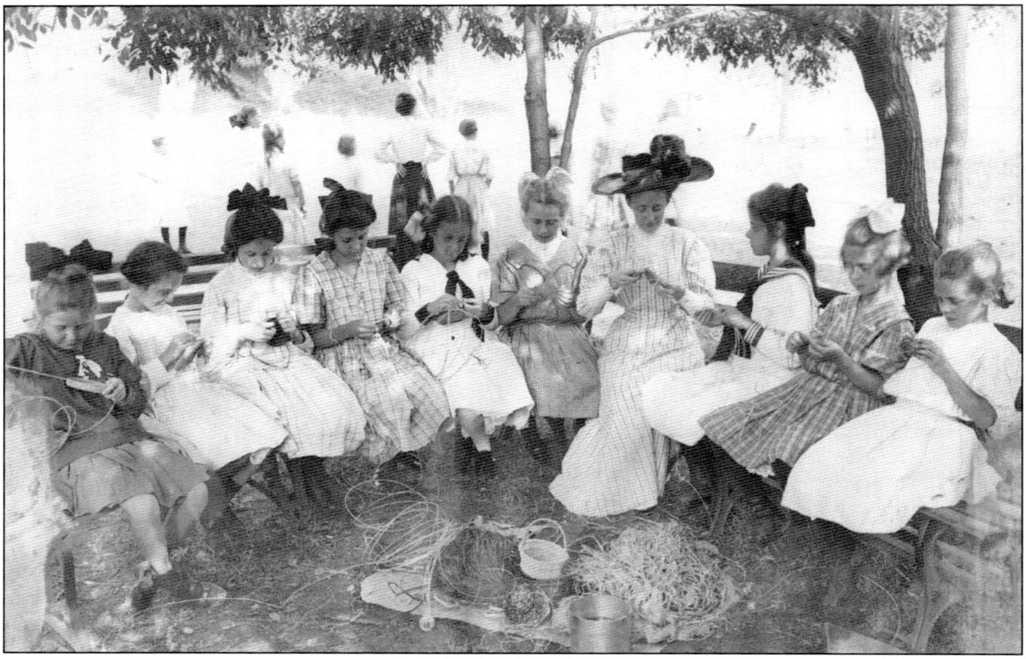

The girls' campground on McCormick's aimed to not only thoroughly develop the young ladies in athletics, but also provide them with activities and education in the domestic sciences. Advanced classes in cooking and baking, sewing, embroidery, and making raffia baskets (seen here), along with instruction in folk and fancy dances were provided to the girls.

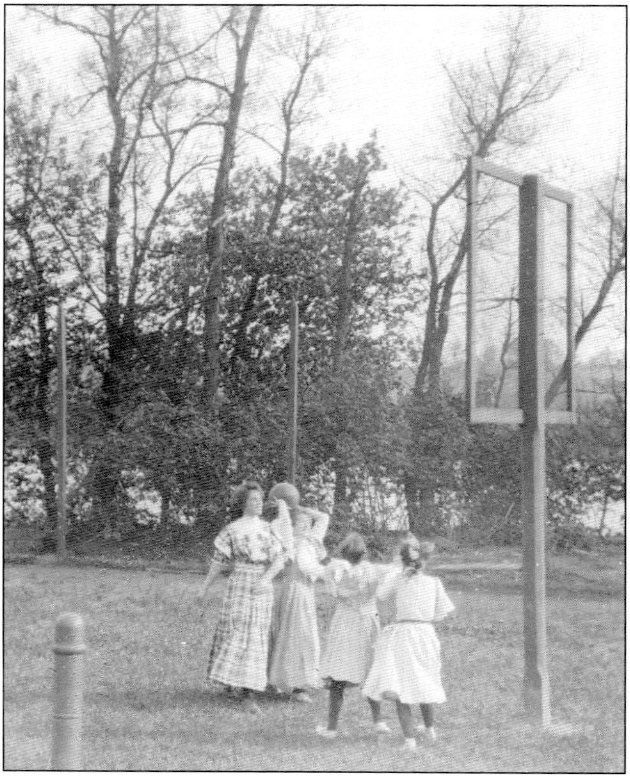

Around 1912, four young ladies enjoy a leisurely pickup game of basketball on the grounds at Kamp Kaughtinrein in this photograph taken by J. Horace McFarland. Surprisingly, the uniforms of organized girls' basketball teams did not differ much from those seen in this image. A typical uniform of this time consisted of a long-sleeved blouse and a full-length skirt or bloomers and stockings.

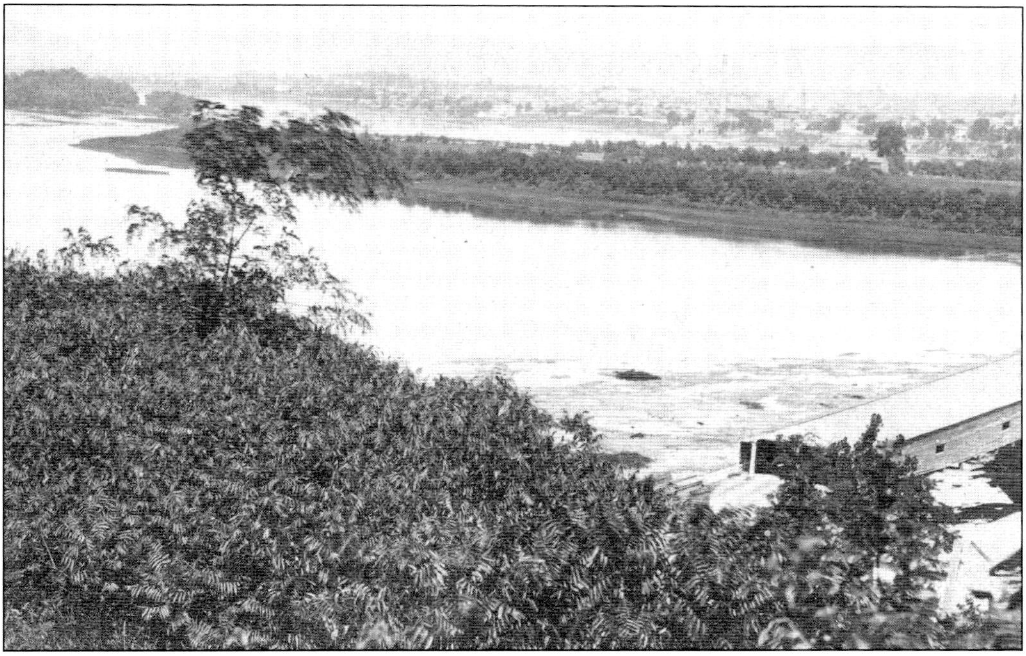

The large island that lies opposite the city of Harrisburg has been known by many names over the years. During the life of John Harris it was called Turkey Island, most likely as it served as a nesting ground for the wild fowl. The island would later take the name of its owners as it passed from the Penn family. During the 19th century, it would be known as Maclay's, Forster's, Thomas's, Longnecker's, Hargest's, and Westbrook's Island. In 1901, ownership of the island passed to the Harrisburg Athletic Club and ultimately to the City of Harrisburg, giving it the name City's Island. Pictured below is the island residence of John J. Hargest, who was locally renowned as a truck (vegetable) farmer who sold his island crops at Market Square.

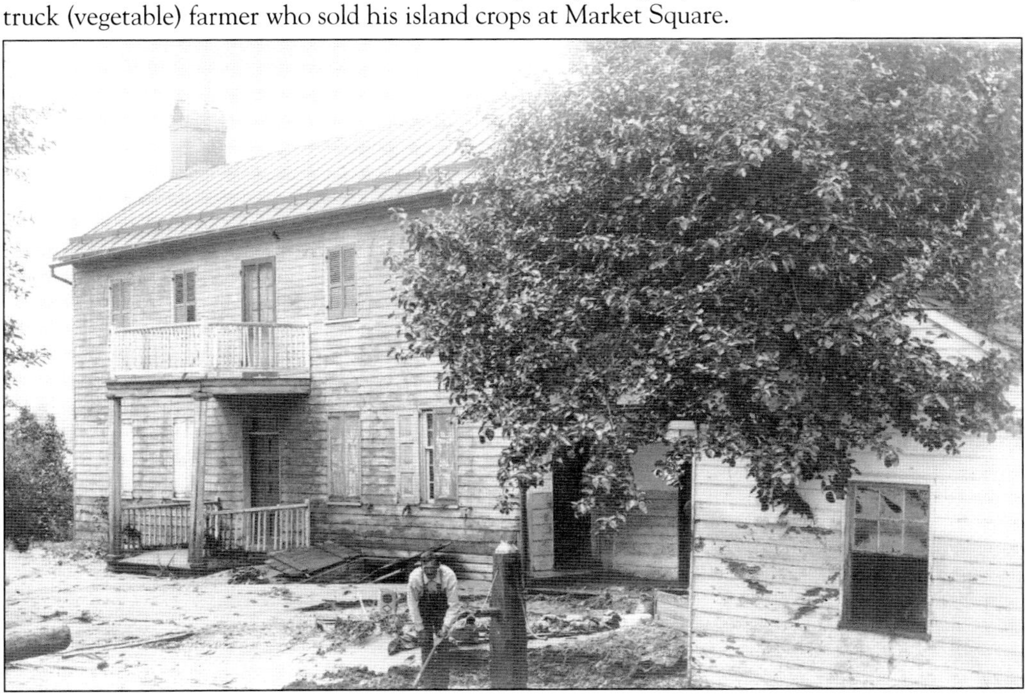

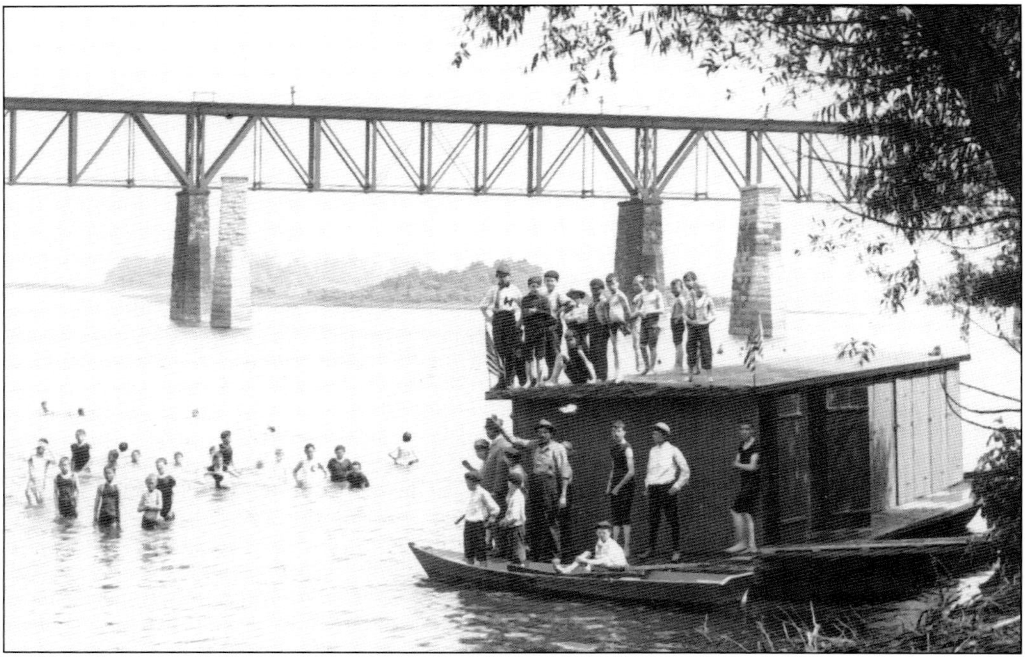

In June 1907, the Harrisburg City Park Commission opened a municipal beach with a floating bathhouse at the southern end of Island Park. In the first year, only men and boys were able to make use of the facilities, since, as the June 20, 1907, *Harrisburg Telegraph* reports, the commission did "not look favorably upon the mingling of men and women on the beach," as the commissioners had "witnessed the antics at Atlantic City and Coney Island."

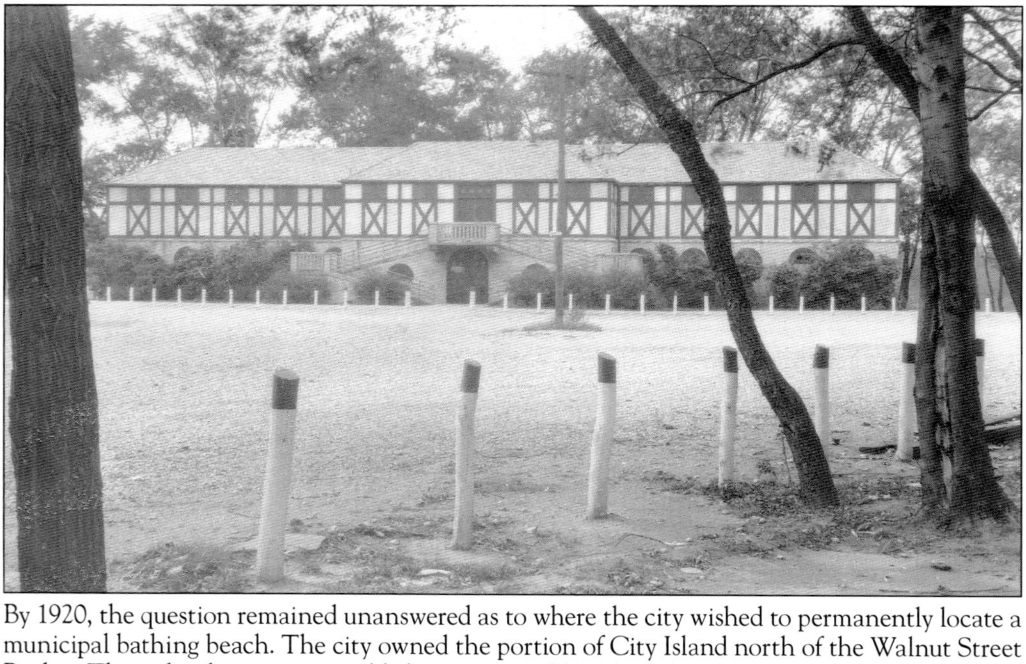

By 1920, the question remained unanswered as to where the city wished to permanently locate a municipal bathing beach. The city owned the portion of City Island north of the Walnut Street Bridge. Thus, the decision to establish a municipal beach and a permanent bathhouse on the northern end of the island was made in January 1920, with the completion of the bathhouse by the spring of 1921.

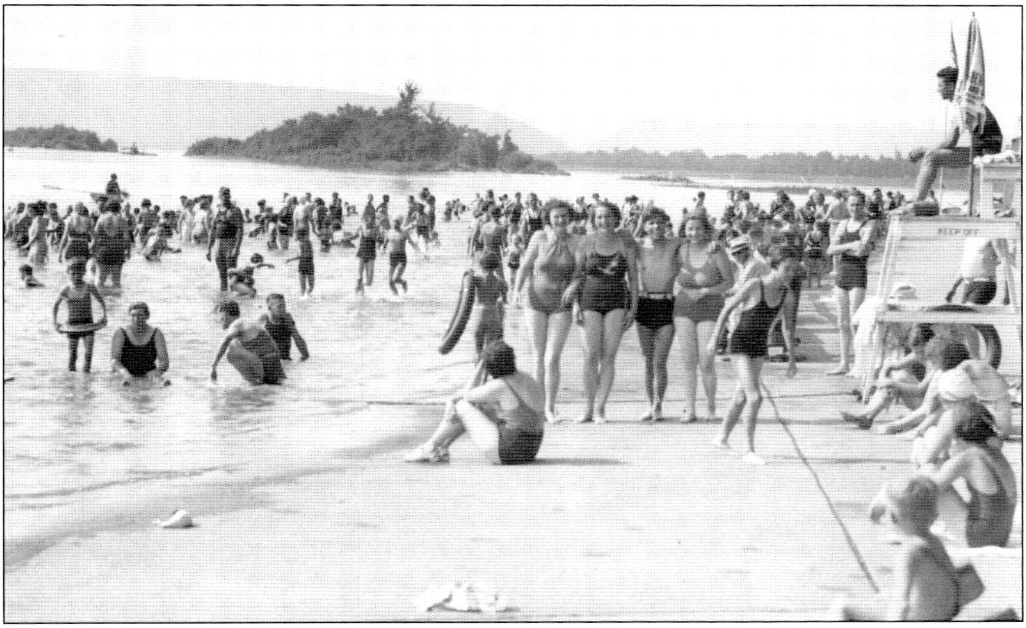

One of the problems that the city's park commissioners faced with the new location of the municipal beach was the yearly spring floods and floes of ice that eroded the northern end of the island. In 1925, it was decided that the beach would be paved with concrete to eliminate this problem. However, the beach still incurred damage and had to be repaired and repaved after the first winter.

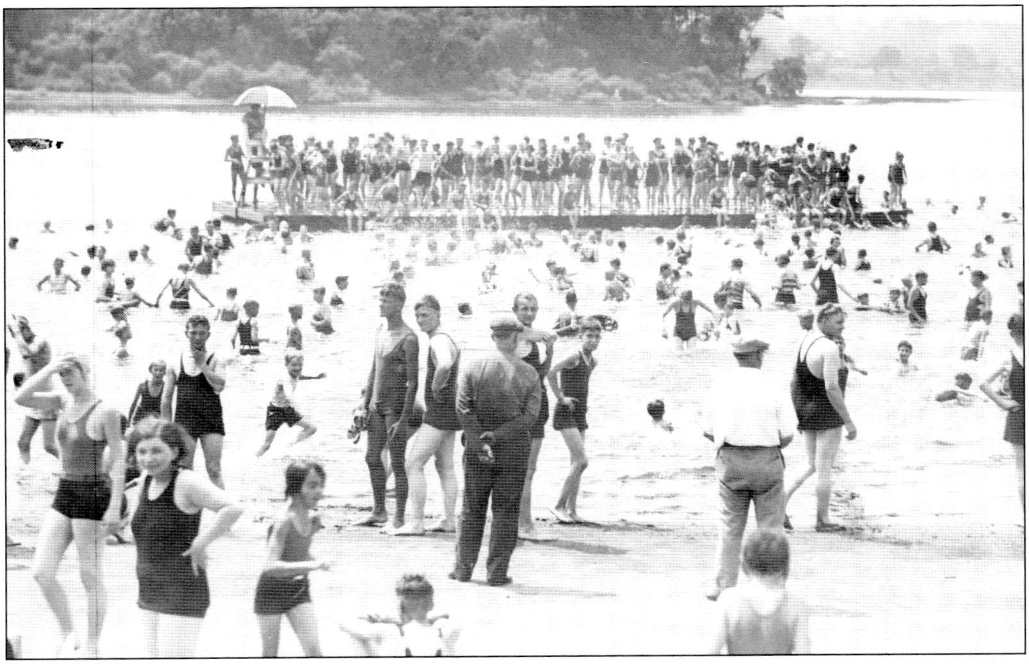

It did not take long for the City Island bathing beach to become a popular warm weather destination, as seen in the image taken for the August 15, 1931, issue of the *Evening News*. Added attractions such as an offshore pier, night swimming, and a real sand beach that was added around the bathhouse brought in thousands of swimmers and beachgoers each day to the island.

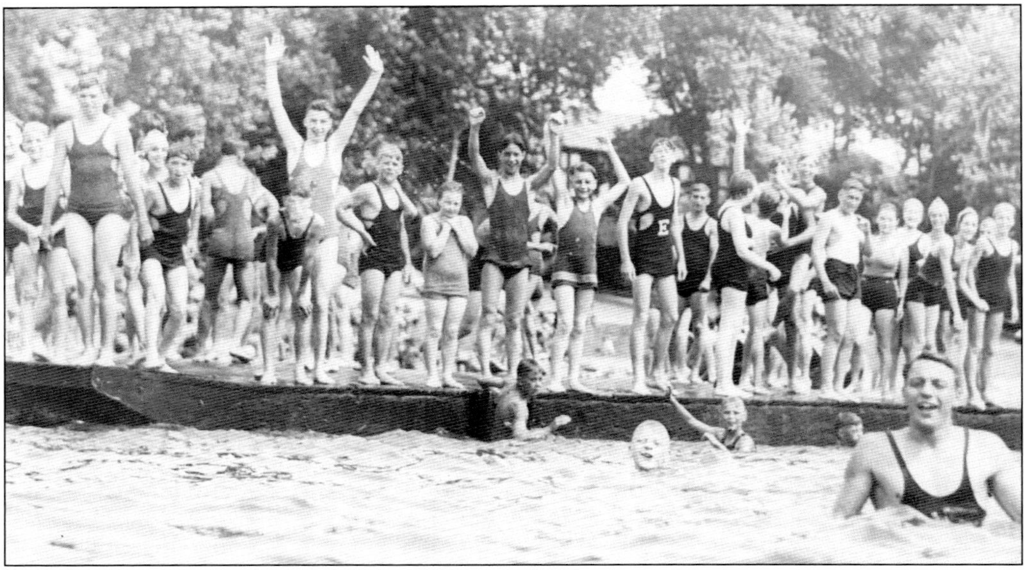

The appeal of the island bathing beach, as seen here in the image above from July 2, 1932, was appreciated largely by the children and young people of the city. It provided a relatively safe summer camp-like environment at a relatively low cost, which consisted mainly of the bridge tolls to access the island. Programs such as aquatic meets and competitions were designed to strengthen the young swimmers and keep them safe in the river currents. In contrast, the photograph below, taken on July 3, 1974, shows the same island beach after the crowds had disappeared over the years. Following World War II, many Harrisburg families left the city for the suburbs, and community swimming pools replaced the old swimming holes.

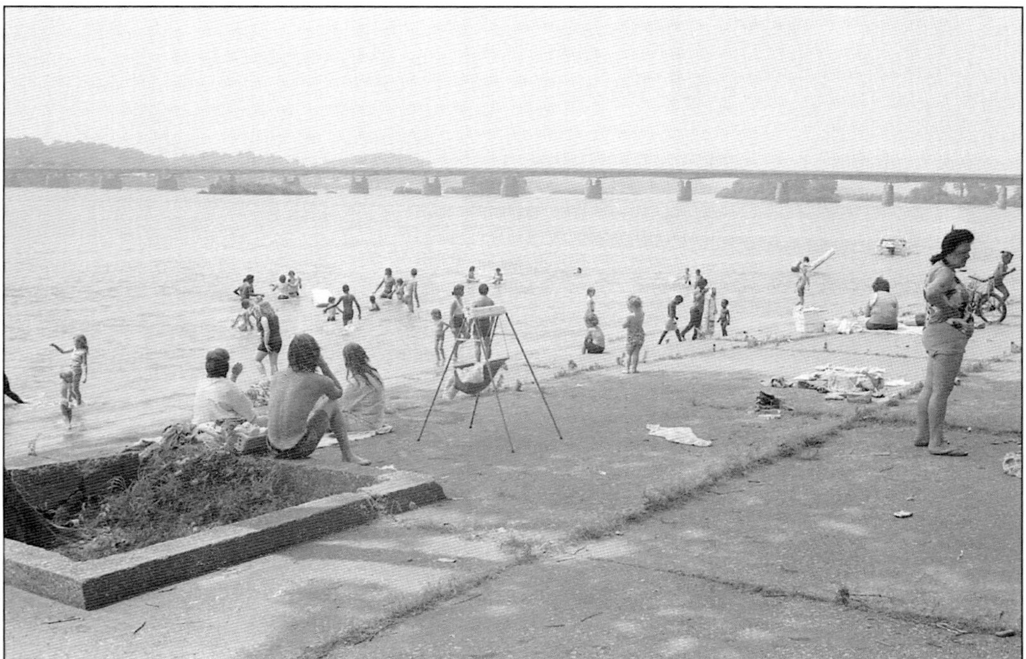

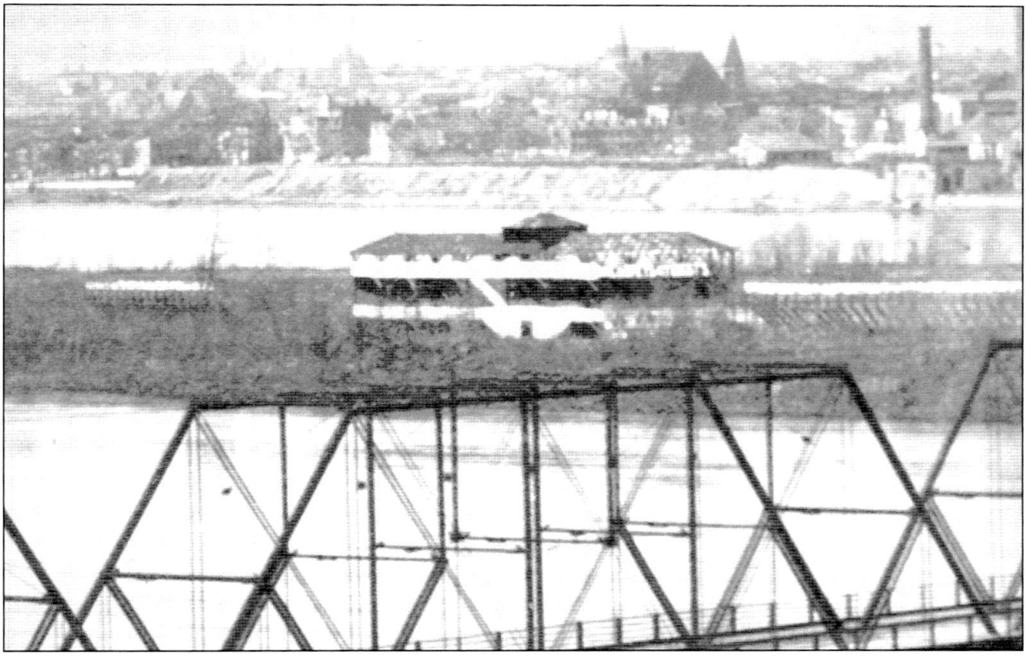

In 1889, as the Walnut Street Bridge was still under construction, plans were being laid to bring a baseball club to Westbrook (City) Island. Under the auspices of the Harrisburg Athletic Association and the Island Park Association, baseball did not take hold on the island in the late 19th century. However, by 1893, a field was laid out and a double-decker grandstand was built, as seen above. The grandstand was short-lived and was removed by 1895. It was dismantled and reassembled at the Carlisle fairgrounds. In 1901, a new grandstand and field replaced the failed first attempt as the Harrisburg Athletic Club took control of the northern end of the island. About the same time, baseball fields were built on the southern end of the island for use by leagues and local pickup games, as seen below around 1905.

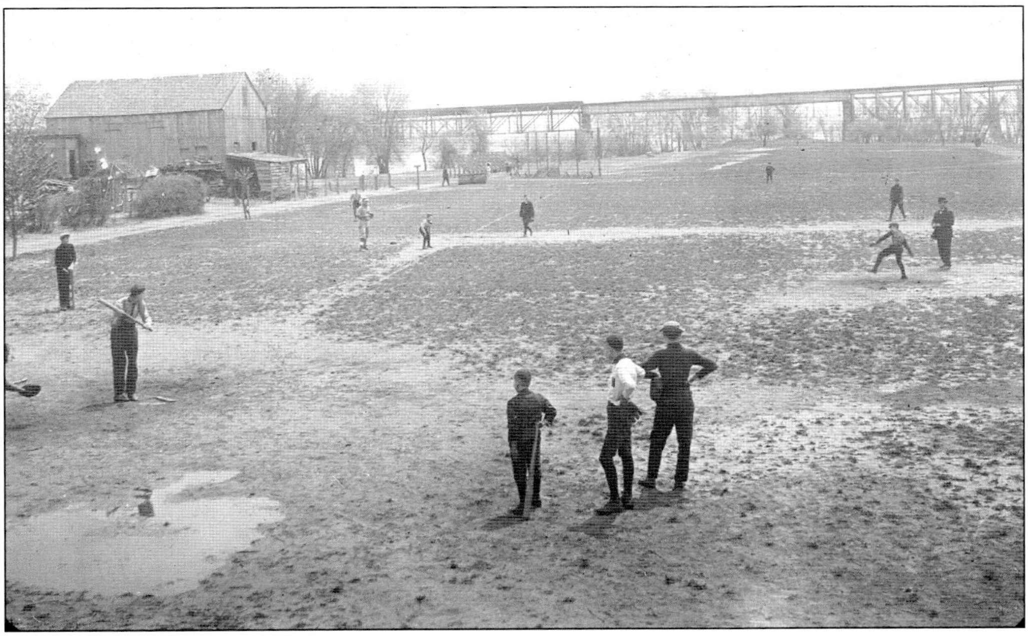

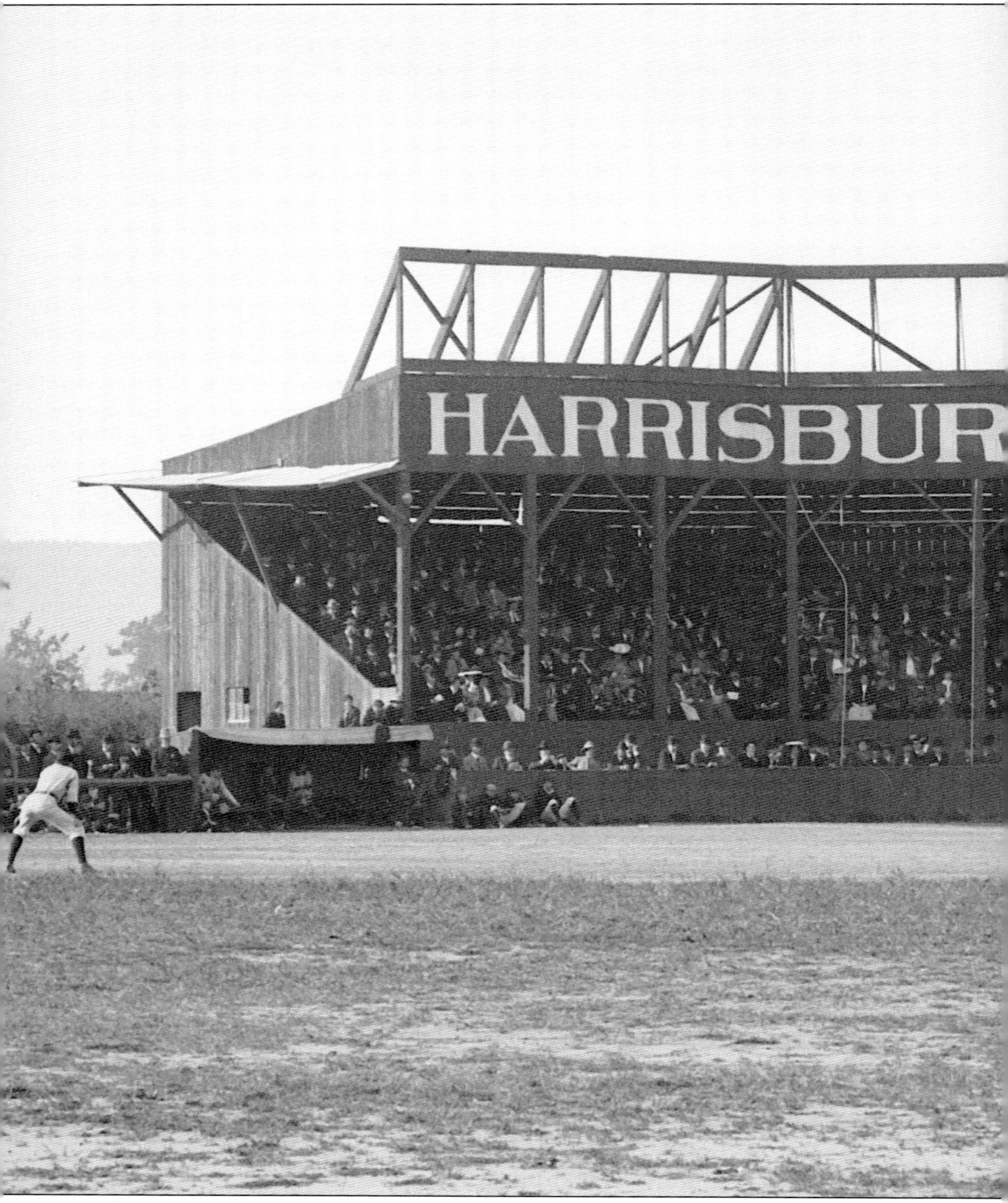


This image was taken at Island Park on Thursday, September 22, 1904, where the Harrisburg Athletic Club played the Washington Senators of the American League in an exhibition game. Seen here, the Harrisburg Athletic Club is in the field, with center fielder Charley Malay in the foreground of the image, "Matty" Broderick at shortstop, Charley Hilbert pitching, and Connie Murphy behind the plate. The Washington Senators would win the contest 6-2. They were

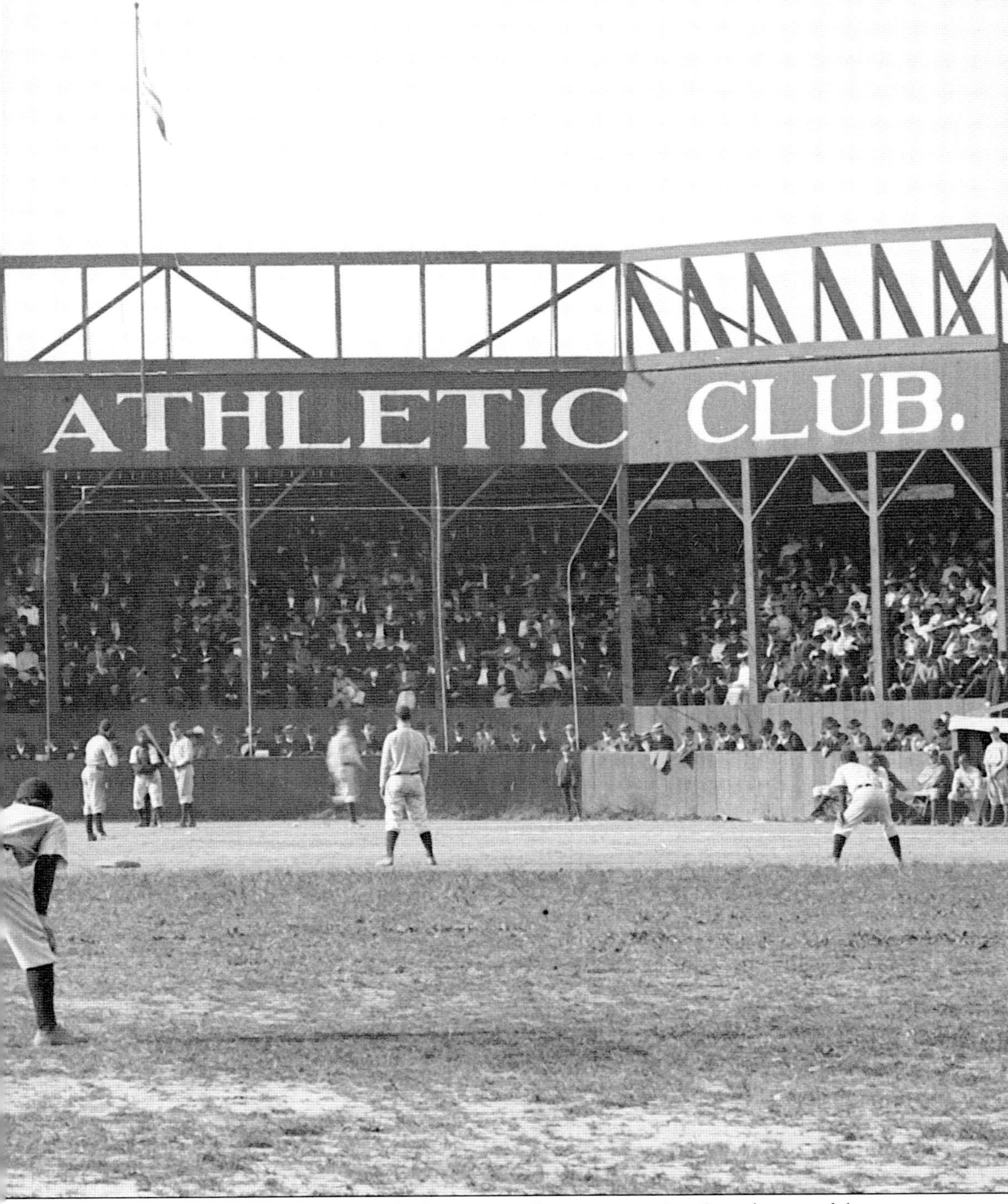


largely aided by the Harrisburg team, which committed seven errors. Joe Cassidy, one of the stars of the Washington club, was a local Pennsylvania product who played shortstop for Harrisburg the previous season. Cassidy would only play two seasons with the Washington Senators, as he tragically died of malaria on March 25, 1906, at the age of 23.

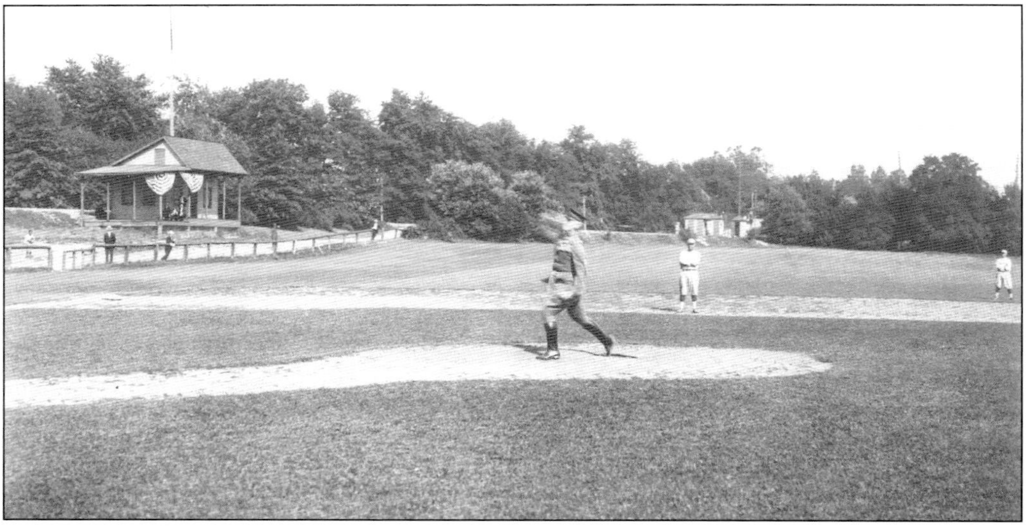

A US Army officer throws a pitch from the mound in this photograph taken about 1917. In July 1917, Company D of the 8th Regiment of the National Guard camped at Island Park and received training before it was set to leave for Georgia for additional training before the men left for their ultimate destination, France.

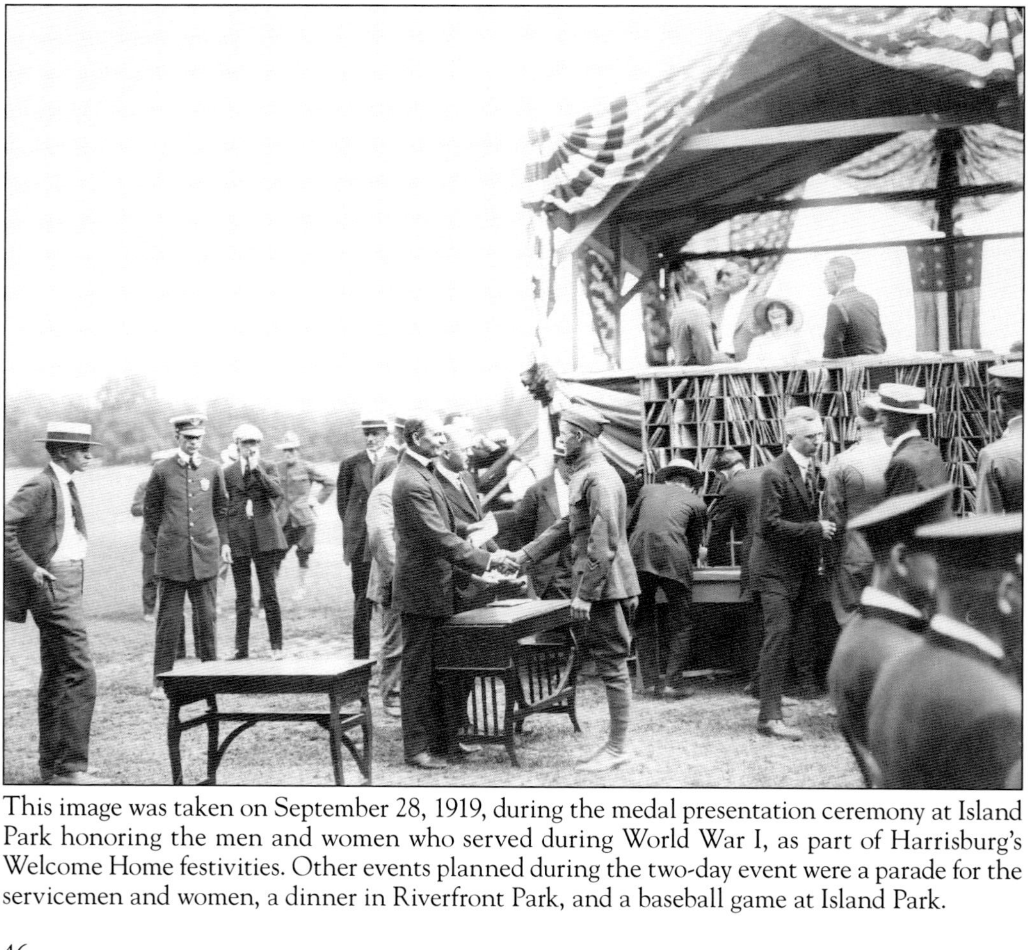

This image was taken on September 28, 1919, during the medal presentation ceremony at Island Park honoring the men and women who served during World War I, as part of Harrisburg's Welcome Home festivities. Other events planned during the two-day event were a parade for the servicemen and women, a dinner in Riverfront Park, and a baseball game at Island Park.

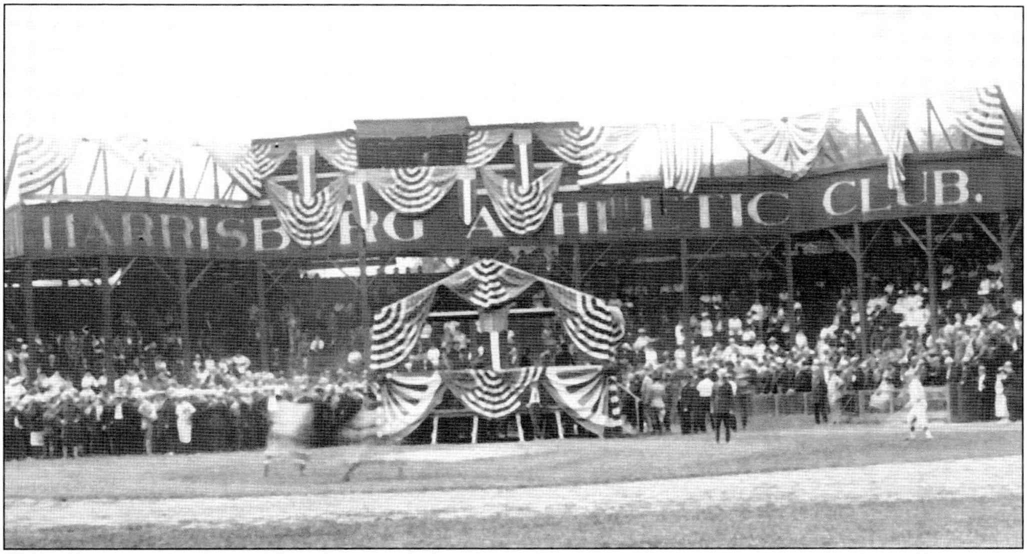

In 1919, Harrisburg did not have a semiprofessional team of its own playing at Island Park. To fill that void, the Klein Chocolate Company Team from Elizabethtown played a series of exhibition games at Island Park against teams from the major leagues. One of these games was against the Washington Senators on September 29, 1919, and billed as part of the welcome home event for soldiers. Hall-of-Famer Walter Johnson pitched the first three innings and was relieved on the mound by fellow legend Sam Rice. The Senators would lose the game in 12 innings to the Klein team. On September 25, the Klein team would play Babe Ruth and the Boston Red Sox. The photograph below was likely taken during that game.

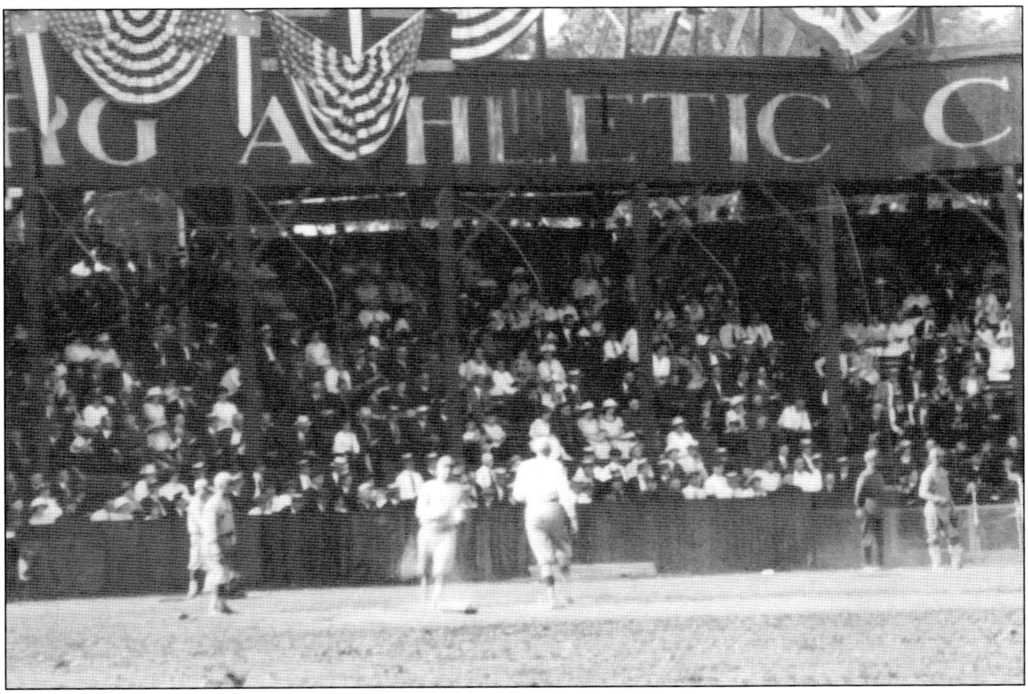

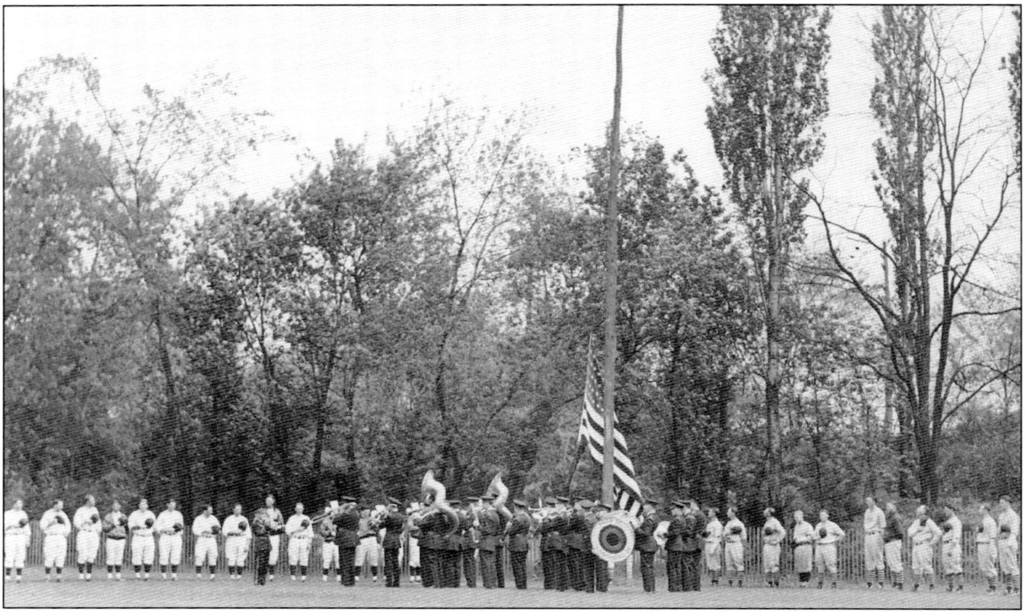

In this photograph, the flag is raised on opening day of the 1930 baseball season at Island Park. The Post 27 Band plays, presumably the national anthem, as the Harrisburg Senators and their opponents from York look on. Of particular note is the flagpole, which would snap and kill 15-year-old John Backenstoe of 1920 Forster Street during a football game between Camp Curtain and Edison on November 21, 1931.

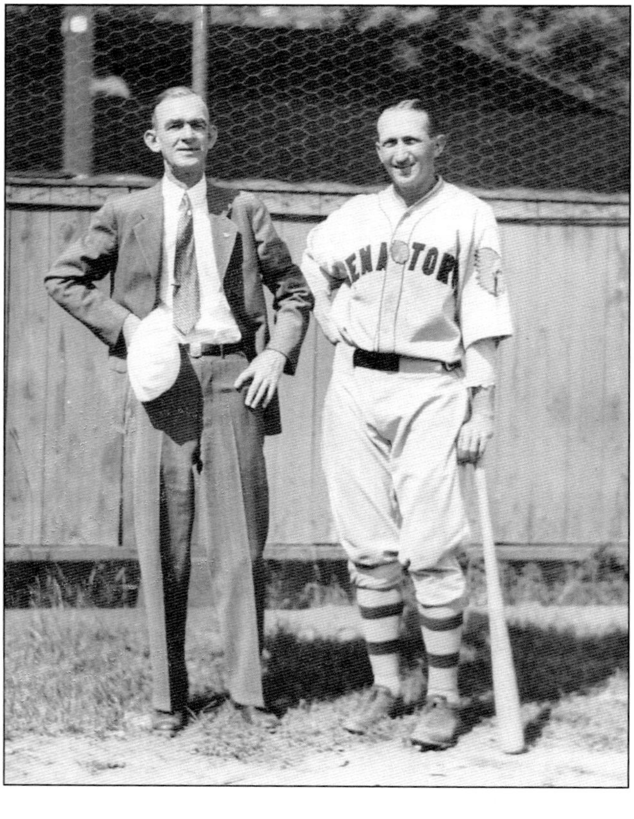

Seen here in 1933 alongside Senators superfan Robin Hood, is William "Cy" Morgan, who joined the Harrisburg team during the 1931 season. Morgan would later manage and scout in the Philadelphia Phillies' farm system, becoming chief scout and field director of the farm system in 1947. He would also scout for the Baltimore Orioles and New York Mets. He passed away on August 13, 1969, at the age of 70.

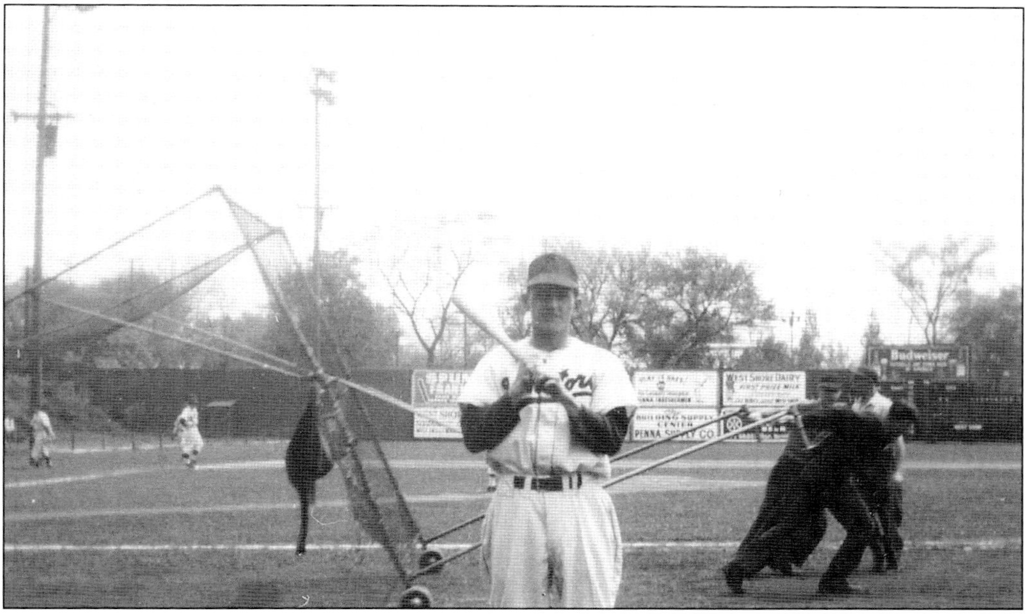

On this page are two images taken prior to a Harrisburg Senators game in 1946. That year, the Senators had become affiliated with the Cleveland Indians in the Class B Interstate League. The team would win the Interstate League title by beating the Philadelphia Phillies affiliate team, the Wilmington Blue Rocks, four games to one in a best-of-seven series. That year's team had several players who would go on to play in the major leagues, with the most successful being catcher Joe Tipton, pictured here (right). A native of McCaysville, Georgia, Tipton would go on to spend seven seasons in the major leagues, playing for the Cleveland Indians, Chicago White Sox, Philadelphia Athletics, and Washington Senators. He was a member of the 1948 World Champion Cleveland Indians squad and filled the role of backup catcher.

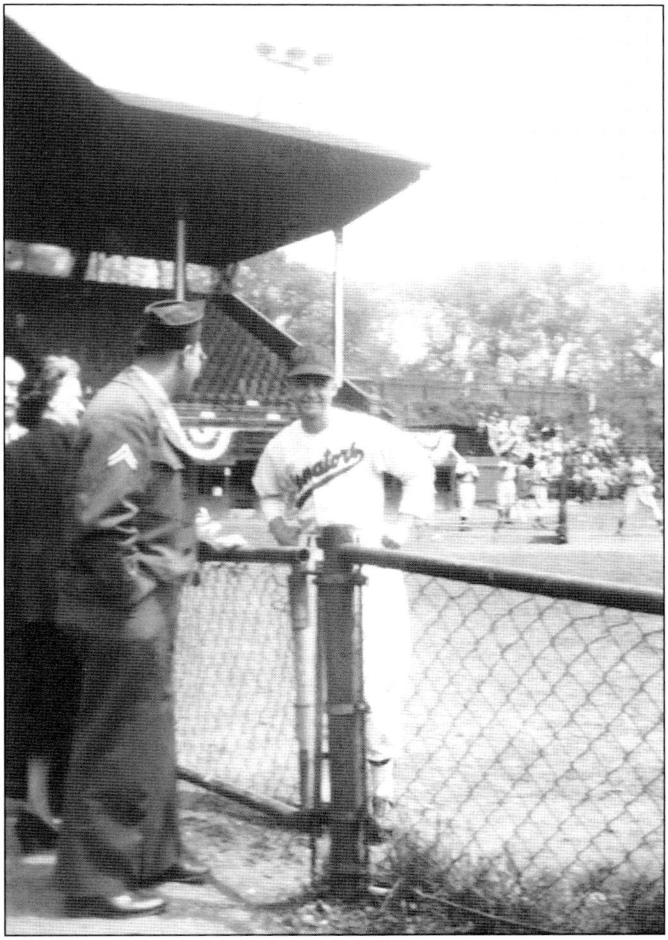

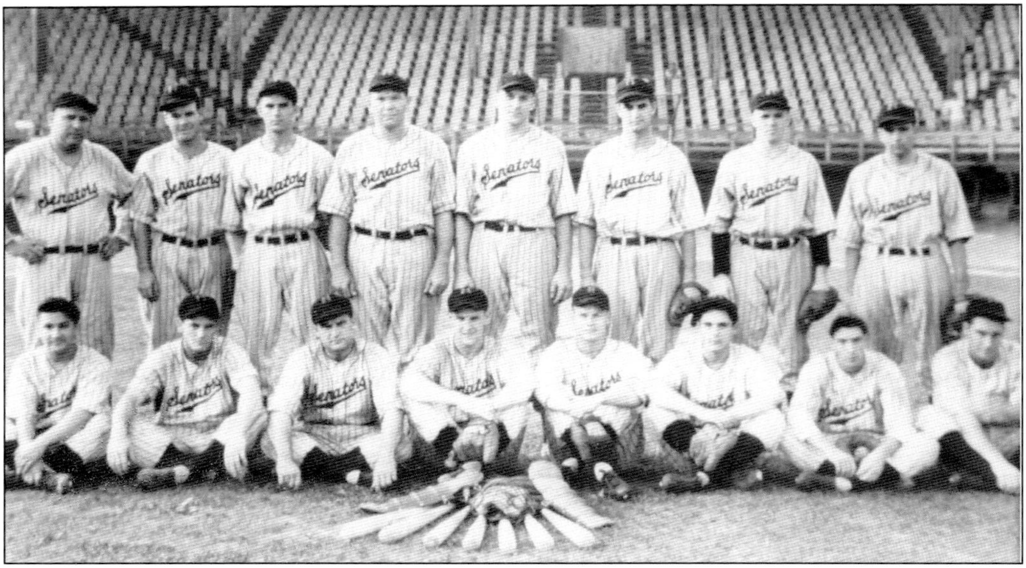


The 1940 Harrisburg Senators pose for a team picture in front of their new grandstand. The flood of 1936 destroyed the old grandstand, and the team had not played on the island since the flood's arrival. The 1940 squad is notable for its star infielder Billy Cox (front row, second from right), a native of Newport. Cox would go on to play 11 years in the big leagues and was a fixture playing third base for the Brooklyn Dodgers in an infield that included Gil Hodges, Jackie Robinson, and Harold "Pee Wee" Reese. To Cox's left is Harrisburg native Danny Tomaso, who pitched for the Senators for four years during the 1940s. In the image below, the final preparations are being made as workers grade the warning track of RiverSide Stadium prior to the first opening day in 1987.

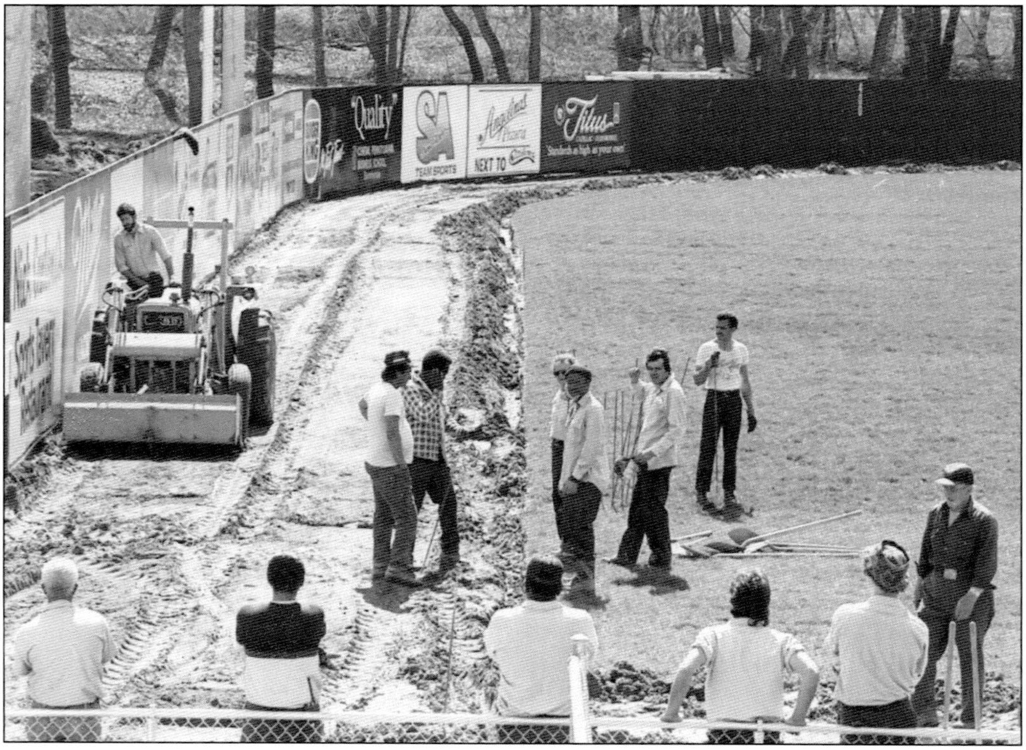

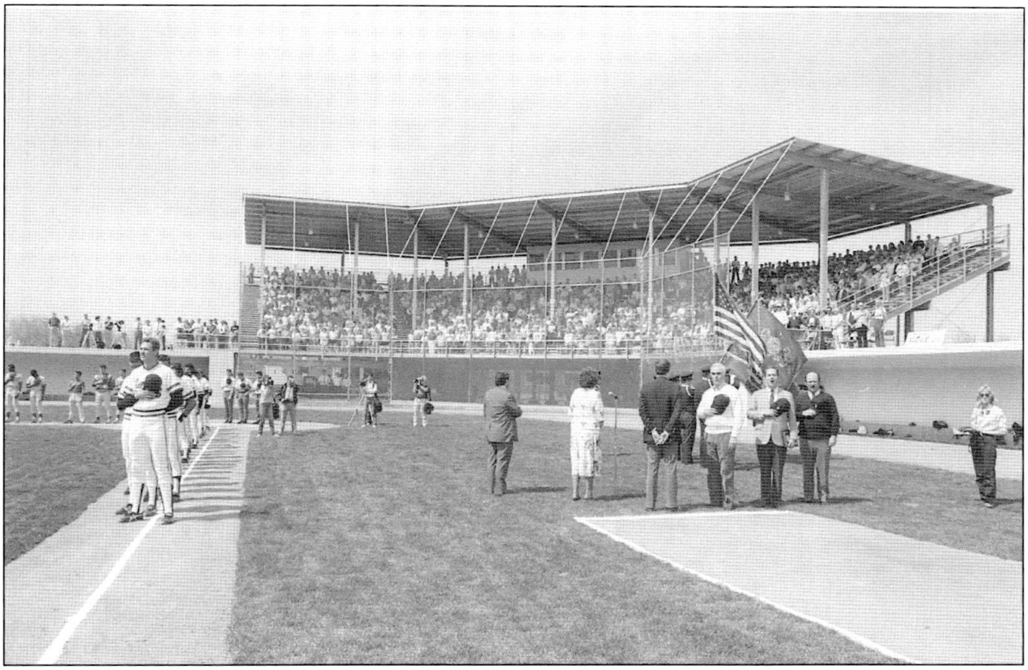

April 11, 1987, was opening day at RiverSide Stadium, as professional baseball returned to Harrisburg after an absence of 35 years. Pre-game ceremonies included Mayor Stephen Reed throwing out the first pitch and introductions of past Senators players, including Harrisburg's own Jimmy Deshong. Pictured standing in front of the American flag during the singing of the national anthem are Gov. William Casey (in white sweater) and former governor Dick Thornburgh (in tan jacket). The Vermont Reds would spoil the festivities, winning the game 11-5.

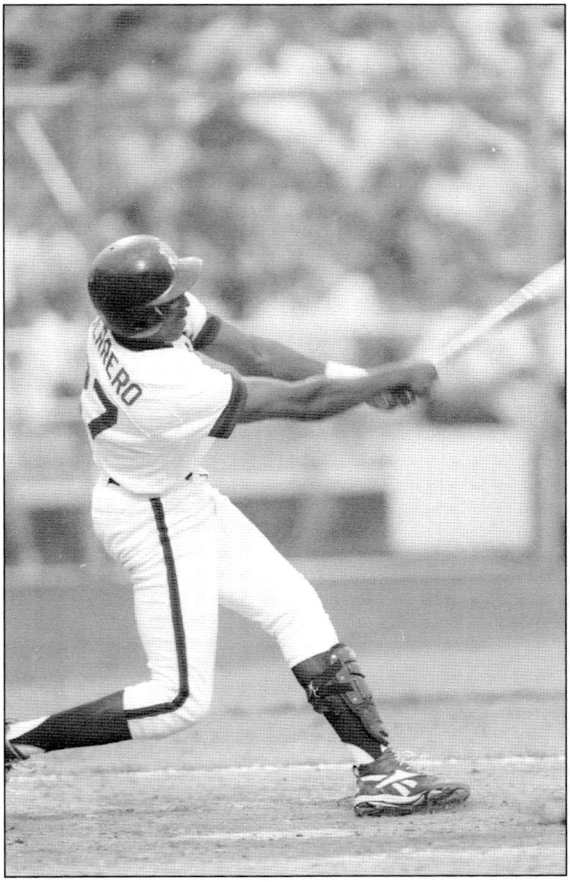

Vladimir Guerrero, known for his unorthodox approach to hitting, played for the Harrisburg Senators during the 1996 season and won the Eastern League Player of the Year award. He would go on to play 16 seasons in the major leagues with the Expos, Angels, Rangers, and Orioles, winning the American League MVP award in 2004. His career achievements include nine all-star appearances, a .318 batting average, and 449 home runs.

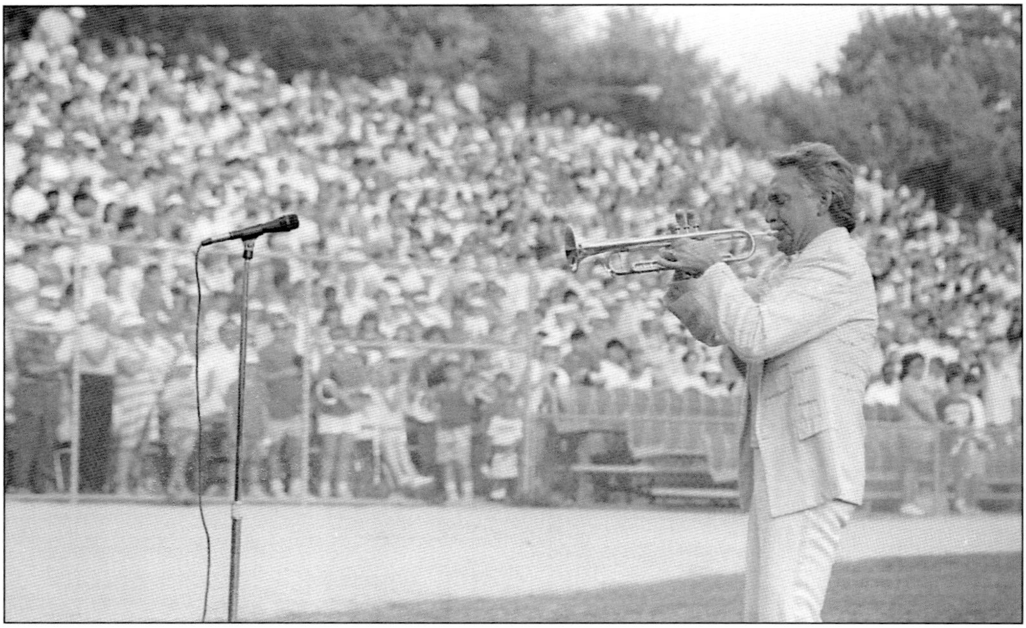

Doc Severinsen plays the national anthem before a seemingly sold-out crowd at RiverSide Stadium on August 15, 1988. Severinsen is most well known as the bandleader for the Tonight Show Band. He played with them for 30 years, from 1962 until Johnny Carson's retirement from the show in 1992.

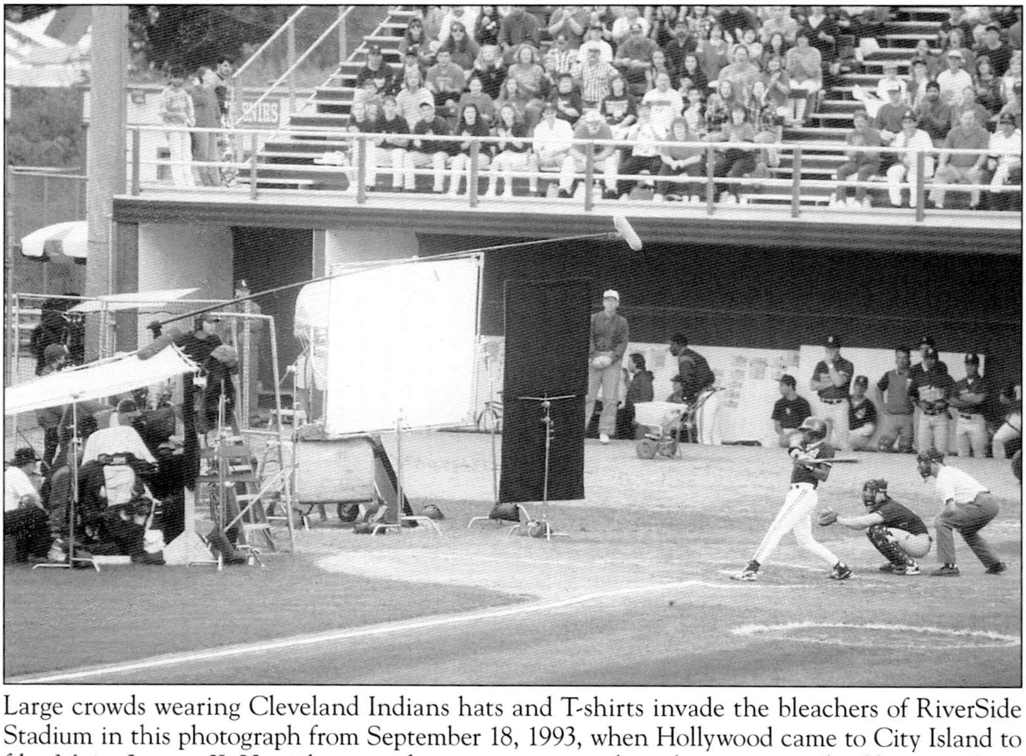

Large crowds wearing Cleveland Indians hats and T-shirts invade the bleachers of RiverSide Stadium in this photograph from September 18, 1993, when Hollywood came to City Island to film *Major League II*. Harrisburg residents were recruited to play extras in the film, mainly as spectators in the bleachers and to cheer on their temporary hometown Indians.

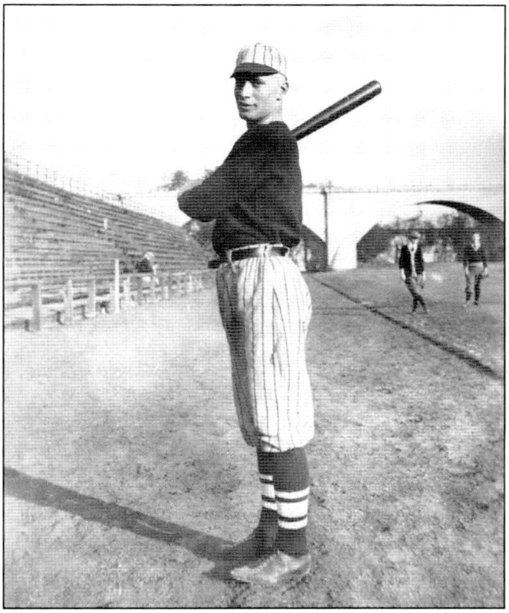
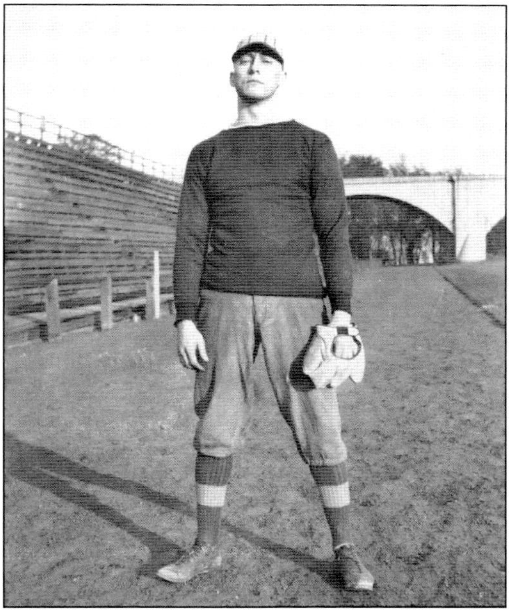

Amateur baseball thrived in Harrisburg during the early 20th century, and leagues abounded. The Zion Lutheran Men's Bible School team won the Sunday School League in 1922. At the Island playground field are "Biff" Gottshall (above right) and Ross Garber (above left). A scrapbook compiled by the Men's Bible Class at Zion Lutheran Church contains the following about Gottschall and Garber: "Gottshall at the bat, with three men on . . . the players are in suspense . . . Biff goes for a long drive and the game is over . . . Garb struck the first three men out who faced him in 1-2-3 order, about as quickly as it takes to tell it." A quote referring to pitcher George Balmer (below left) claims that "one particular ball that he pitches has whiskers on it which makes it impossible for the hitter to see." A quote about second baseman Lucian D. Wilson (below right) states that "everybody calls him lucky 'Luce' and when they do it means one less cigarette in the pack." (All, courtesy of Zion Lutheran Church.)

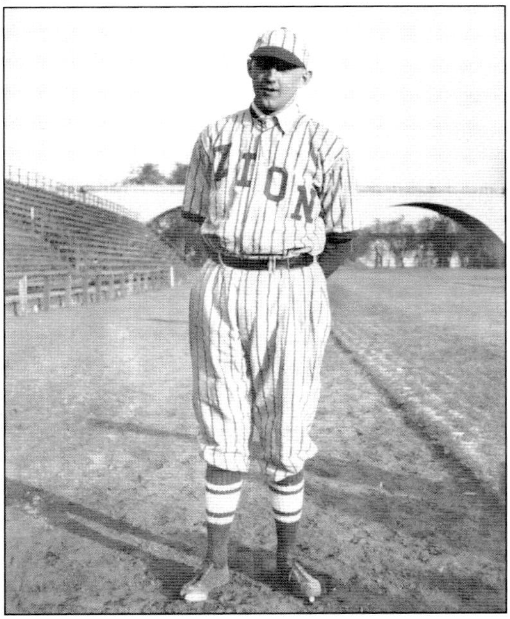

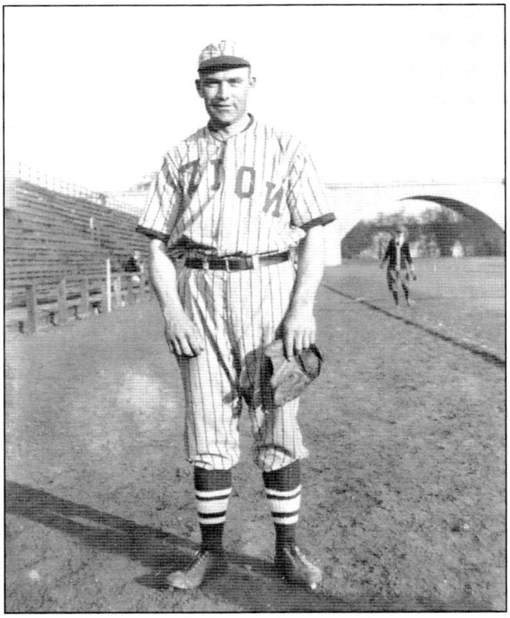

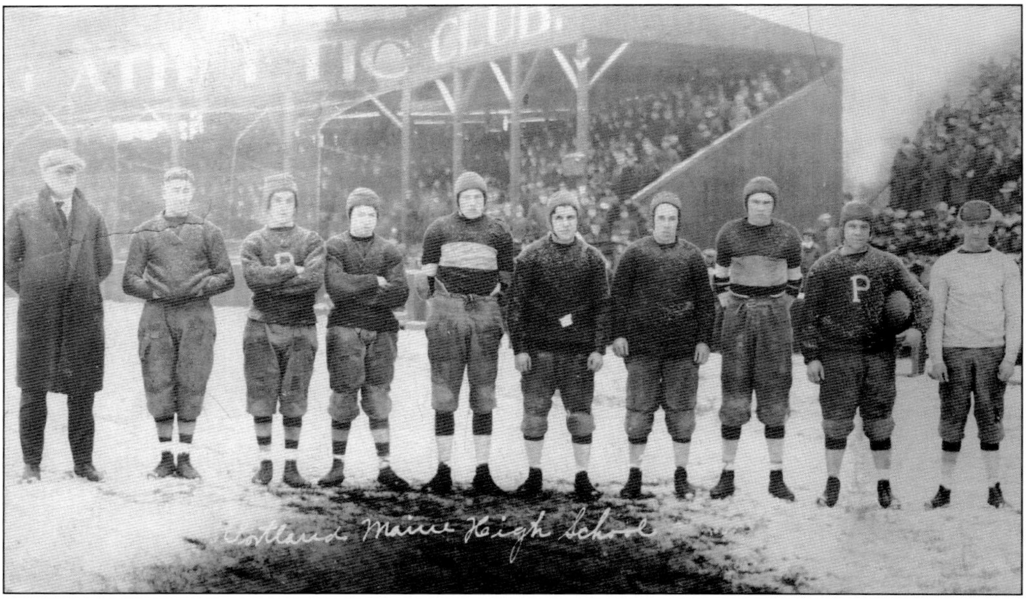


The football program at Technical High School of Harrisburg existed only from 1905 to 1925. At times, the program seemed doomed to fail from the start, as the highlight of its 1907 season was a 0-0 tie versus Marysville. The team failed to score a single point in that relatively short five-game season. However, by 1917 the team had become a Northeast powerhouse, including a 117-31 victory over Easton High School.

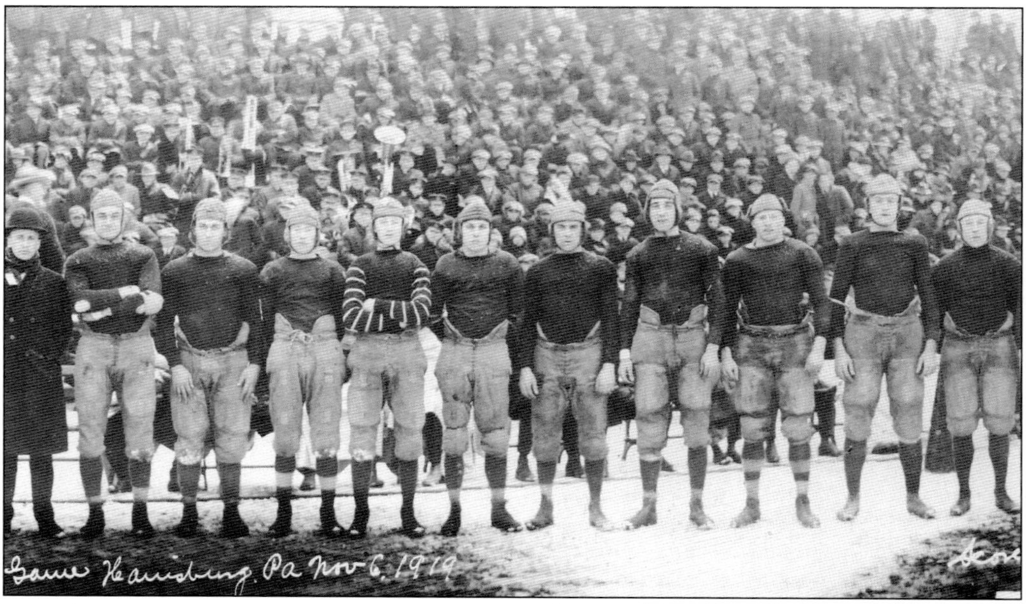


Later that year, the team began a 30-game win streak that ultimately ended in 1920 when it was defeated 20-7 by the freshman team of the University of Pittsburgh. During the undefeated run, the 1918 squad outscored its opponents 724-10 over the course of the 11-game season, which included a 76-7 beating of Johnstown High School for the state championship. The Technnical High School team was ultimately voted national champion.

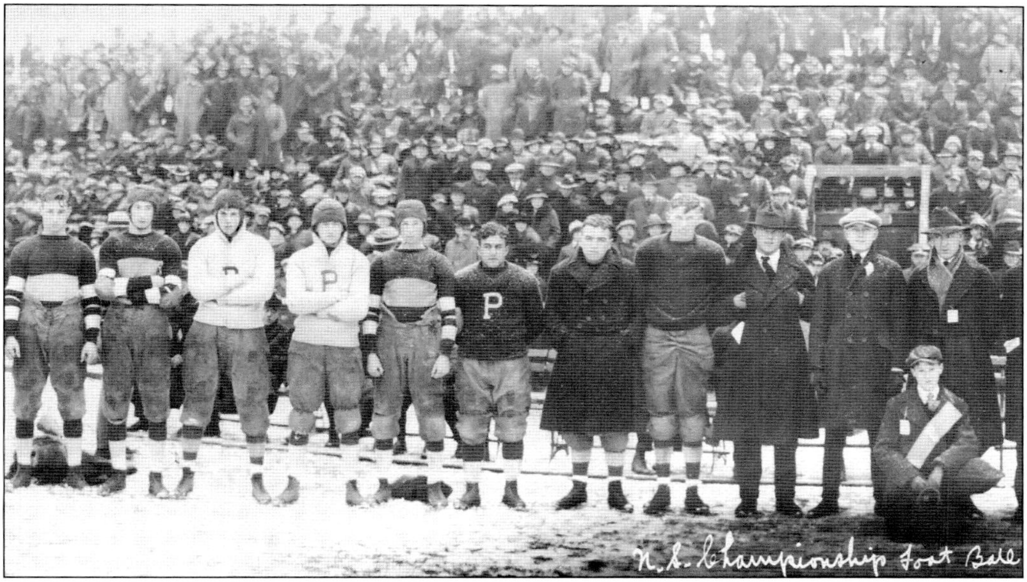


The 1919 Tech squad followed up a nearly flawless 1918 season with simply one of the greatest seasons ever put together by a football team on any level of competition. In 12 games, it outscored opponents by a combined score of 701-0. A second consecutive national championship season was capped by a 56-0 thorough beating of the visiting Portland Maine squad at Island Park Stadium on December 6, 1919.

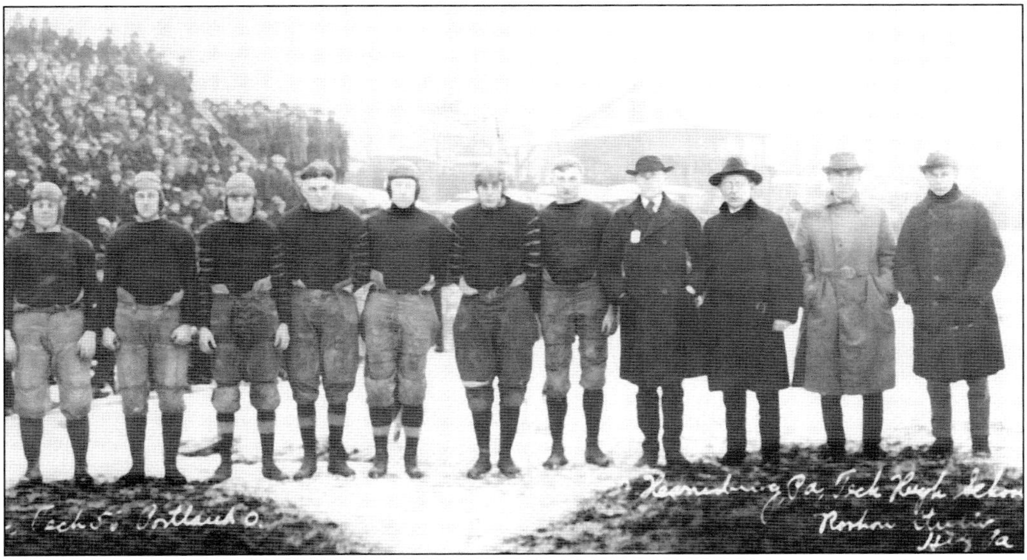


The star player of the squad was Carl Beck, seen third from right on the bottom of the previous page. Beck was a star three-sport athlete and drew comparisons to Jim Thorpe. Beck would go on to play college football at West Virginia and Vermont before playing professionally for Altoona, Trenton, and the New York Giants. Note that the photograph incorrectly gives a November 6 date for the game.

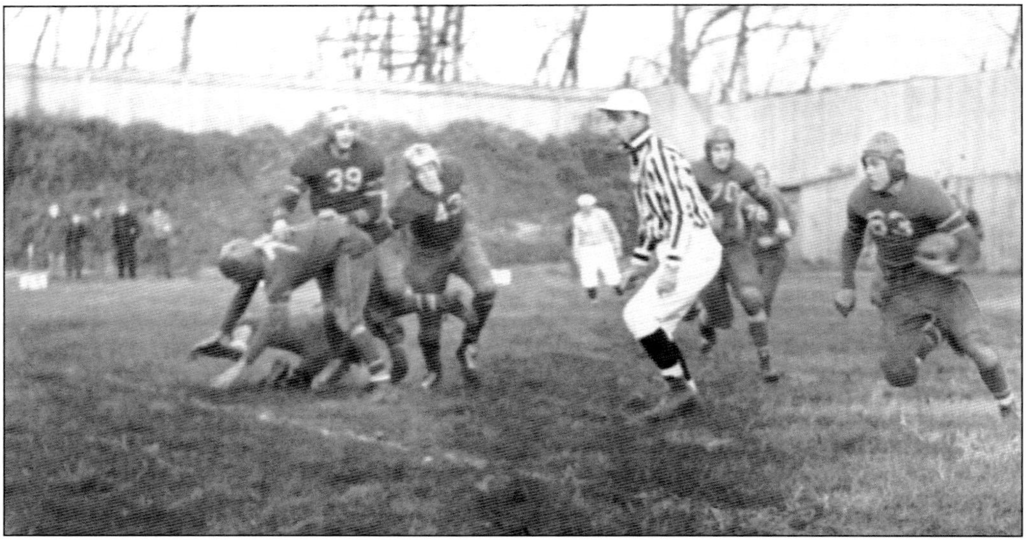

Pictured here are two views of a high school football game played on November 23, 1946, at Island Park between Lower Paxton and Susquehanna Township High Schools. The Susquehanna Township team, wearing gold helmets, would win the contest 13-0. Lower Paxton High School played its home games at Island Park during the 1940s, many of which were night games, against other local high school teams such as Lemoyne, New Cumberland, Hummelstown, Susquehanna Township, and Duncannon. The Island Park field also served as the site for the annual Thanksgiving Day game between John Harris and William Penn High Schools to determine Harrisburg's football supremacy.

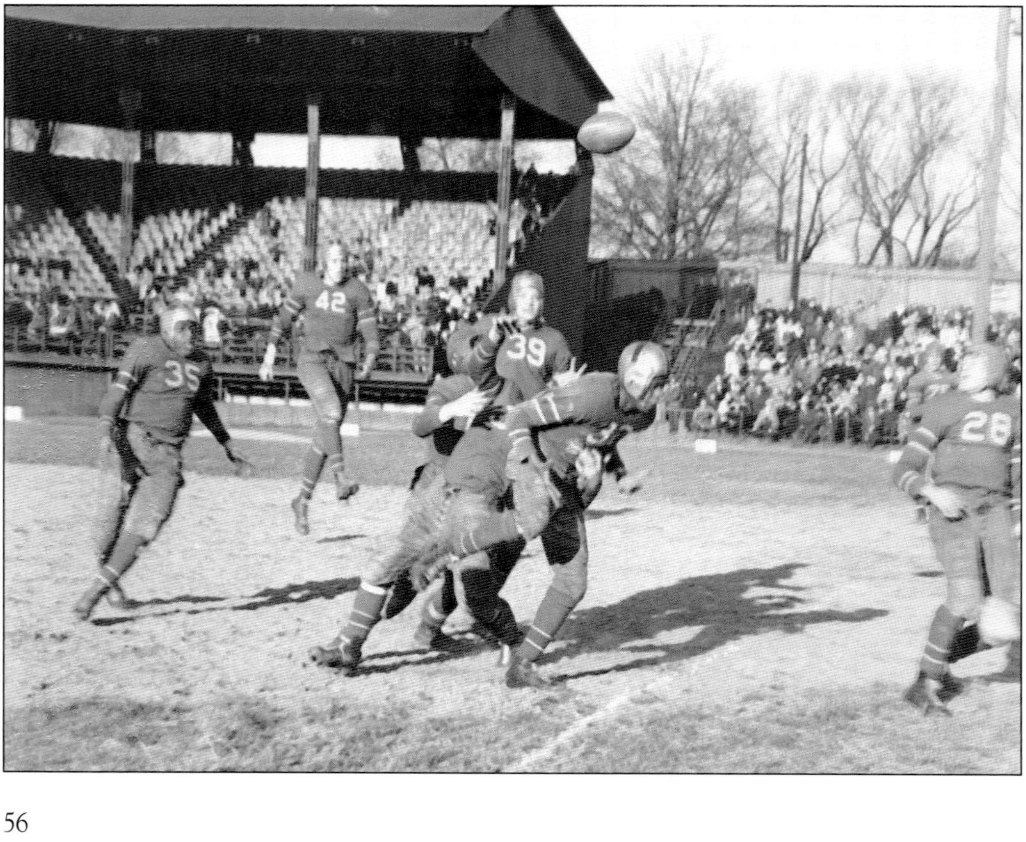

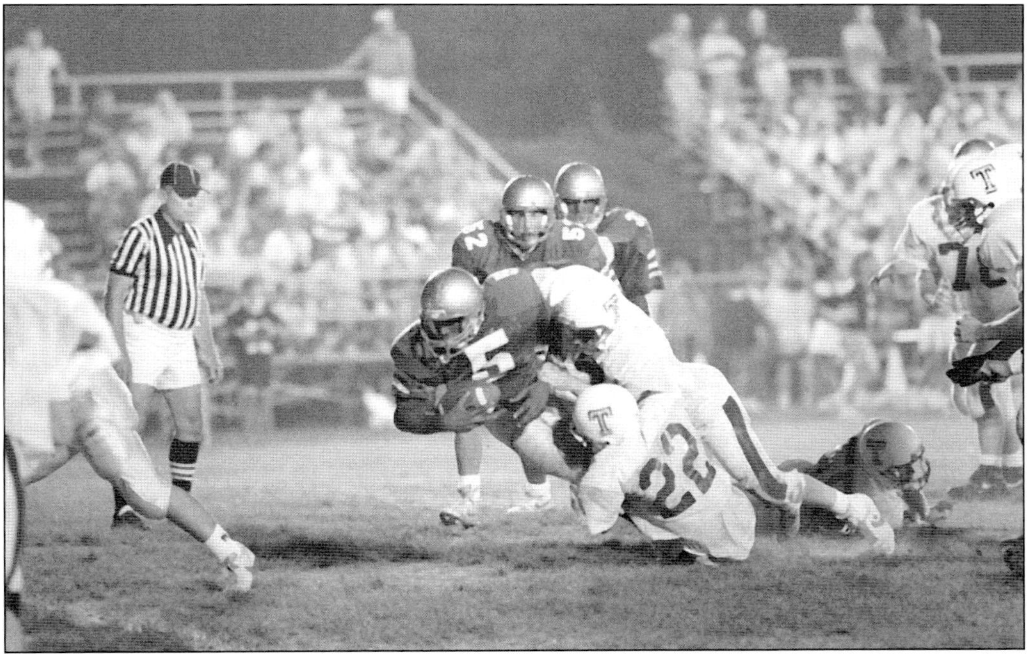

Bishop McDevitt running back Dwight Henry is brought down by two Trinity High School defenders at a game played on September 6, 1990, at the Skyline Sports Complex, the former site of the old city filtration plant on City Island. Bishop McDevitt would go on to win the game by a score of 28-14.

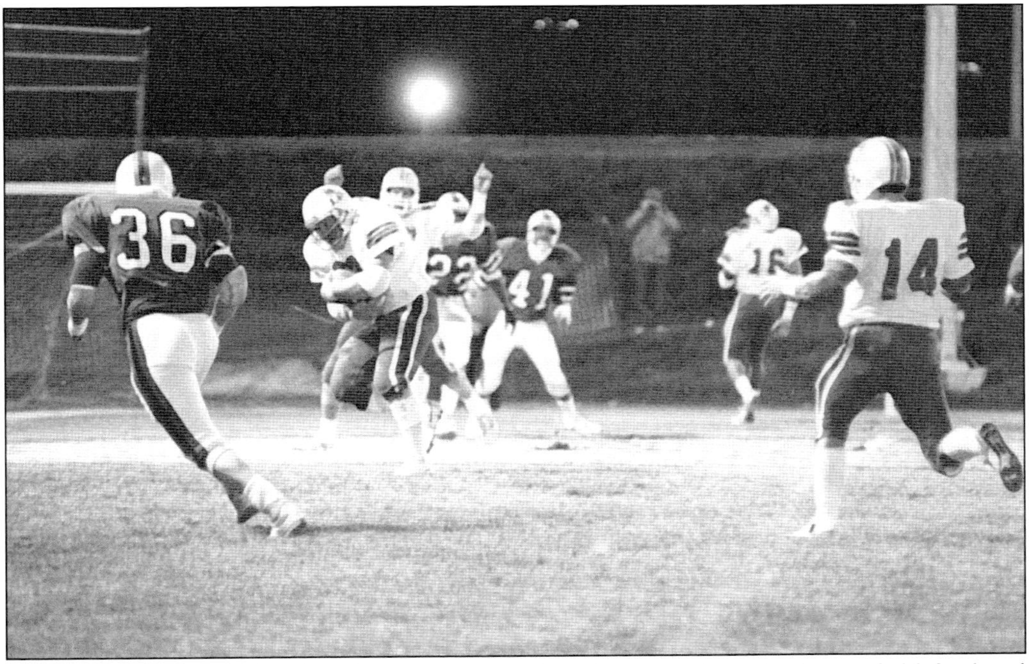

During the 1980s and 1990s, Skyline Sports Complex served as the home field for local semiprofessional football teams such as the Harrisburg Patriots and later the Piranhas. Here the Patriots take on Frederick in the championship game in the Continental Interstate Championship League on December 3, 1988. Frederick would ultimately win the contest by a score of 24-14.

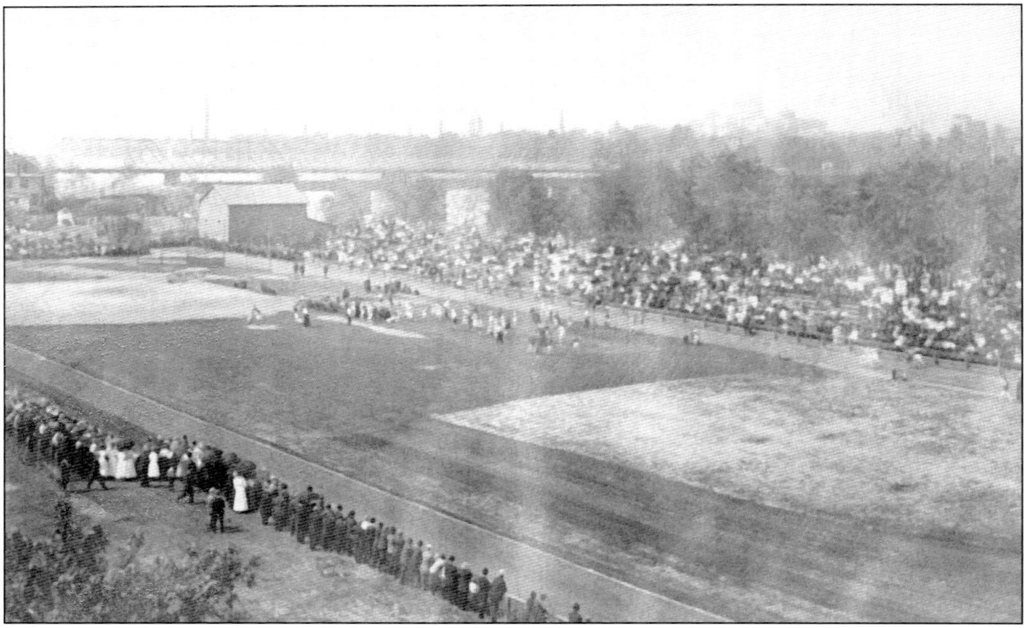

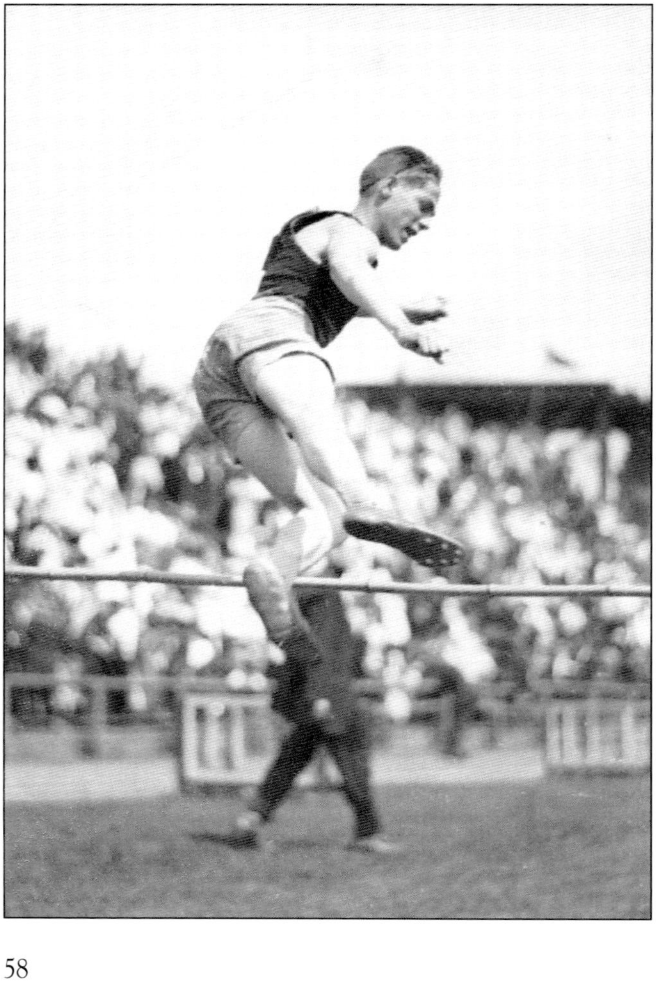

The Island Playground track, completed in May 1906, was a quarter-mile cinder track that was asymmetrical in shape in order to fit within the available space on the island. The turn at the southern end had to be laid out around a pier of the Cumberland Valley Railroad Bridge to keep the length of the track at a quarter mile. In 1908, the main bleachers on the track's front stretch were installed and had a seating capacity of 2,900, which allowed for total crowds of over 4,000 to view the events at the track. In the image at left, a contestant leaps over the bamboo crossbar during the high jump competition, around 1908. Jim Thorpe set the island record for the event in 1908 with a jump of six feet.

In 1906, when the Island Playground track was newly completed, it consisted of a loose cinder base that was 2.5 inches deep. The cinders were brought from the pumping station of the Harrisburg Water Department on Front Street and were derived from the remnants of the river coal that was burned at the plant.

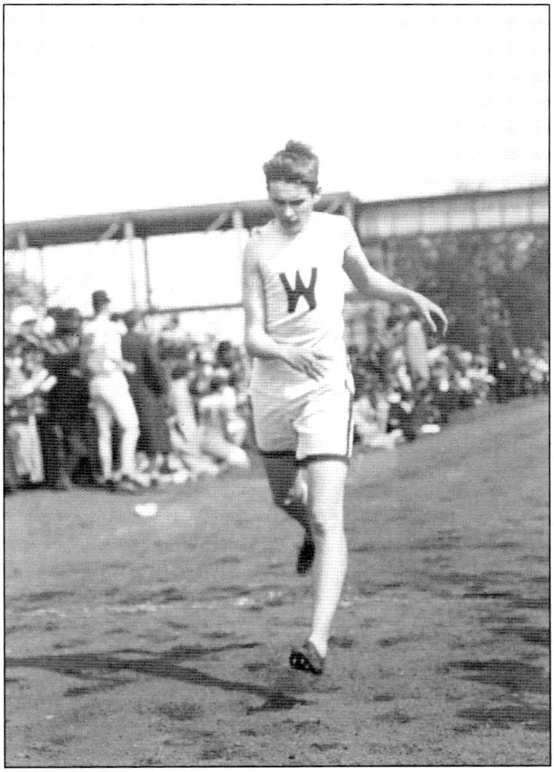

In this image, a contestant clears the crossbar during the pole-vaulting event at an Island Park track meet, about 1908. In 1908, a height of 11 feet was cleared by Charles Mitchell of the Carlisle Indian School to set an island and school record in the event.

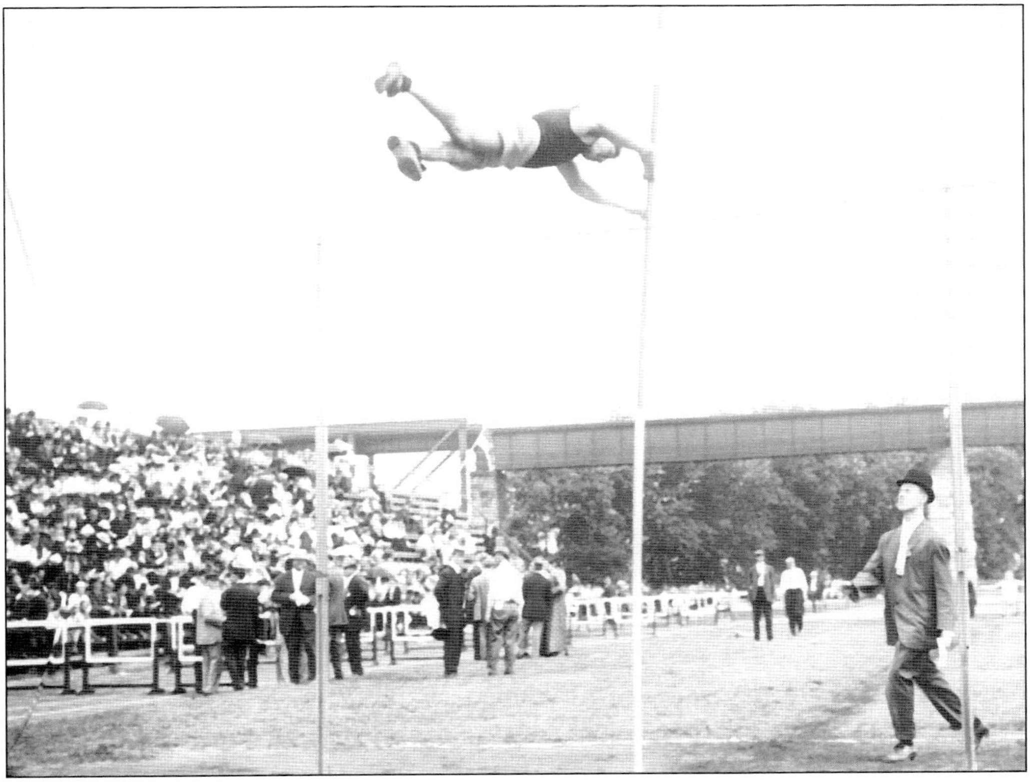

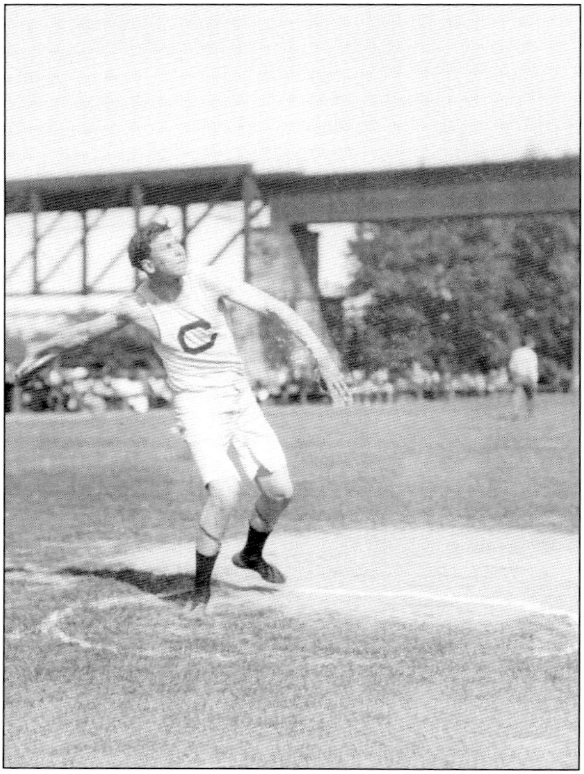

In this image from about 1908, an unnamed competitor winds up to throw the discus at an Island Park track competition. Devoid of modern facilities at the new track and field complex, the competitors at the early meets were obliged to use the barn that stood adjacent to the track as a locker room.

The 1908 Harrisburg Technical School Track team is pictured here at the Island Park track. The team includes, from left to right, (first row) ? Kauffman, Jeff Hargest, and Howard Stewart; (second row) Roy Howard, Robert Karle, Howard Brine, and Fred Payne; (third row) Dave McConnell, ? Long, Paul Bitner, Leroy Young, ? Shisler, ? Hemperly, and ? McPherson.

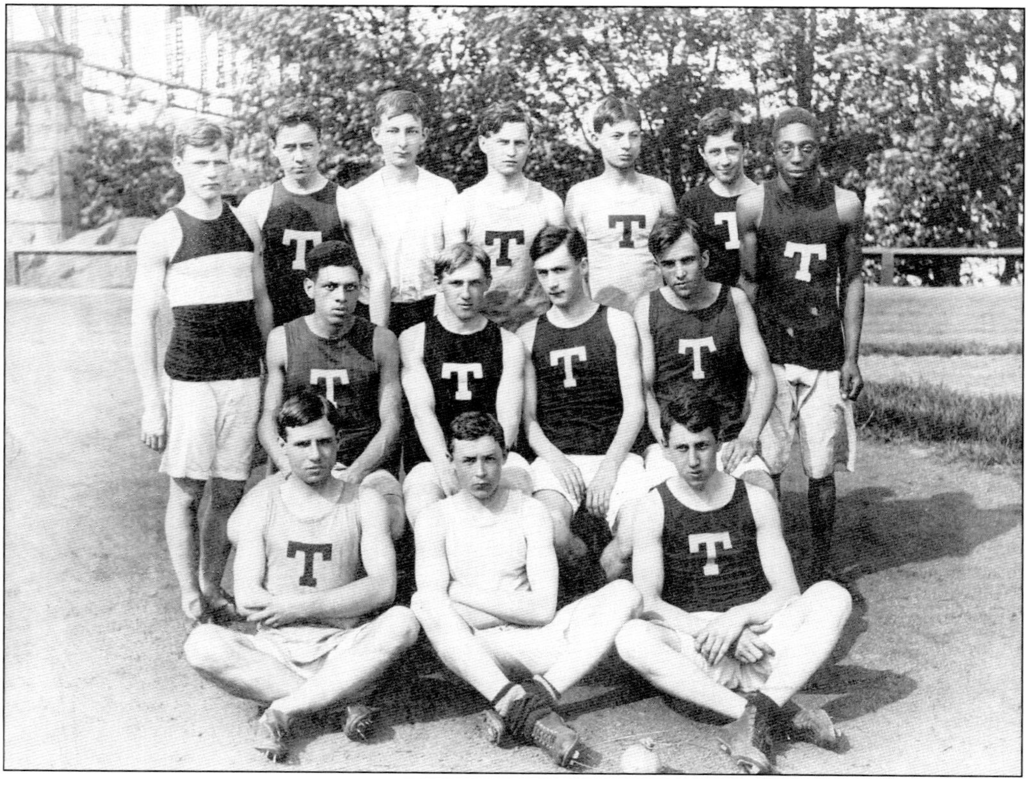

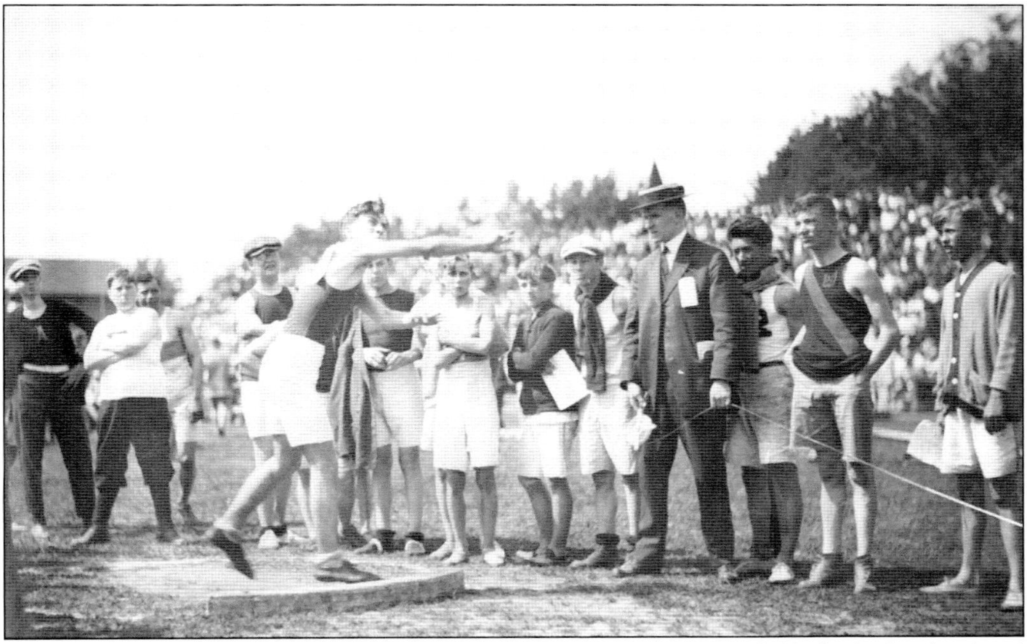

In addition to the track-and-field meets held at the Island Playground fields for high school and college athletes, the site was also used for annual meets to showcase the talents of boys from the city grammar schools and the city playgrounds. As seen in these two photographs from around 1915, these younger athletes were given a chance to perform on the island's big stage. The competitions at city playground meets divided the boys into weight classes of for each event. Lightweights had to be less than 75 pounds, middleweights were between 75 and 90 pounds, and the heavyweights were over 90 pounds. In addition, all entrants for the city park meet had to be less than 16 years of age. The playground meet began in 1908 and was dominated in the early years by the team from the Sycamore playground.

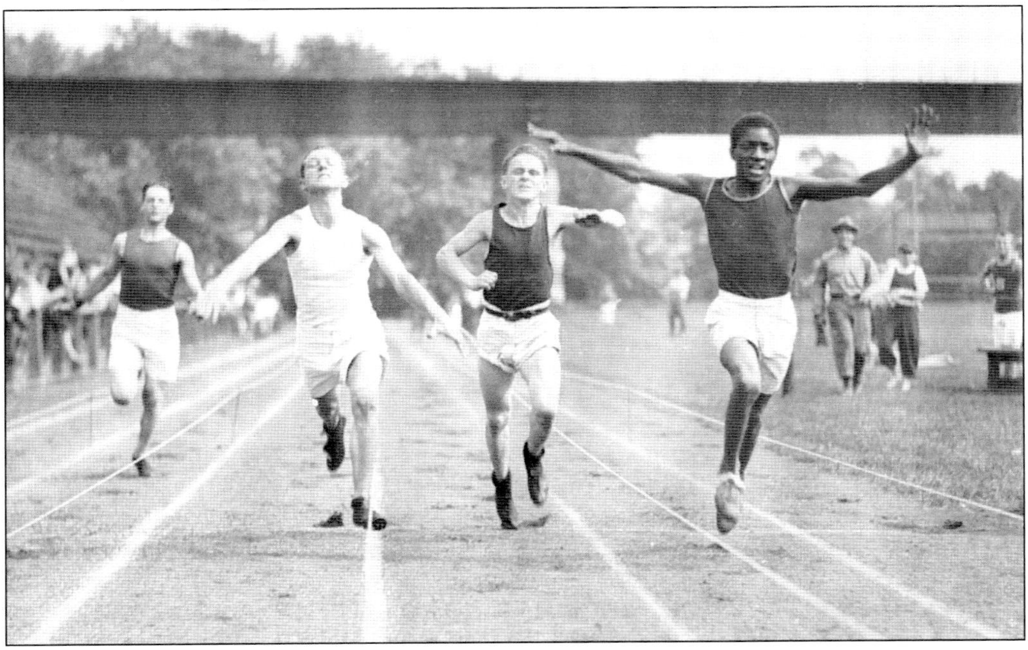

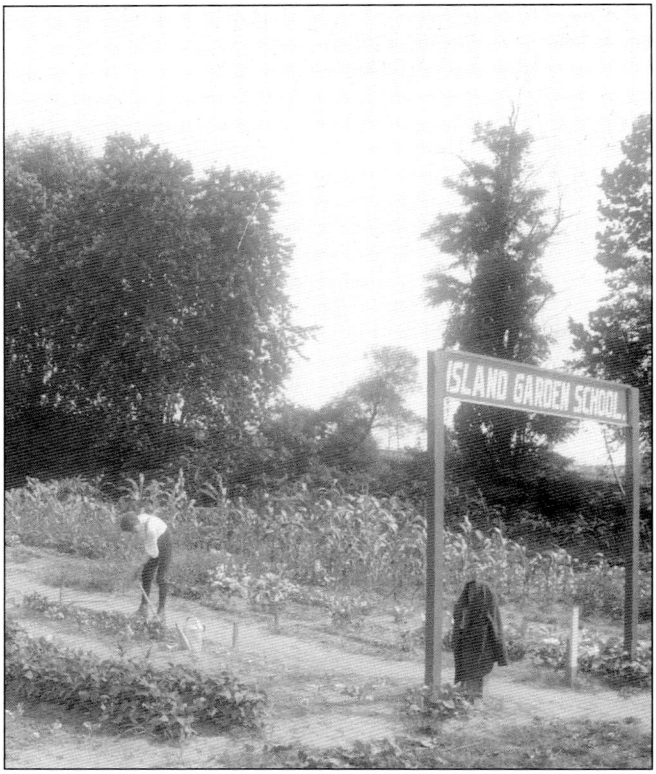


The Garden School was a program introduced by the Harrisburg Civic Club where children could tend to a small plot of land for free or with minimal cost to cover the purchase of seeds. Seen here, the Garden School was held on Island Park during 1906 and 1907 on a plot of land located between the Market and Walnut Street Bridges. There were 104 plots of land measuring 10 by 15 feet offered to the children for use. While the plots were free to use, the children had to pay the bridge tolls each day to visit the island school. As a result, only 60 plots were utilized throughout the season. In later years, the garden school relocated to a four-acre plot between Second and Third Streets, a short distance above Senaca Street.

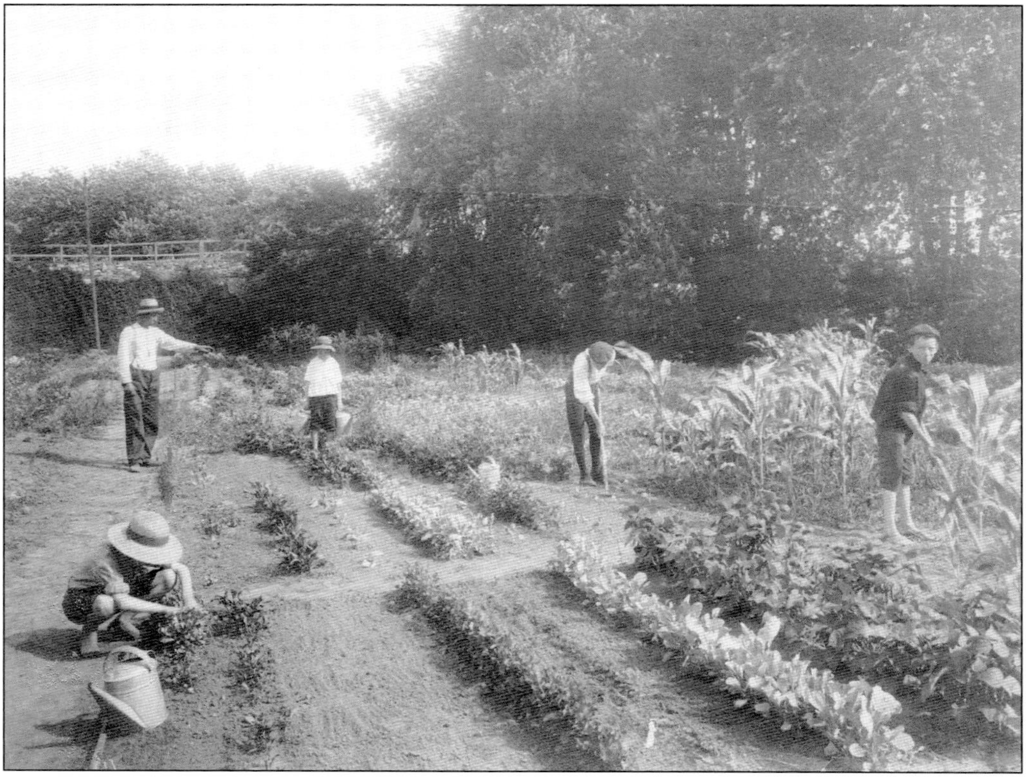

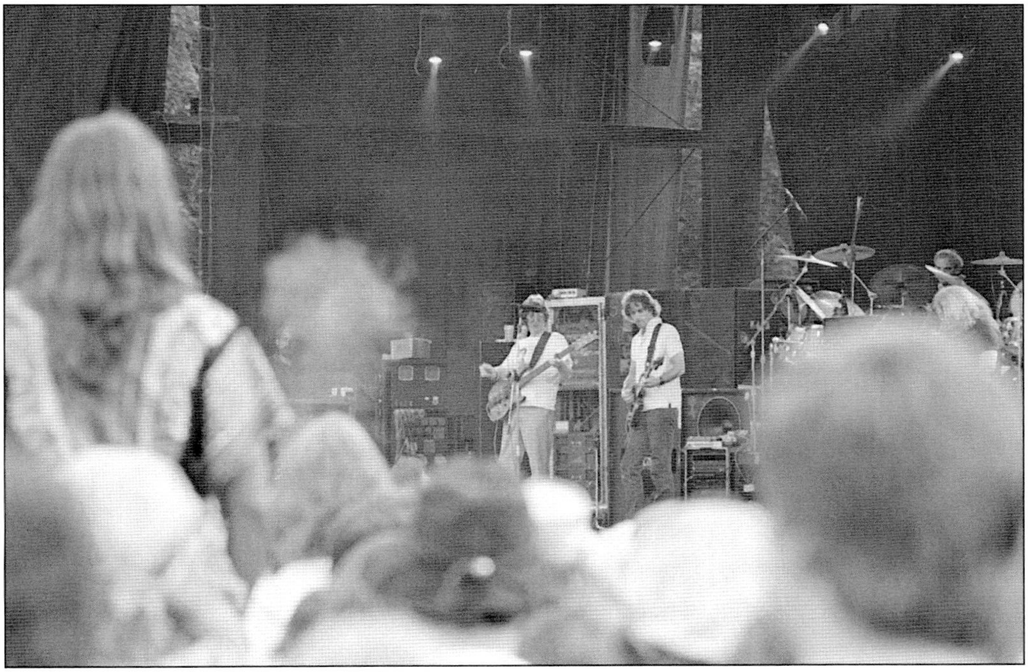

Above, Phil Lesh (left), Bob Weir (center), and Jerry Garcia (partially obscured at right) of the Grateful Dead can be seen performing through the crowd and smoky haze of City Island on June 22, 1984. Jerry Garcia, partially obscured, is seen at right. During the summer months of 1983 and 1984, national acts such as the Grateful Dead, the Beach Boys, Judas Priest, the Cars, Blue Oyster Cult, and Def Leppard performed on the old baseball field grounds on City Island. The concerts were eventually stopped due to complaints of excessive noise and what was perceived as general rowdiness. The concerts would be revived in 1989 at the Skyline Sports Complex, where Kiss, Metallica, Bob Dylan, Willie Nelson, and Public Enemy, to name a few, played through 1990, when the shows were largely stopped for the same reasons as in the past.

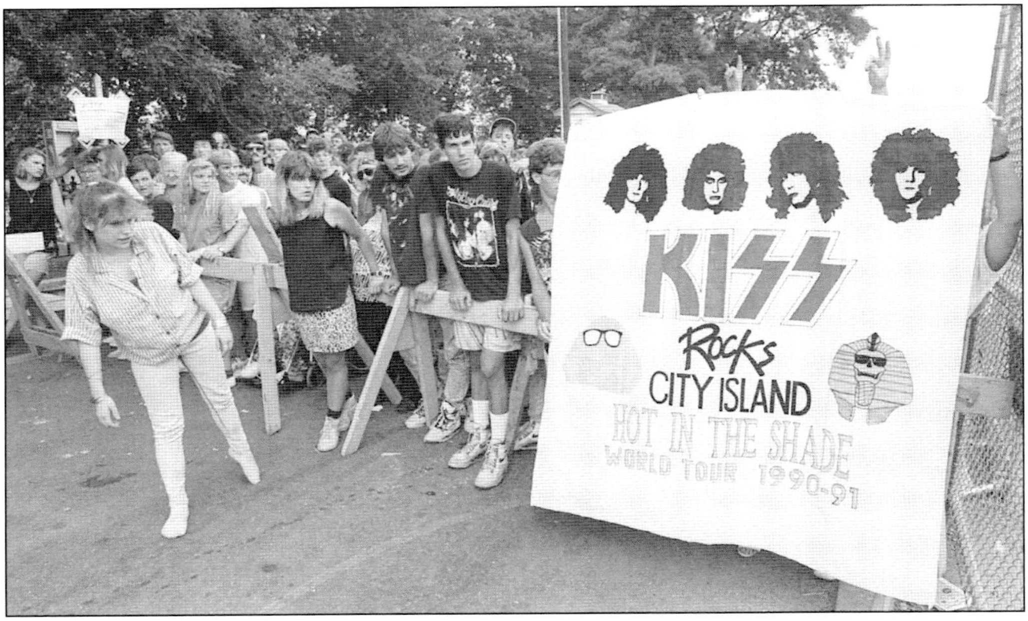

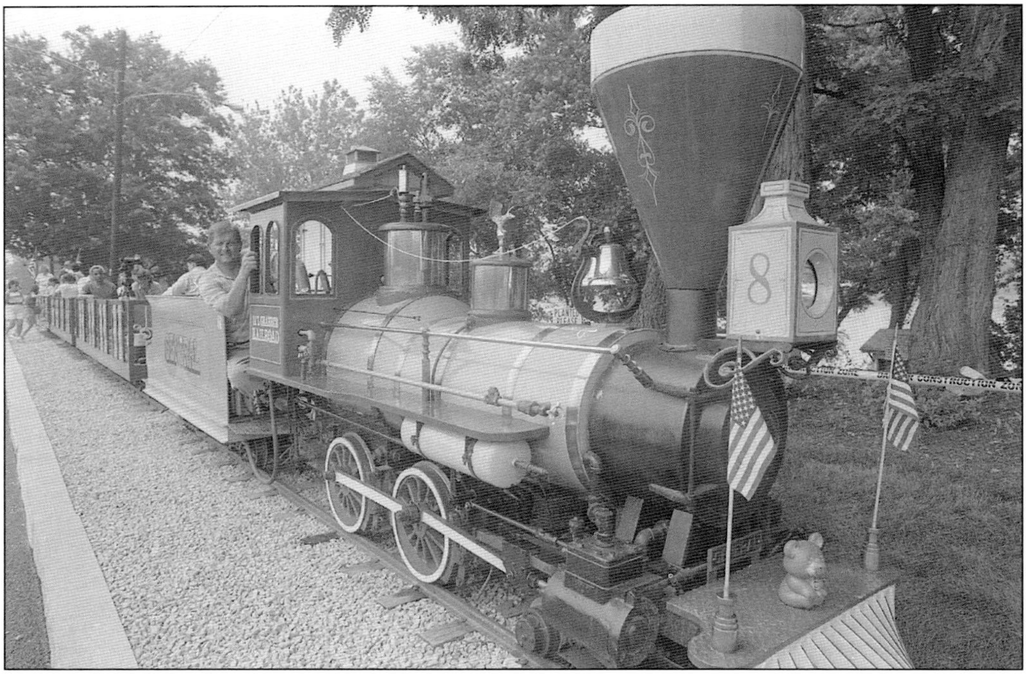

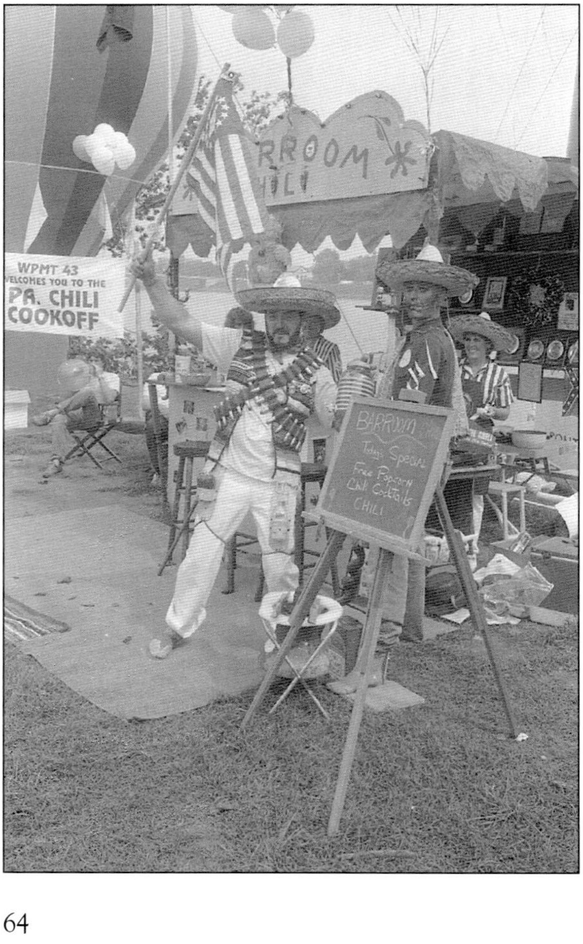


Part of the revitalization of City Island was to reimagine the grounds as an entertainment complex with broad appeal for kids and adults. On June 27, 1989, the Li'l Grabber Railroad made its first test run on the eight-tenths-of-a-mile track that runs around City Island. Piloted by owner Mike Trephan, the small engine is a scale replica of *The General*, a Civil War–era steam engine. Also during this time, the Riverside Village Park was constructed, beach volleyball courts were installed, and the island played host to a diverse array of events including the Bentley Brothers Circus and the annual Chili Cook-Off competition.

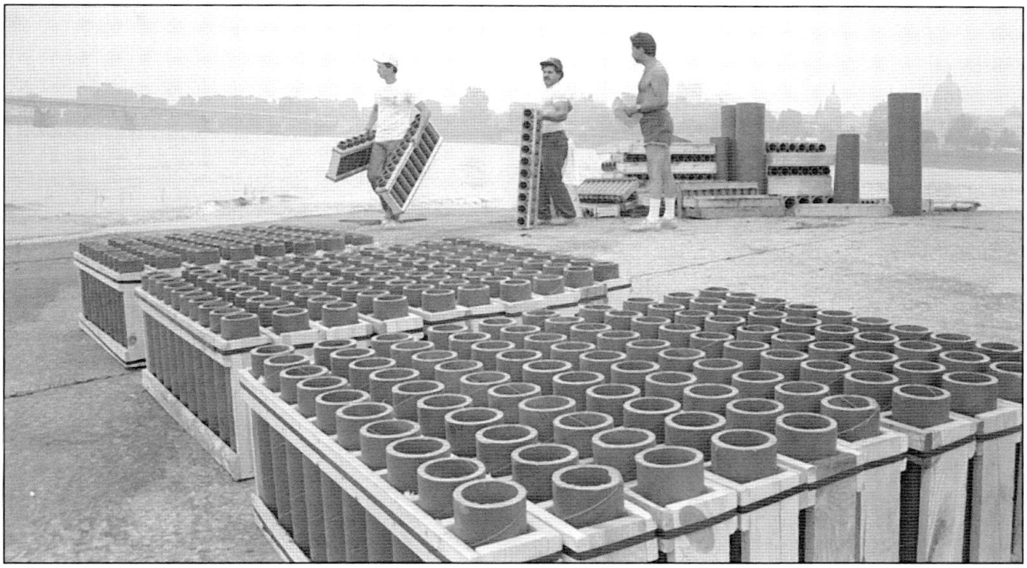

In the image above, Gino Volpe (right), of the Zambelli fireworks company, oversees the setup of the 300 tubes holding the pyrotechnics to be set off during the July 4, 1989, celebration on City Island. Fireworks displays have been a staple of celebrations in Harrisburg dating back 200 years. Historian William A. Kelker recounted how on December 8, 1814, fireworks were set off from the then unfinished piers of the Camelback Bridge in honor of the men returning from service in the War of 1812.

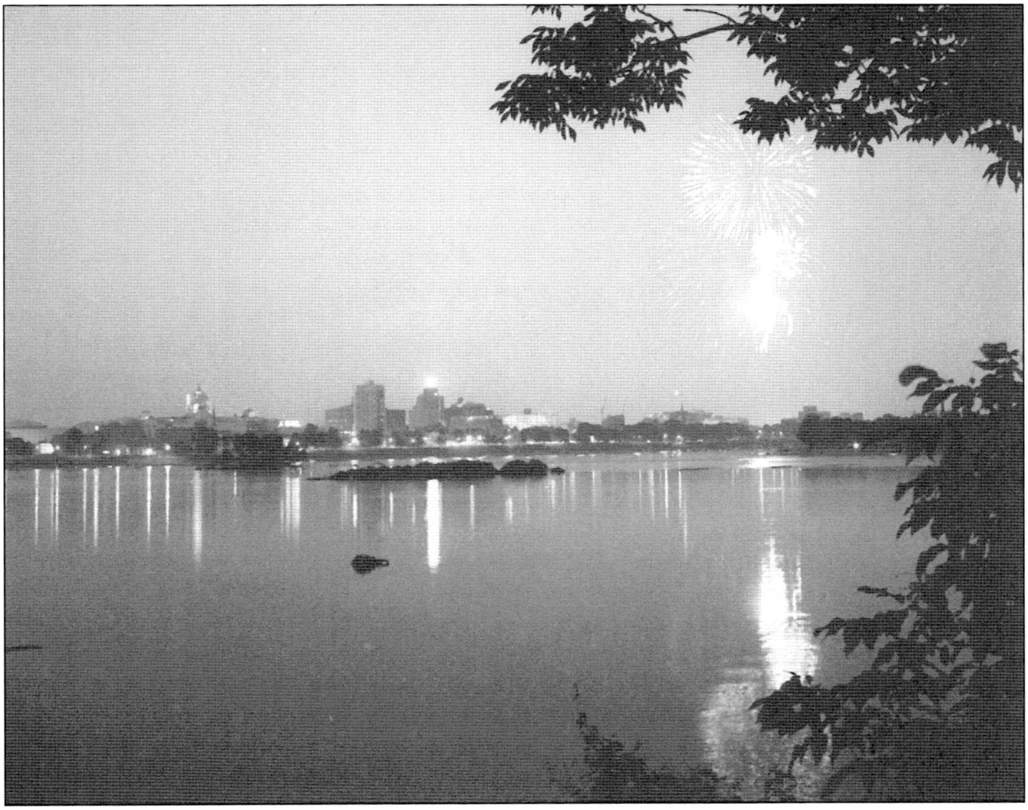

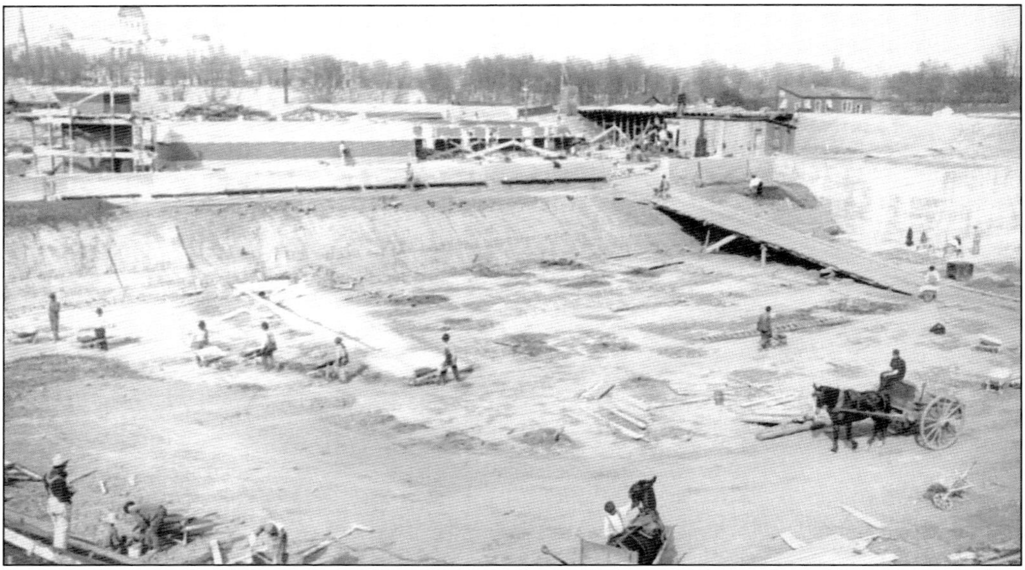

Construction of the Filtration Plant, which included the excavation of the sedimentation basin as seen here, began in the summer of 1904 on the northern end of Island Park. The Filtration Plant became operational by October 1905 with the capability of providing 12 million gallons of clean, filtered water daily under normal conditions. The plant operated by drawing in water from the river through an intake pipe on the eastern side of the island. The water was brought into the sedimentation basin (seen below), where sediment was filtered out of the water. The water was then processed through a series of filters before being pumped across the river to the pumping station and from there out to the reservoir at Reservoir Park. The plant remained operation until 1972 when it was damaged from the flooding from Tropical Storm Agnes.

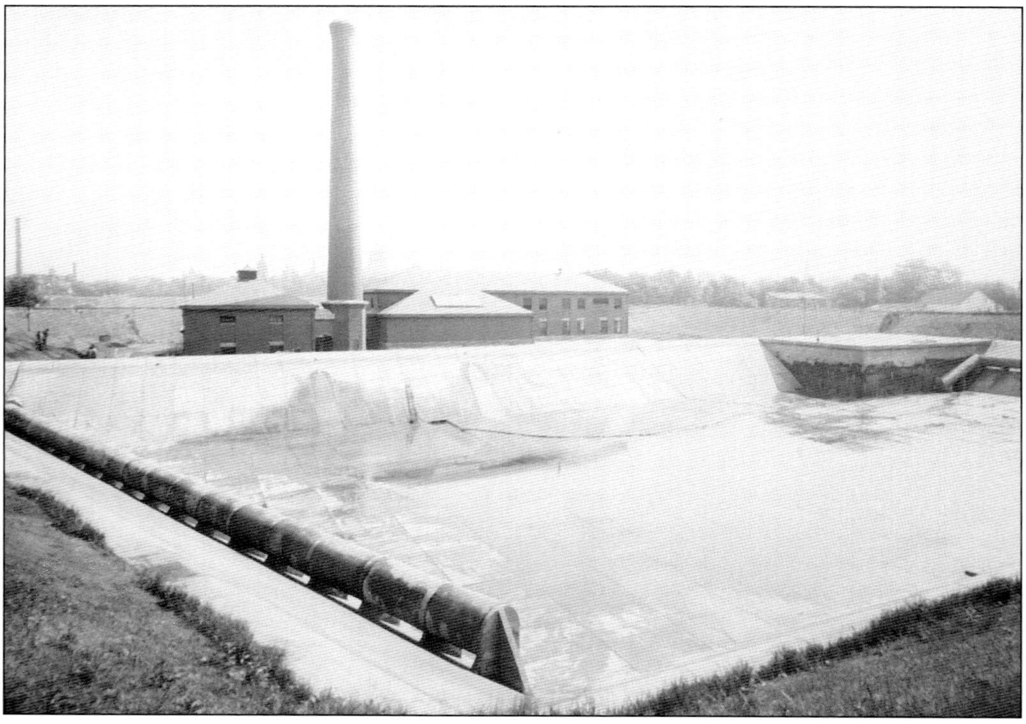

# *Four*

# The River Beautiful

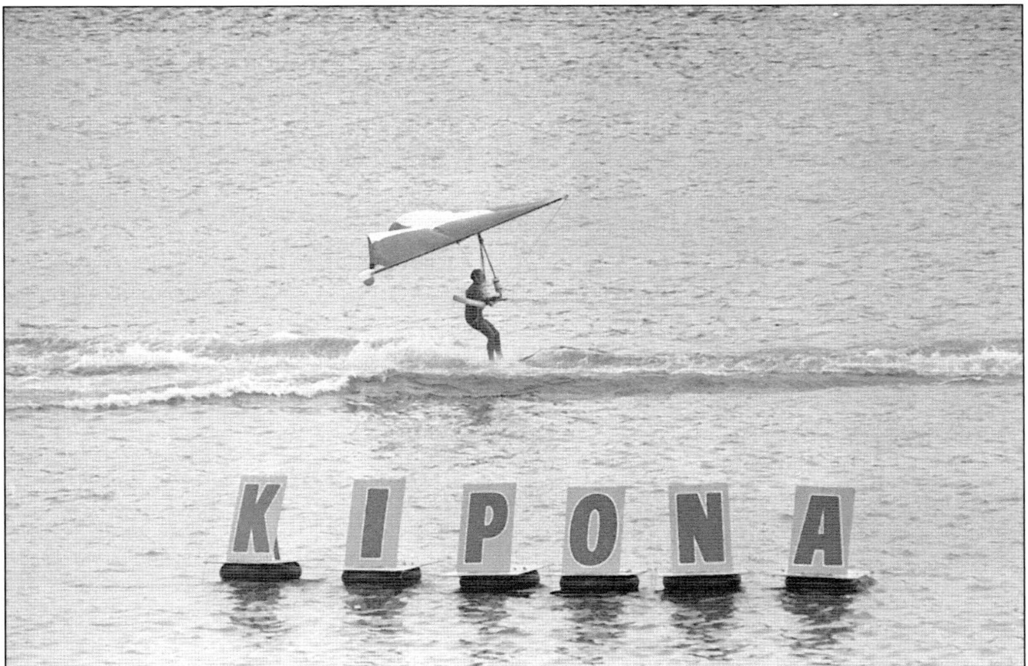


During the 19th century, the Susquehanna River became a force of nature to be conquered and exploited for its resources. Raw materials were dredged from its shallow depths, and raw sewage was dumped into its currents. By the dawn of the 20th century, a movement began to look at the river as a source of beauty and a destination designed to keep the local residents, and their money, at home. Here, during 1972 Kipona festivities, Dick Myers from Conestoga Marine is on the Susquehanna in his delta wing hang glider.

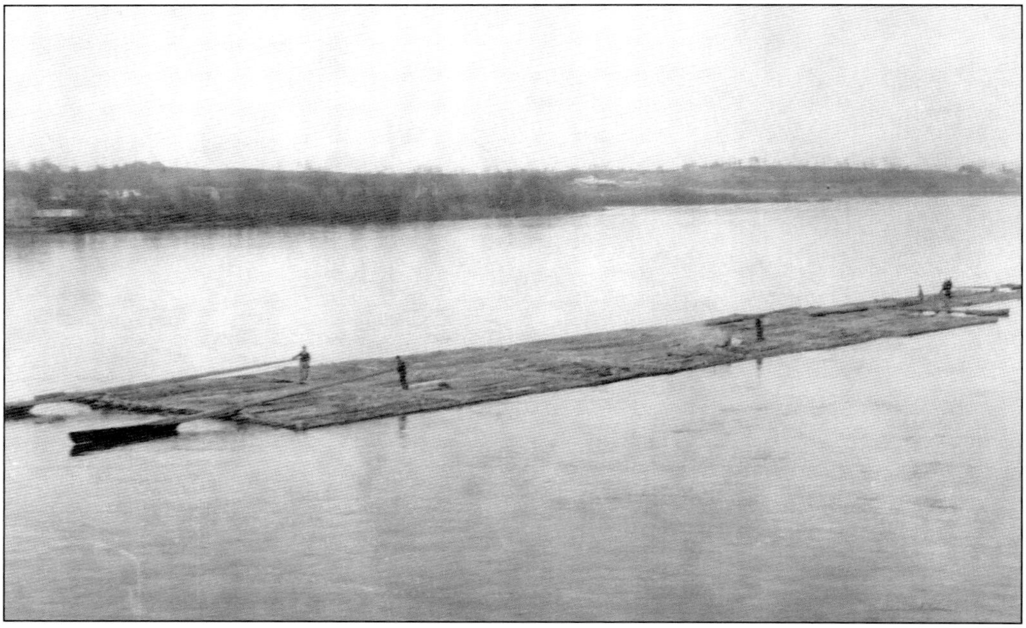

The Susquehanna River, given the right conditions, provided an economical means of transporting lumber and other goods to market by means of rafts. Prior to the proliferation of railroads, it would not have been uncommon to see large numbers of vessels floating down the river in the springtime to destinations of Harrisburg or other points south. One account from April 1841 estimated that 300 rafts passed the Camelback Bridge in one day. However, these rafts did not travel on the river without a small measure of peril. The raftsmen were often subject to torment from local youths who would rain stones down on them as they slowly drifted by on the river's currents or raid their caches of goods when they left their docked rafts in search of prospective buyers for their wares.

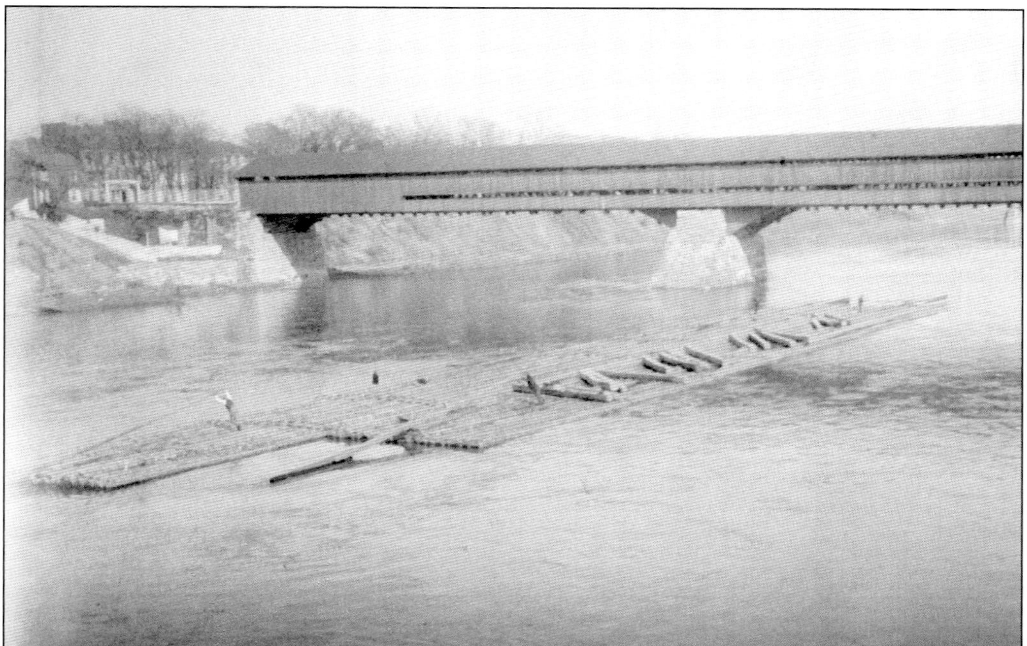

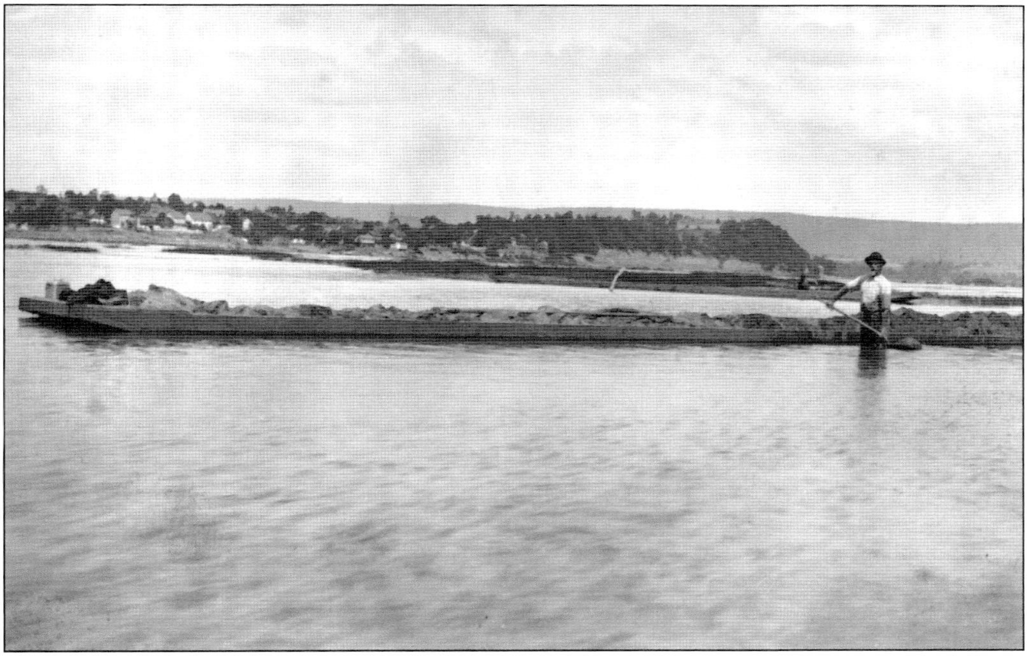

In the photograph above, men load river sand by hand onto flat-bottomed boats in the shallows of the river opposite West Fairview. These men were often referred to as "sand-flatters" and would extract sand from the river's bottom that was deposited there from upstream sources by the swiftly moving currents. This manual method of extracting sand was replaced in the late 19th century by siphon extraction, which yielded a more streamlined, less labor-intensive process. As seen in the photograph below, the sand was then deposited at a location at the base of Forster Street, where it was carried by wagon from the river's banks. The river sand provided a necessary construction material that was used widely in city building projects, including the current state capitol that was dedicated in 1906.

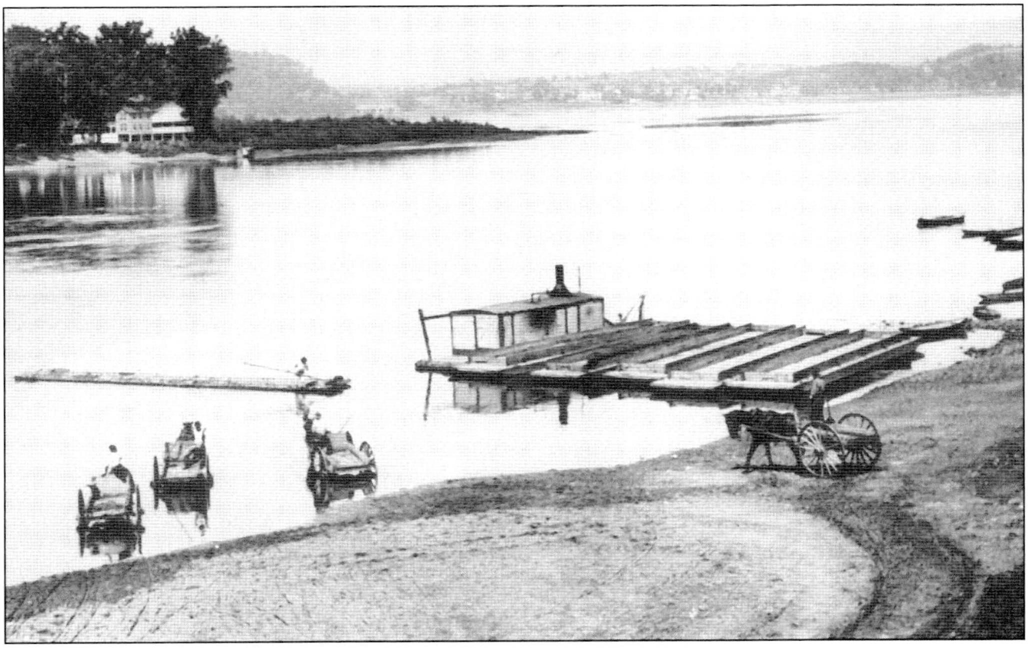

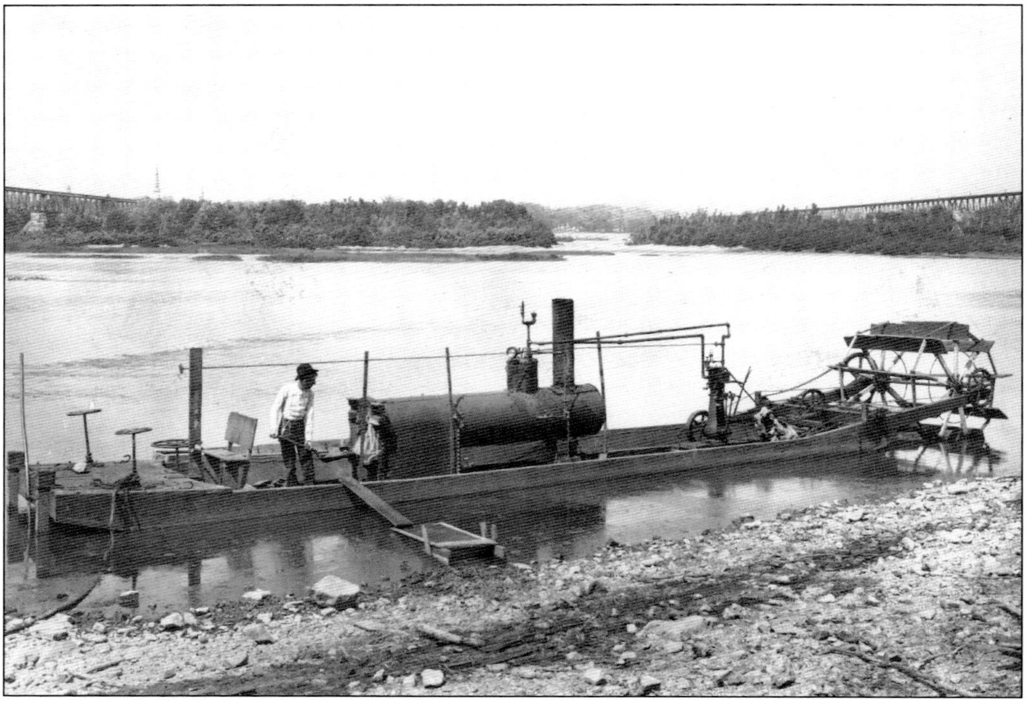

The image above captures a coal-powered steamboat along the western shore of the Susquehanna, between the Cumberland Valley and Philadelphia & Reading Railroad Bridges, about 1900. These types of boats were instrumental in obtaining river coal from the Susquehanna. River coal was coal that washed downstream as far as 100 miles during floods and high waters from the coal breakers at Nanticoke, Plymouth, and Shickshinny. This waste coal introduced a new industry to communities downstream. By 1918, an estimated 100,000 tons were dredged annually. Four years later, an estimated 247,000 tons were extracted from the river. The image below shows the increasing number of barges that began to favor the more profitable loads of coal over sand.

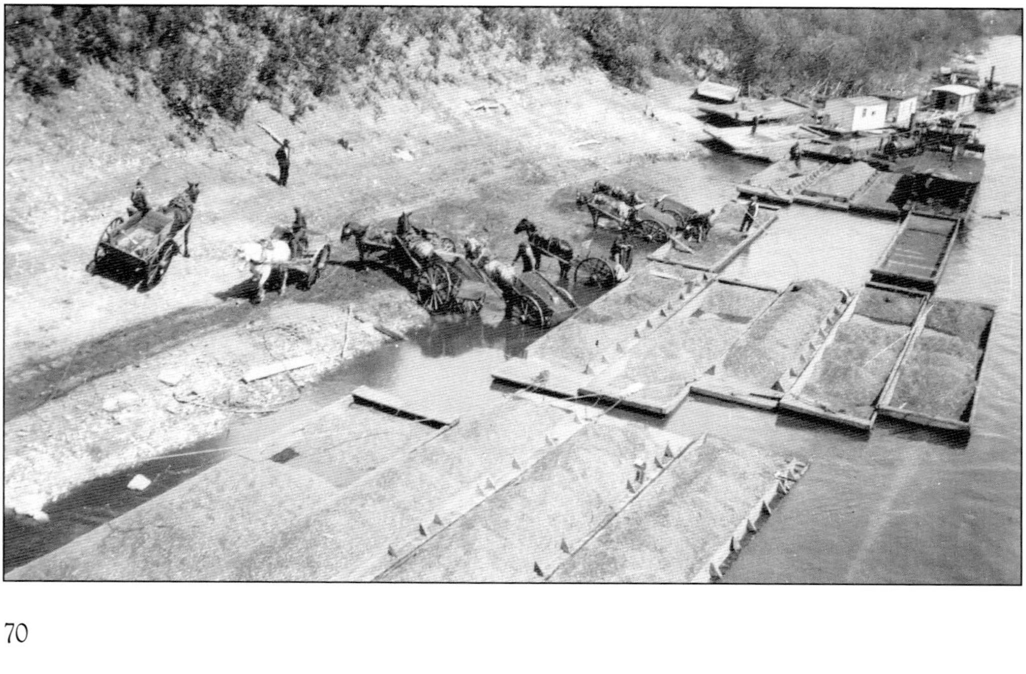

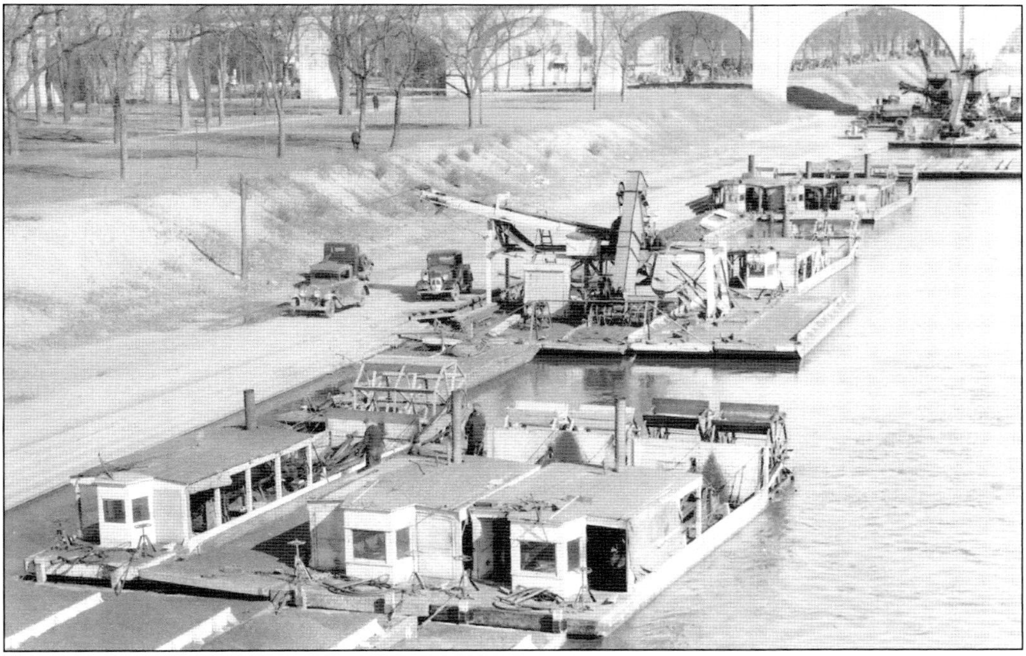

The above and below images show the coal barges along the riverfront during the 1930s and 1940s. During this time, river coal operations were no longer handled by sand-flatters, as the profitability of the industry brought in corporate entities such as Central Construction Corporation, which set up its barges and trucks along the riverfront at Harris Park. This location provided better access to the riverfront for unloading the coal barges, but it also drew the ire of groups such as the Harrisburg Civic Club, which felt the coal company's operations spoiled the beauty of the riverfront. However, the ultimate end to dredging river coal was not due to public pressure, but rather state legislation that prohibited disposing of industrial waste, such as the river coal from anthracite mining operations, in the rivers and streams.

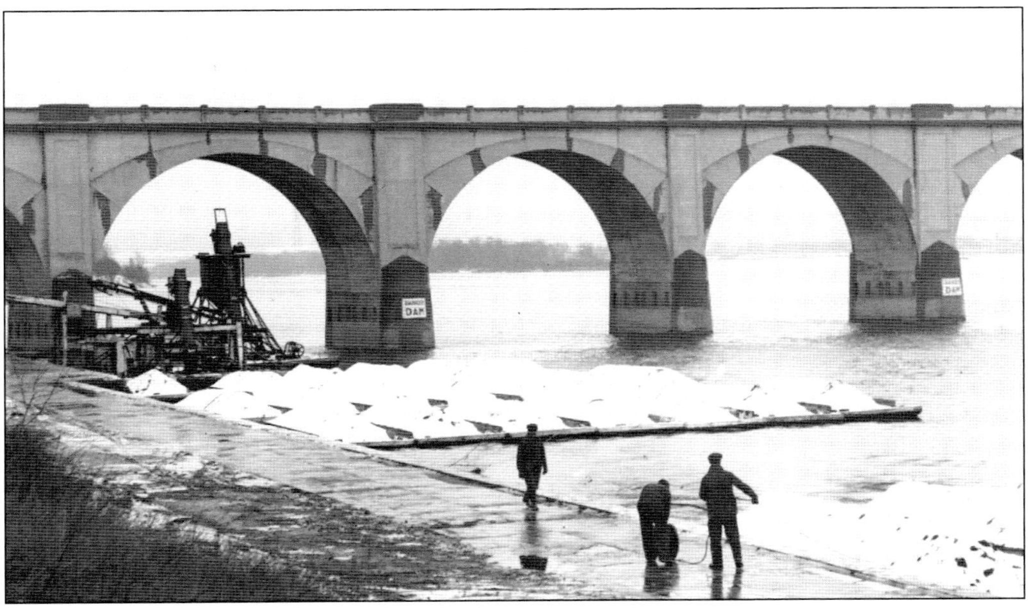

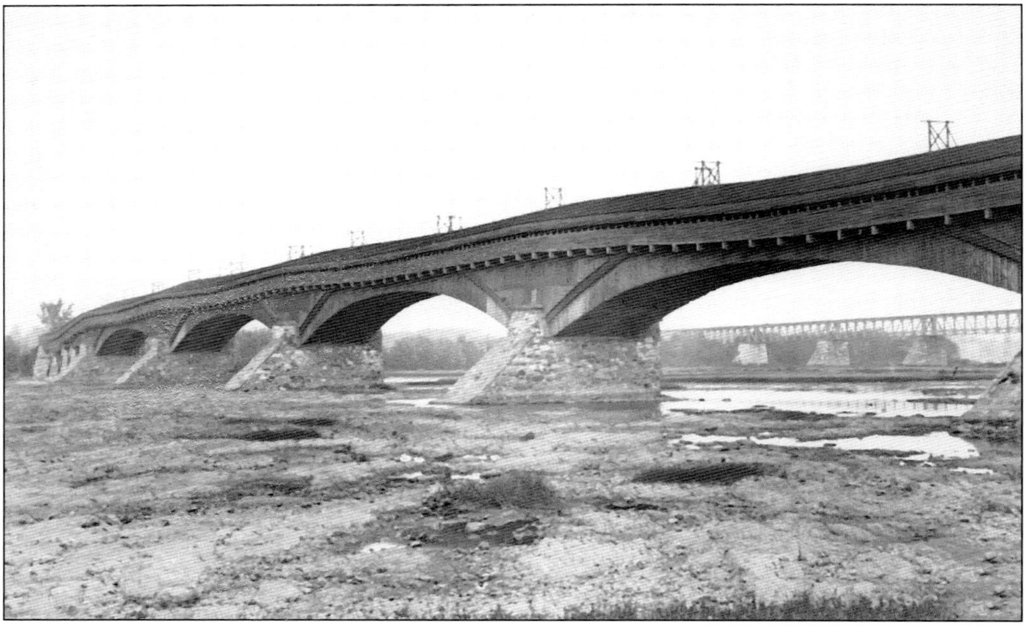

In the summer of 1900, the water level of the Susquehanna River dropped to lows that had not been seen since 1822, or the low watermark observed in 1803 and carved into Maclay's Rock. Here, the above view shows that the western channel beneath the Camelback Bridge is largely dry, except for the occasional pooling of water in lower spots. It was these extremes in the water levels that helped the case for the construction of a dam to control the river's water levels, as the low levels were not conducive to recreational activities such as swimming and boating. The depth problems also presented a serious health hazard, as the raw sewage that was pumped directly into the river would lie in stagnant pools along the river's edge.

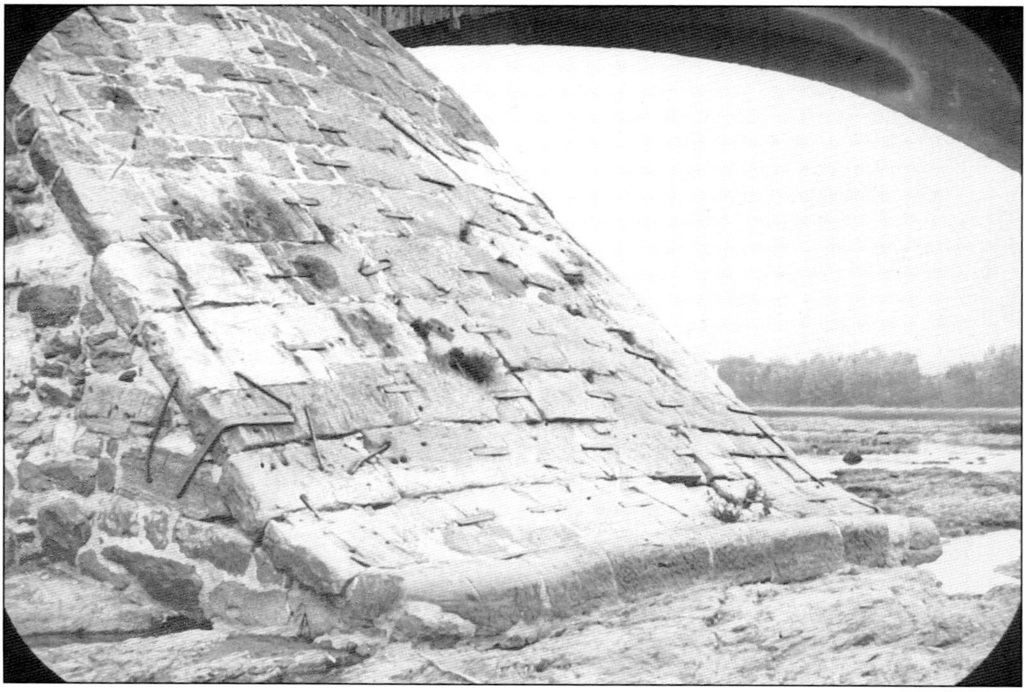

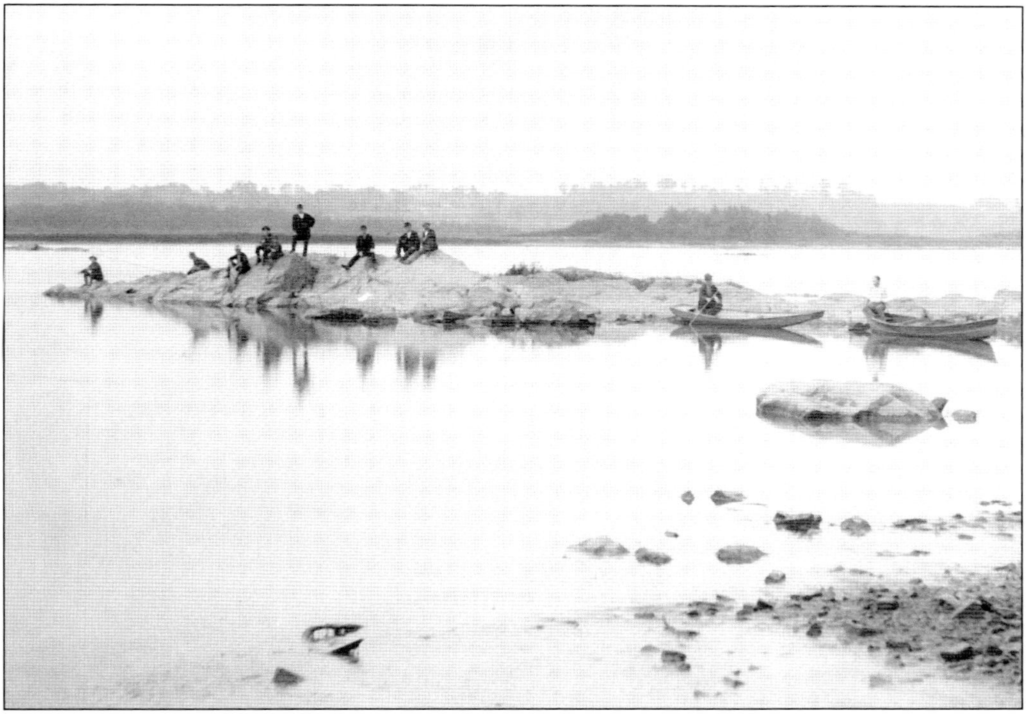

Several well-dressed gentlemen pose for a photograph out on the outcropping known as Maclay's Rock, about 1885. The rock, located at the foot of South Street, is named after Sen. William Maclay, whose residence was nearby. Maclay's Rock served for many years as the official low-water gauge for the river. Baltzer Sees, a local businessman and inventor, carved a line, along with the year 1803, to record the water level at that time. Aside from an observation made by Dr. John Heisley on September 19, 1822, the 1803 low watermark was not surpassed again until 1900, as seen in the photograph below, where the carvings of Sees and various others can be seen above the water line. Maclay's Rock is still visible above the water's surface, but much of it was obscured upon the completion of the Dock Street Dam.

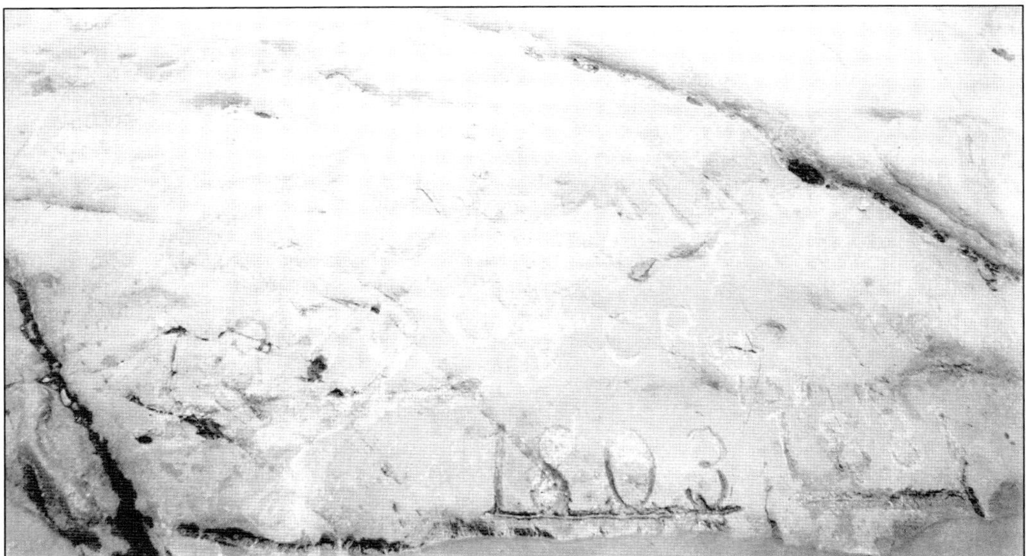

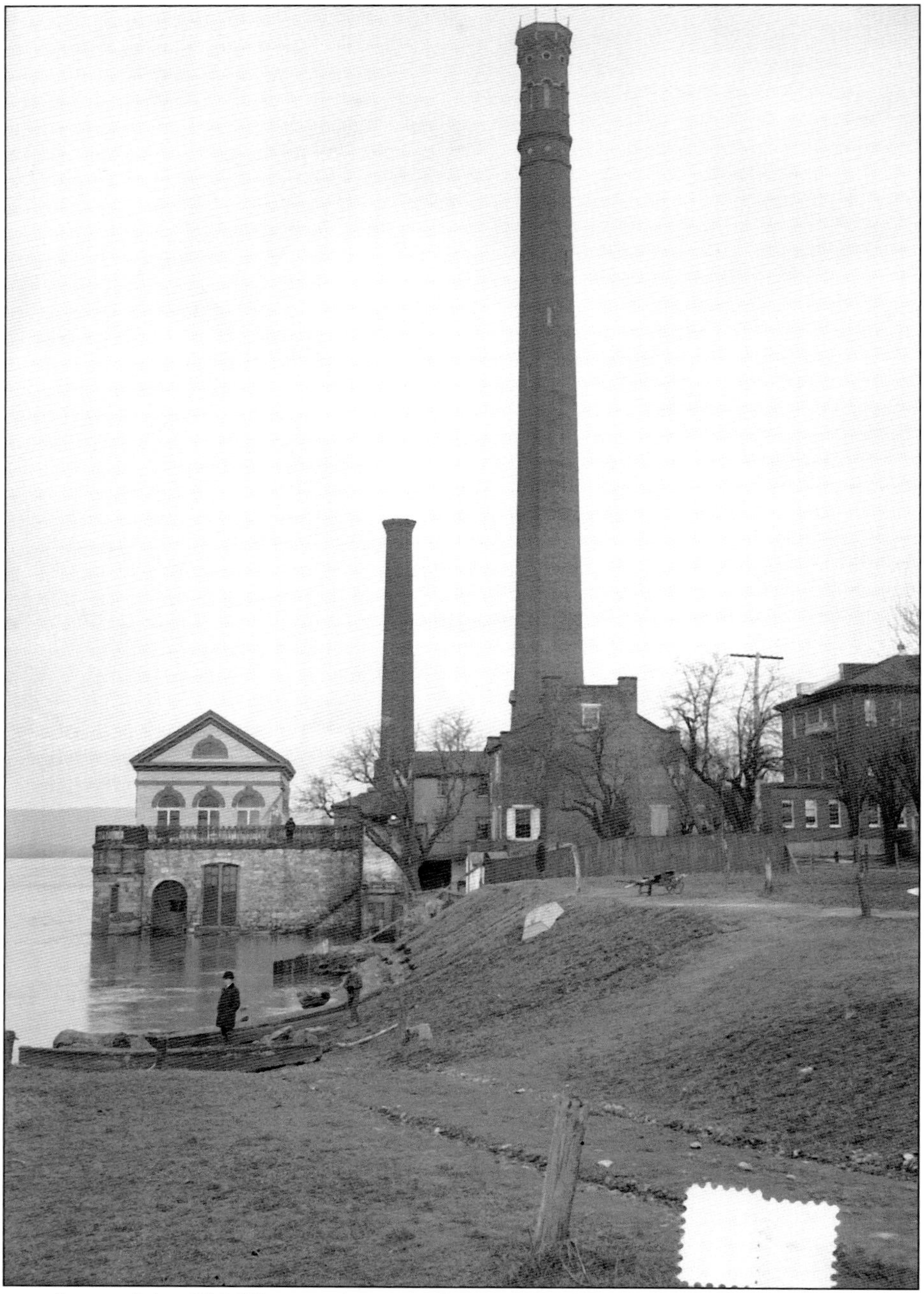

The standpipe of the Old Waterworks was a favorite perch for photographers and sightseers to access an elevated view of Harrisburg and the Susquehanna Valley. The standpipe, completed in 1875, was not a smokestack, but rather contained a 30-inch-wide iron pipe through which water was pumped to a height of 210 feet above the low water of the river. It was then transported back down by gravity and out to the city reservoir that stood at present-day Forster and Commonwealth Streets. In this view, taken during the 1902 flood, the waterworks and the surrounding riverfront landscape can be seen prior to construction of the Fleming Mansion (now the Harrisburg Civic Club), which with its surrounding grounds would drastically alter the riverfront landscape at this location.

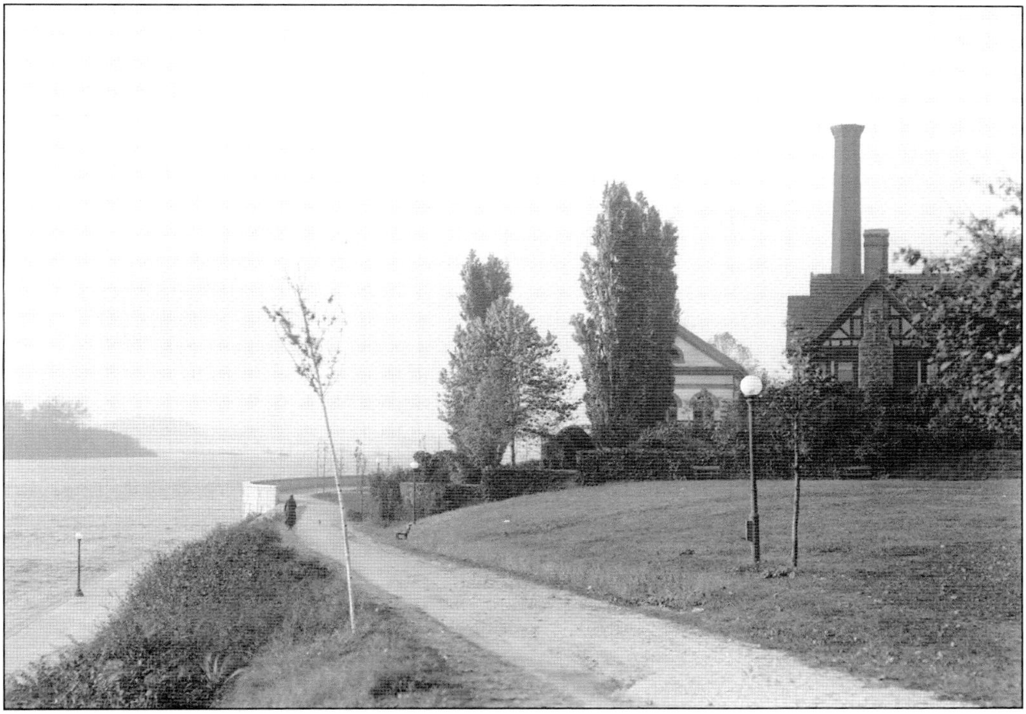

The Old Waterworks is seen above about 1920, after the surrounding grounds have been completely transformed. In 1913, the standpipe was removed as it had become obsolete and was in need of repair. Here also, to the right, stands the Fleming Mansion, also known as Overlook, which was completed in 1904. It was donated to the Harrisburg Civic Club, which took ownership of the property in 1916 from the estate of Virginia Hammond Fleming. In the image below, work crews lay pipe to carry clean water from the Island Filtration Plant to the Old Waterworks, where it will be pumped to Reservoir Park. The large pipe was placed seven feet below the river's surface to insure that it would not be disturbed by ice floes. (Above, courtesy of the Library of Congress.)

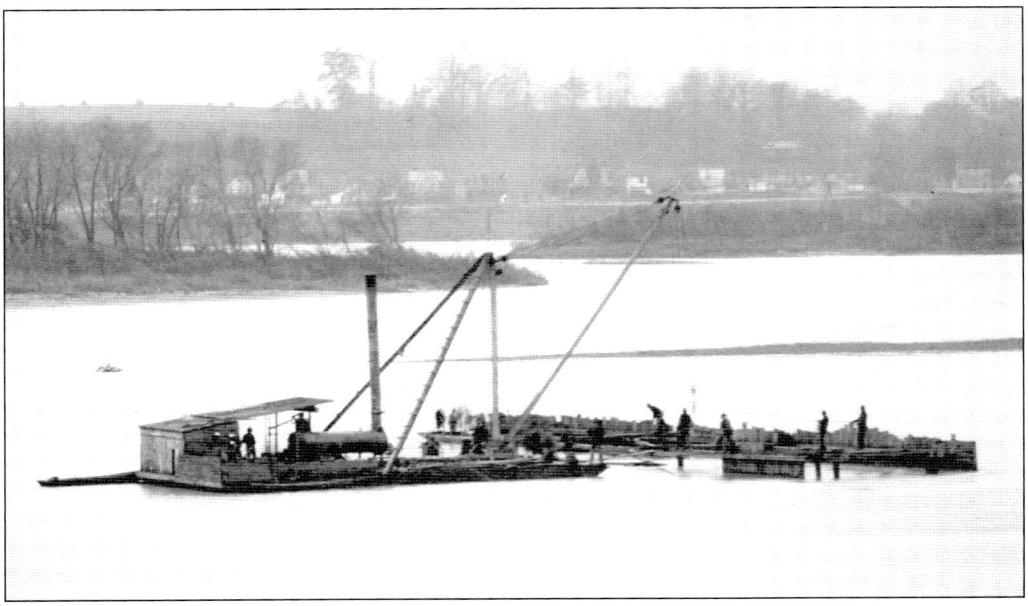

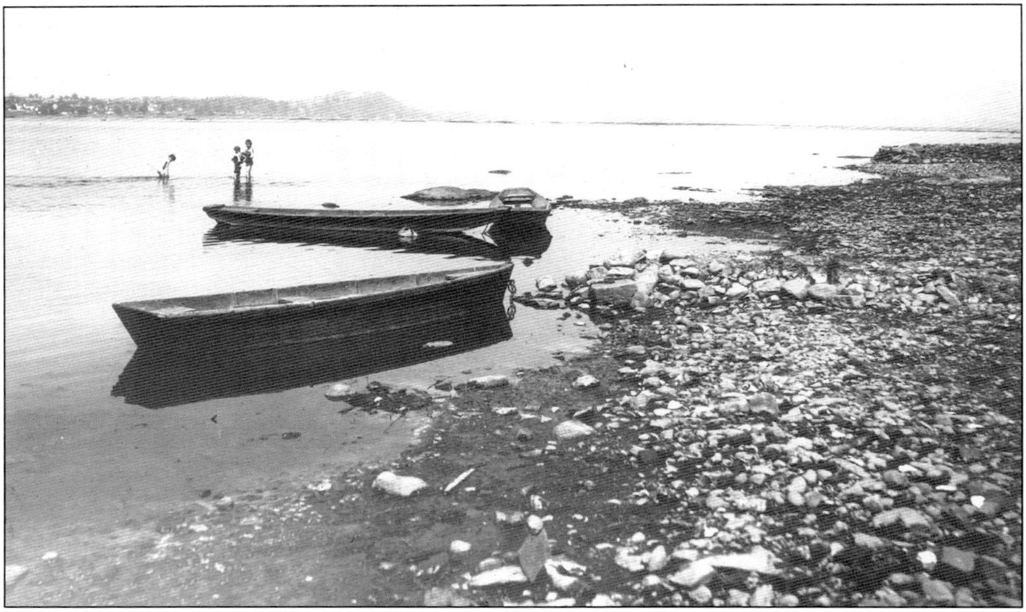

These two photographs were taken by J. Horace McFarland around 1900. Raw sewage was being pumped directly into the river at this location near Forster Street, and when the river was at low levels, it pooled near the shoreline. Amidst outbreaks of typhoid, these images deliberately included children swimming and playing in the contaminated water. On December 20, 1900, Mira Lloyd Dock spoke before the Harrisburg Board of Trade on the City Beautiful movement and how it could pull Harrisburg out of the downward spiral of decay that had gradually overtaken the city during the last century. McFarland and Dock put into motion a plan to revitalize the city, which would focus largely on the riverfront. Over the next 15 years, plans seen and yet unseen would be undertaken to reshape the physical and emotional landscape of the city.

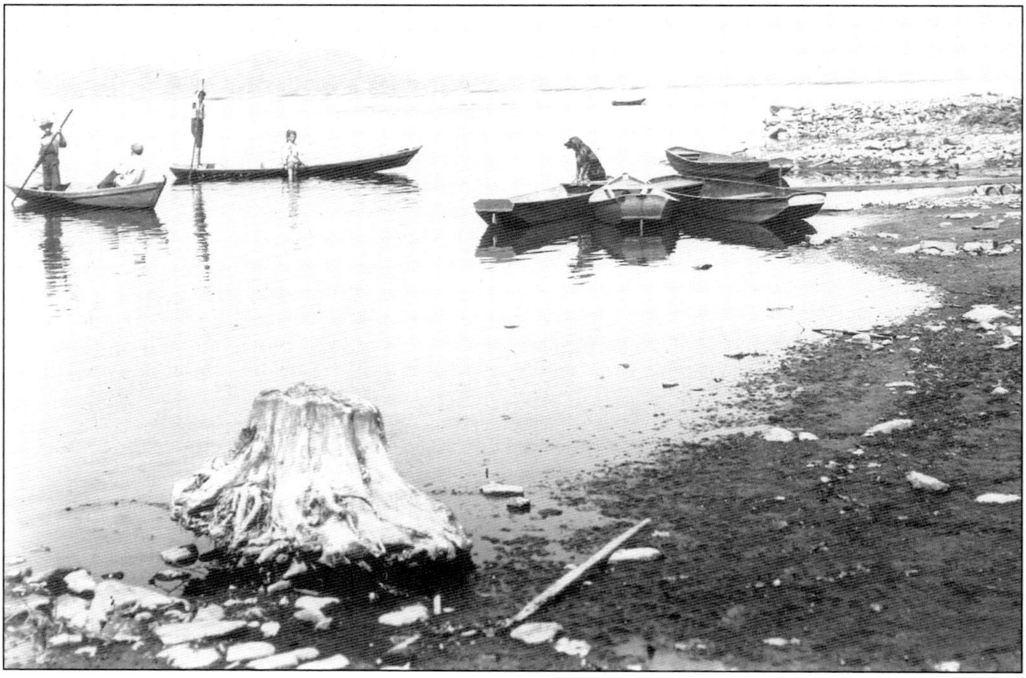

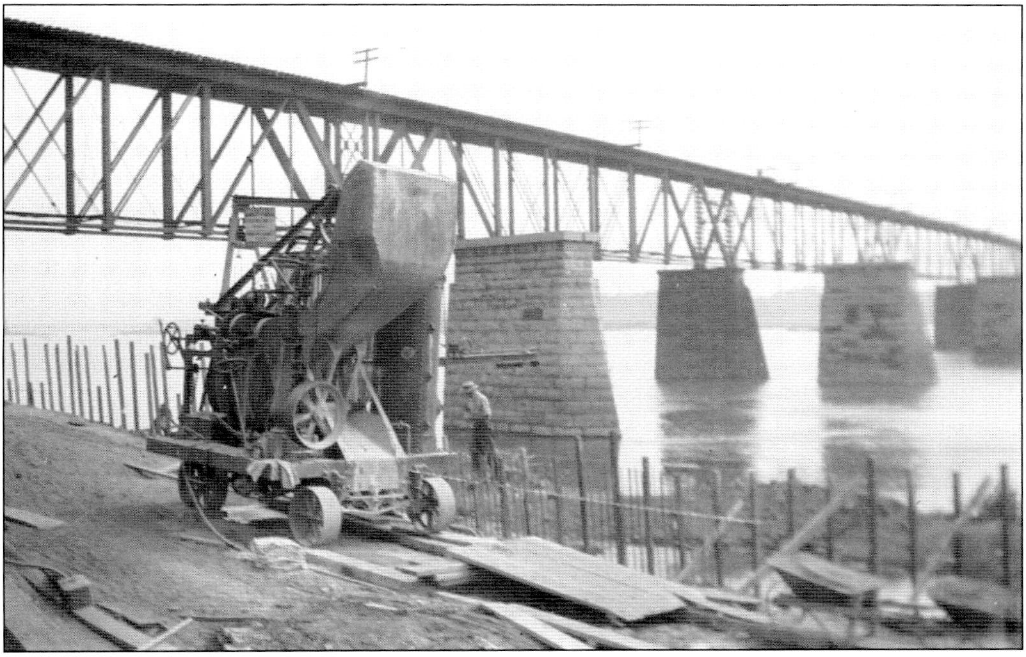

The riverfront steps were a continuation of the municipal improvement initiatives that first started to take shape in 1900. With the completion of the interceptor sewage system, the task of completing a riverfront walkway officially began on July 7, 1913, when the Stucker Brothers Construction Company was awarded the contract to complete the three-mile stretch of steel-reinforced concrete. The image above shows the pouring of concrete near the Philadelphia & Reading Railroad Bridge and Vanderbilt Piers. The image below shows the concrete stringers in place, which were backfilled with earth and ash before the concrete was poured for the steps and walkway. With the exception of a gap that existed in the Hardscrabble district north of Forster Street, the steps would be completed by November 1915.

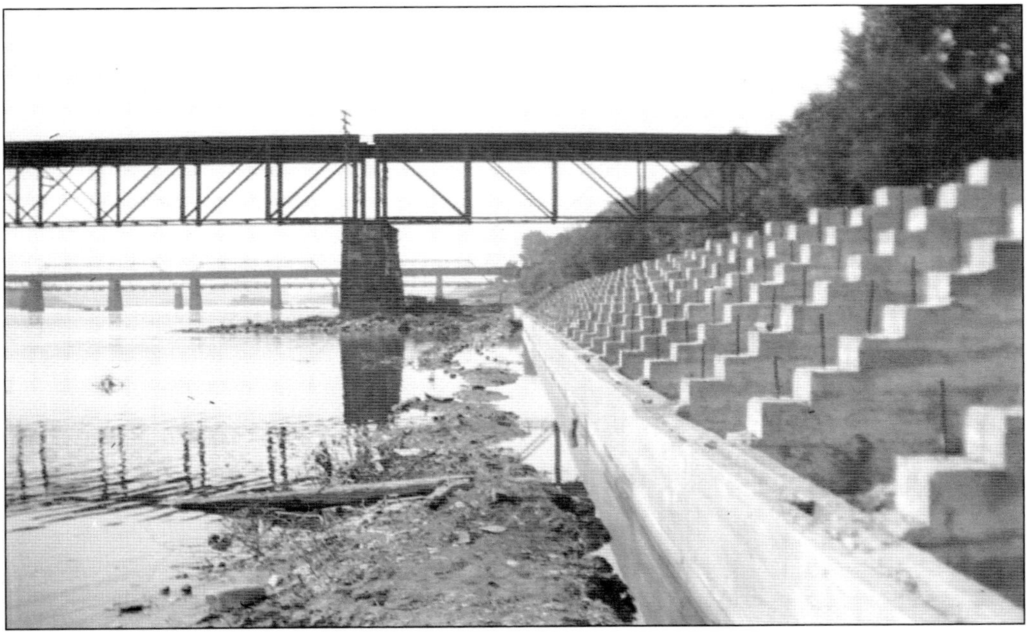

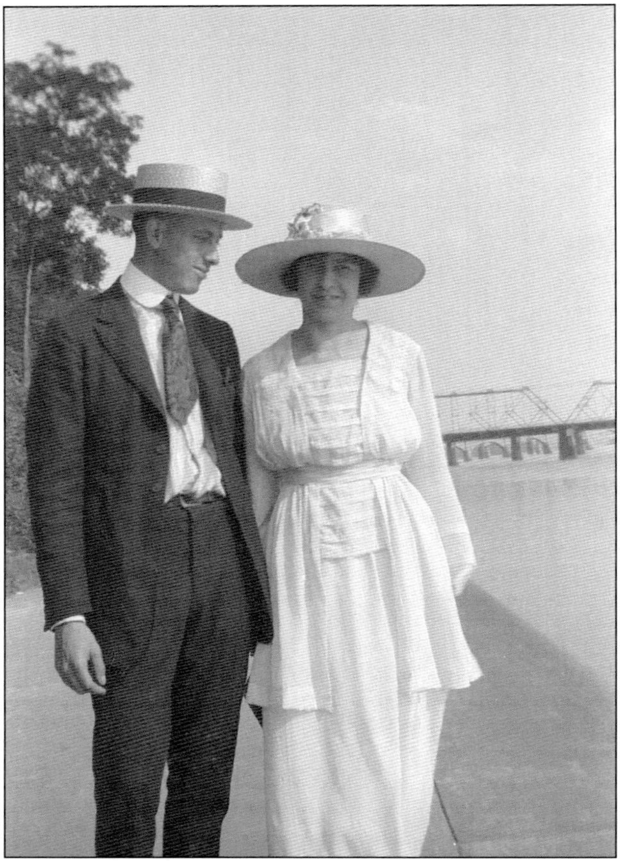

In the image at left, a couple poses on the recently completed riverfront steps above the Walnut Street Bridge. In 1901, a river dam was proposed as part of the solution to eliminating the sewage problem that existed during periods of low water, with sewage collecting along the shoreline instead of flowing out into the river. However, with the building of the interceptor, this issue was solved. There was also a growing sentiment for deepening the river for recreational uses, as boating and swimming were often dictated by the water's depth. As a result, construction of the dam located at Dock Street began in 1913, utilizing concrete slabs spaced between piers secured into the riverbed. By late summer of 1915, construction was effectively completed, which raised the water level four feet at the dam, with a gradual decrease heading upstream.

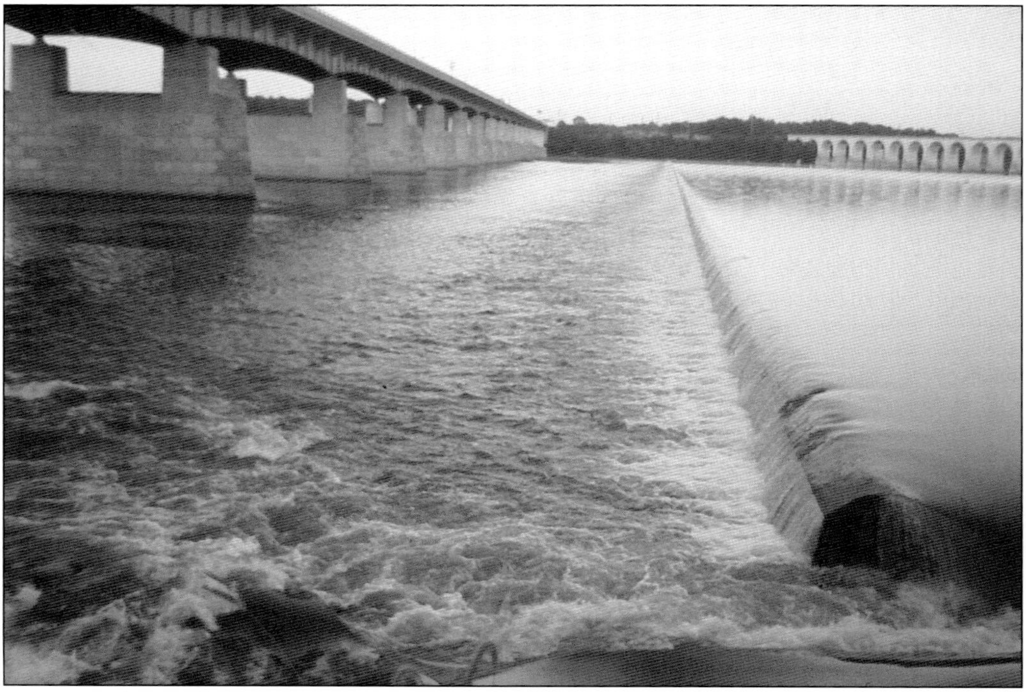

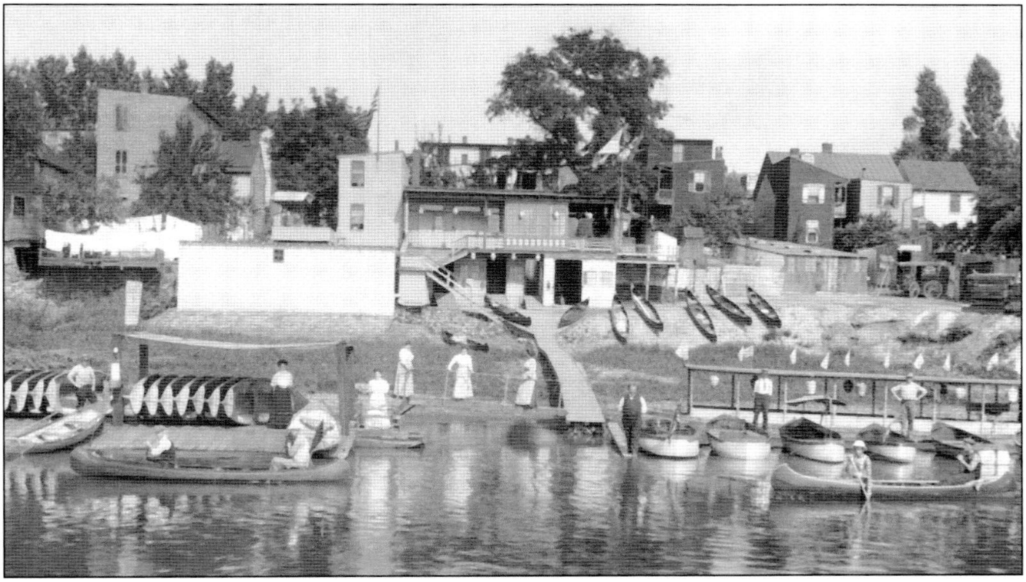

Dintaman's Boat Livery, seen here around 1913, was located at the 1100 block of North Front Street in the Hardscrabble district of Harrisburg. Boasting a wide selection of canoes and steel-bottomed motorboats, Dintaman's ferry benefited from its riverfront location opposite Independence Island by providing boat rentals to the popular river destination.

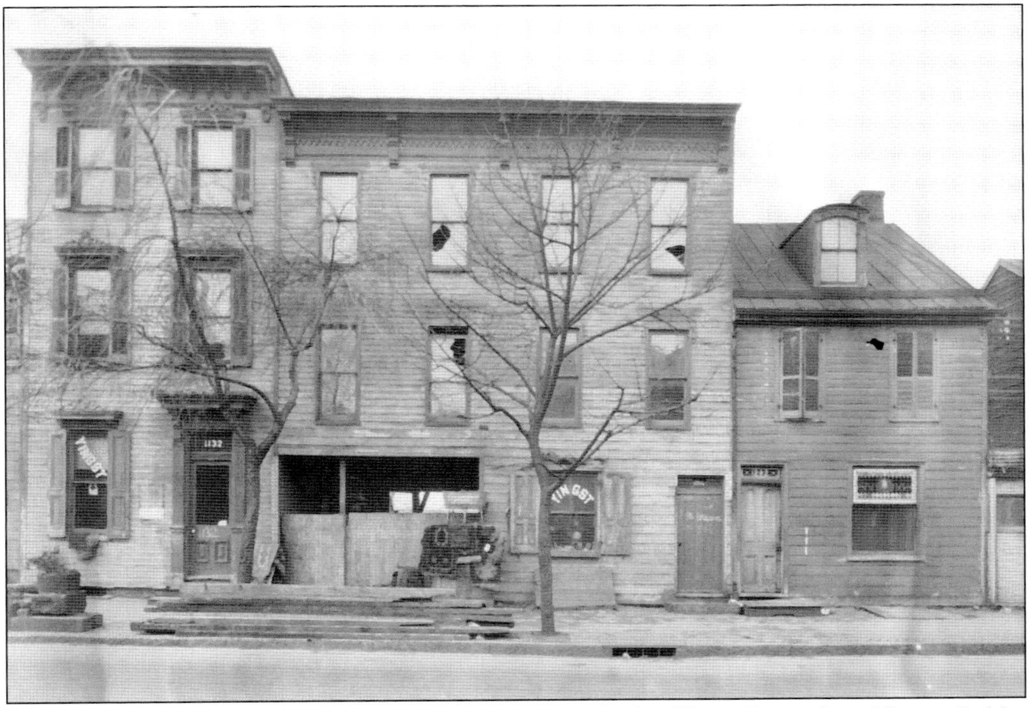

The Hardscrabble district was situated along the western side of Front Street from Herr to Calder Streets. Beginning as a small village in the late 18th century, it has been also been called Hartz Gravel and Pottstown over the years. Consisting of largely frame buildings, Hardscrabble fell into disrepair by the beginning of the 20th century. Considered an eyesore, it fell into the crosshairs of the City Beautiful movement.

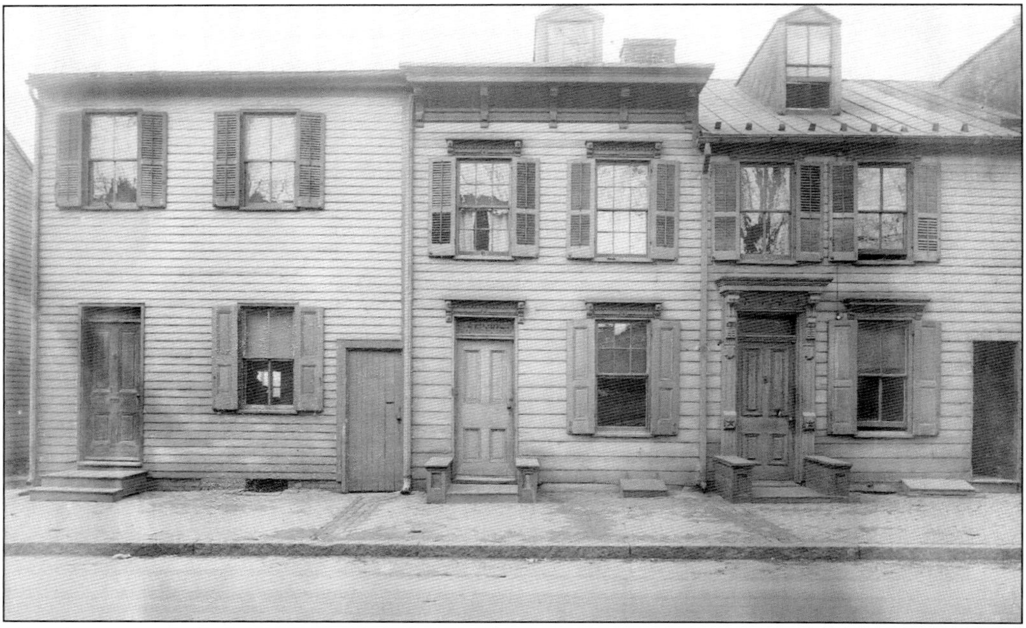

The above image shows a series of buildings in the Hardscrabble district, 1218–20–22 North Front Street. Prior to the Civil War, these building were part of the Jennings Iron Foundry. The structure pictured below was located at 1100 North Front Street and at one time served as the Fox Hotel, or tavern. Built around 1840, the Fox Hotel and the nearby Duck Tavern were favorites of the loggers stopping over on their trips down the Susquehanna. In 1914, the city passed an ordinance taking over the properties of the Hardscrabble district. Litigation over the matter continued until late 1920, but the owners were forced to vacate their premises by April 1, 1921. The stated reason for the takeover was the realignment of Front Street, although it was widely known that the city wished to dispose of the eyesore.

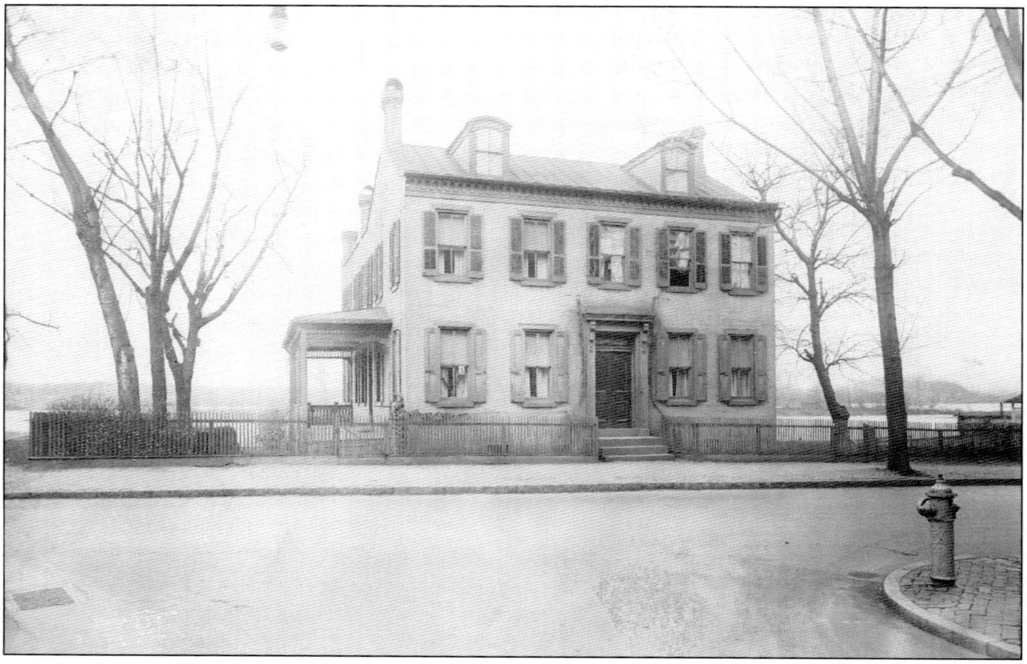

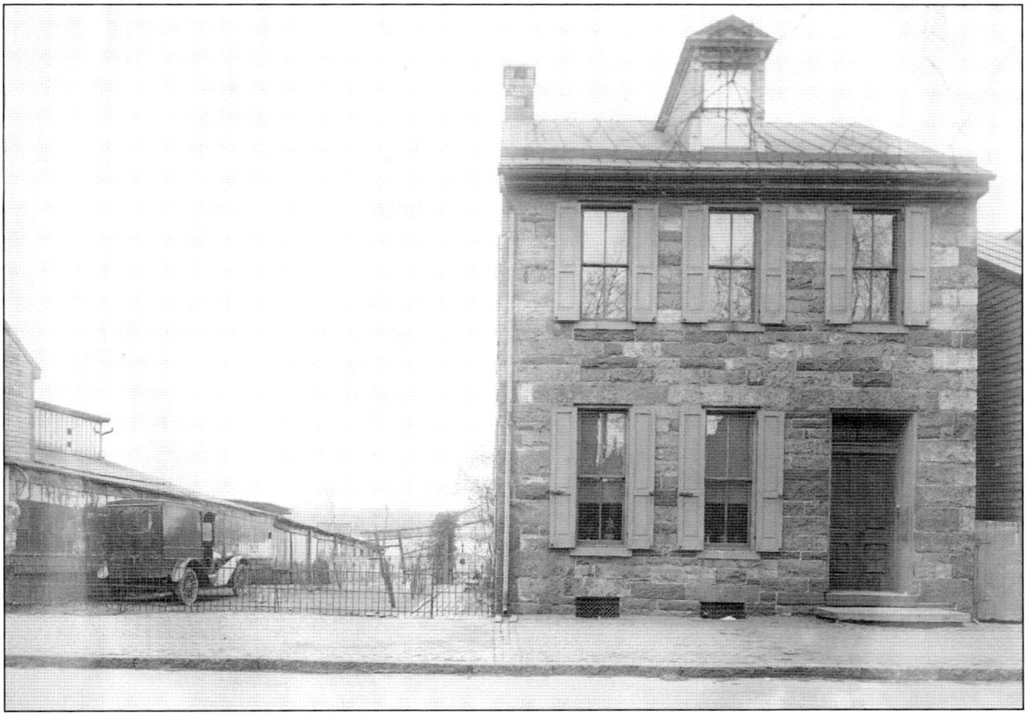

The Hardscrabble properties went to auction in March 1921 for the purpose of reclaiming the building materials from the structures. The Berrier residence, pictured above, was constructed in 1888 from river stone. At auction, its building materials sold for $475. The Fox Hotel sold for $700, and the materials were to be used on a structure built on South Thirteenth Street. After the properties had been razed, the site was utilized for the *Lest We Forget* World War I memorial, which was dedicated on November 11, 1922, and also for the sunken memorial gardens seen in the image below.

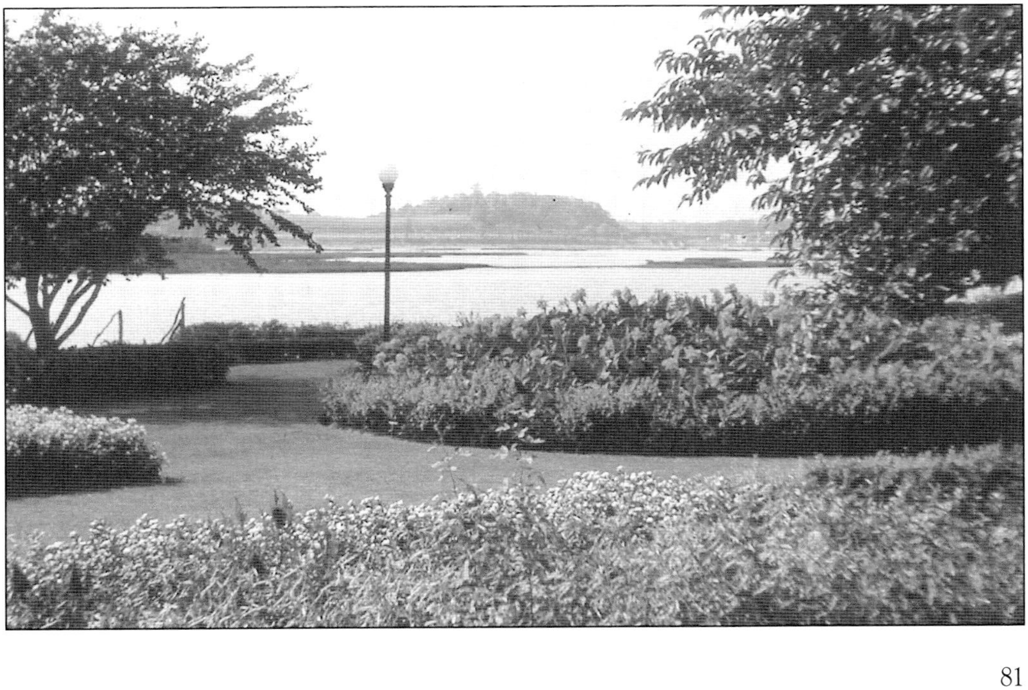

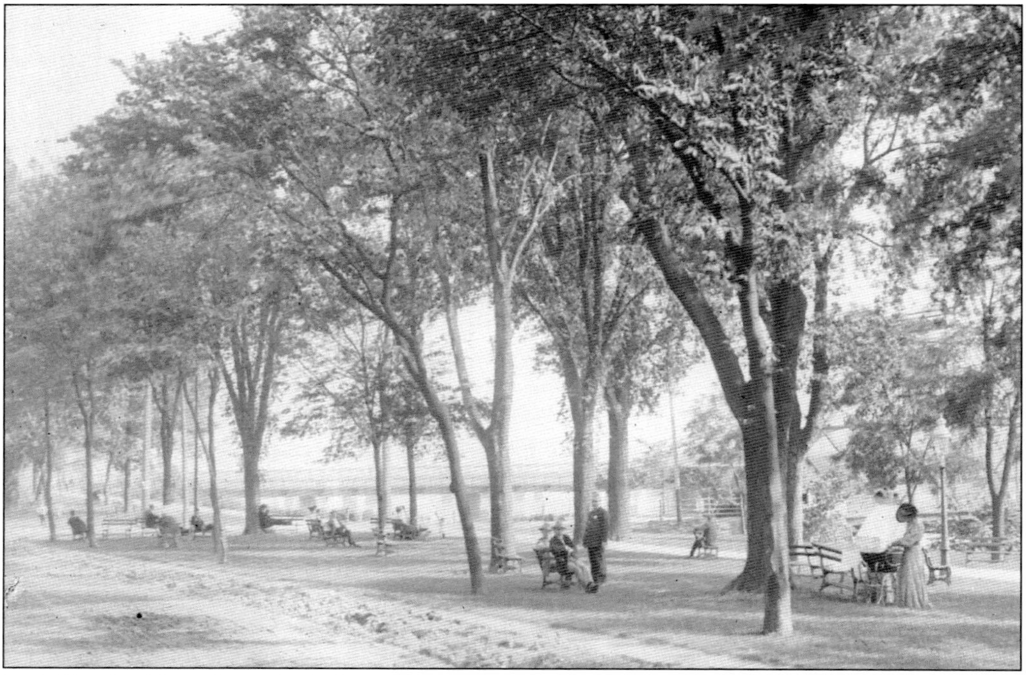

In 1902, the Harrisburg Park Commission was organized, and $250,000 was obtained for the improvement of the city's park system, which included Riverfront Park. The park improvements were spearheaded by Warren H. Manning, who served as landscape advisor, overseeing many of the park projects. In these two images from around 1905, Riverfront Park provides an elevated vantage point to view the beauty of the natural river landscape, which was largely unfettered by buildings and industry.

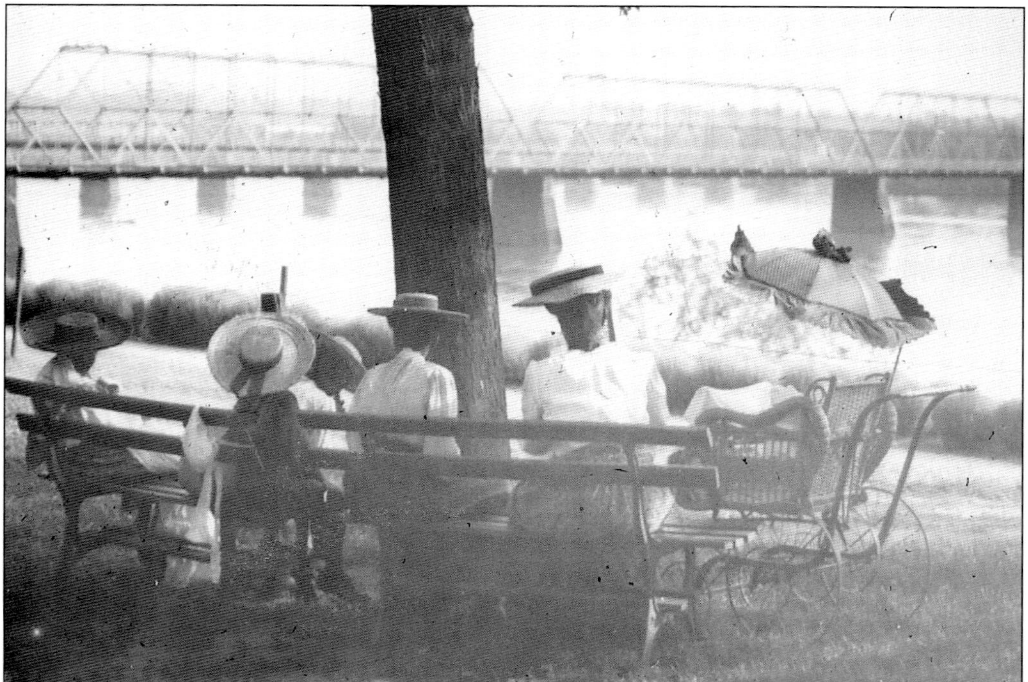

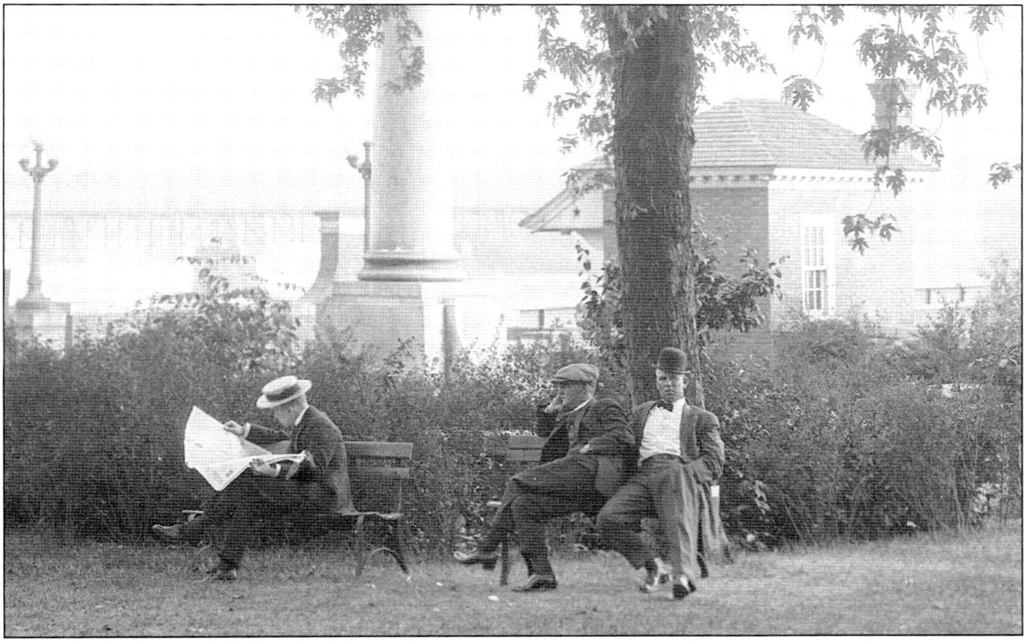

In 1905, the Harrisburg Park Commission purchased 300 park benches to be used from Paxton to Herr Streets; a police detail was assigned to patrol the park, and the park paths were upgraded. Riverfront Park became a destination in which to lounge and relax. It was a place suitable for families, a place to sit under the tall shade trees and read the newspaper or just watch the river roll on by. Front Street also benefited from the improvements of the park, as it too was given a face-lift with new granite curbing and paving of the old dirt thoroughfare.

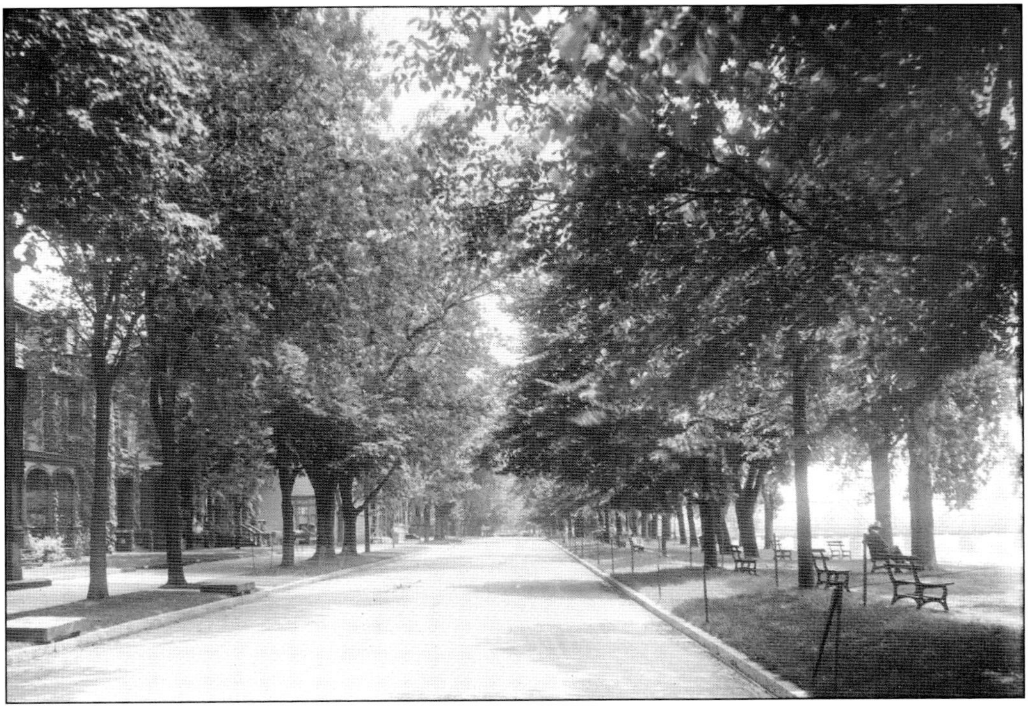

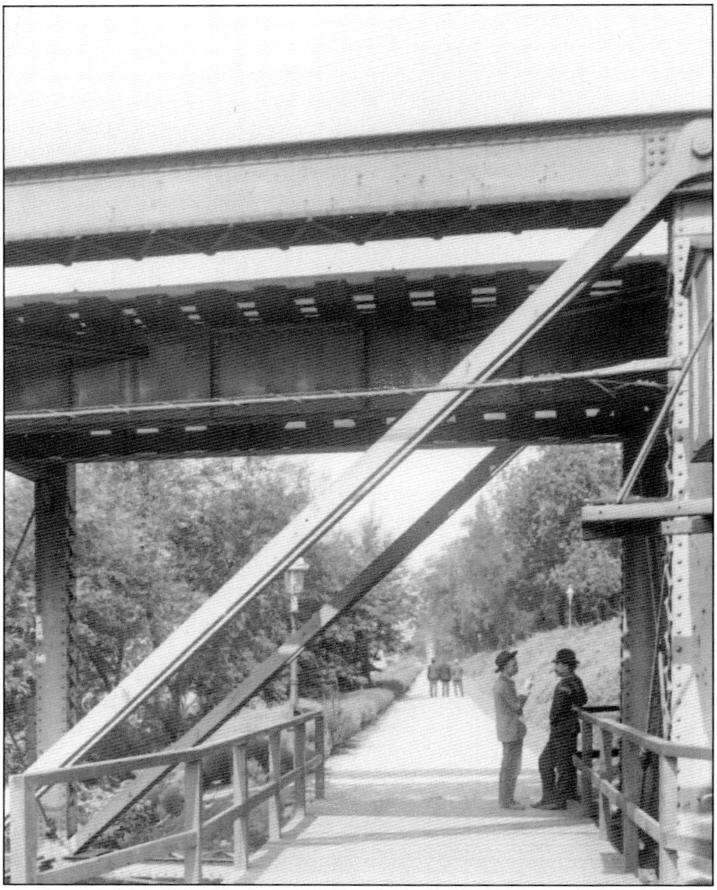

In the image at left, two gentleman stand on the riverfront path in Harris Park beneath the overhead tracks of the Cumberland Valley Railroad Bridge. In the image below, a woman enjoys a view of the riverfront from a bench in Harris Park near the grave of pioneer John Harris, around 1905. In the background loom the Vanderbilt Piers and the Philadelphia & Reading Railroad Bridge. Harris Park consisted of three acres of land that extended from Paxton to Mulberry Streets. It was established by an act of the Pennsylvania General Assembly on March 20, 1859. In 1915, a monument was placed at the foot of Paxton Street commemorating the Harris Ferry.

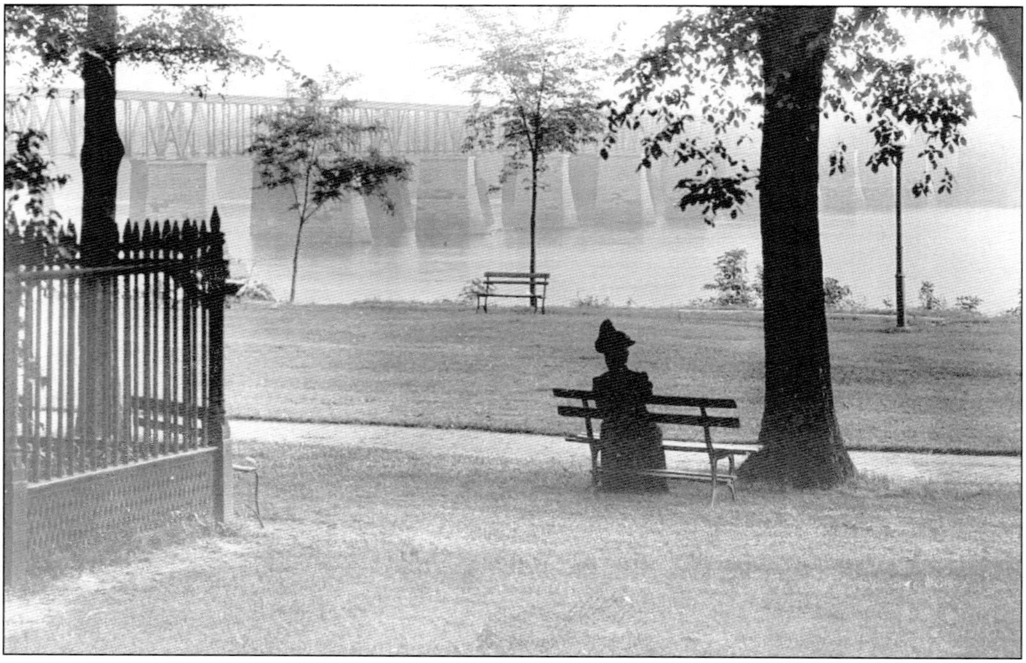

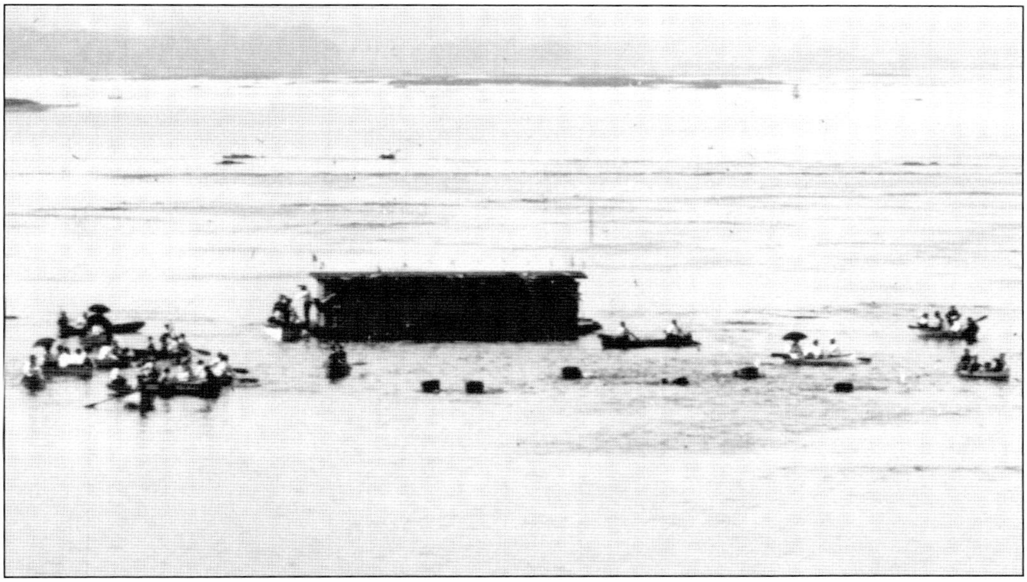

The image above depicts a bathtub race about 1914. Bathtub, plank, and canoe races became regular events on the river starting in the 1870s, as they were often initiated by the Harrisburg Boat Club. In the image below, spectators line the Walnut Street Bridge to get an elevated view of the contests taking place below on the Susquehanna River during the first Water Carnival, Labor Day, September 2, 1907. A full slate of swimming and boating events was held on the river that day, but there were only a small number of events, as the city was virtually shut down to view the spectacle along the river in addition to parades, contests, and picnics in the parks.

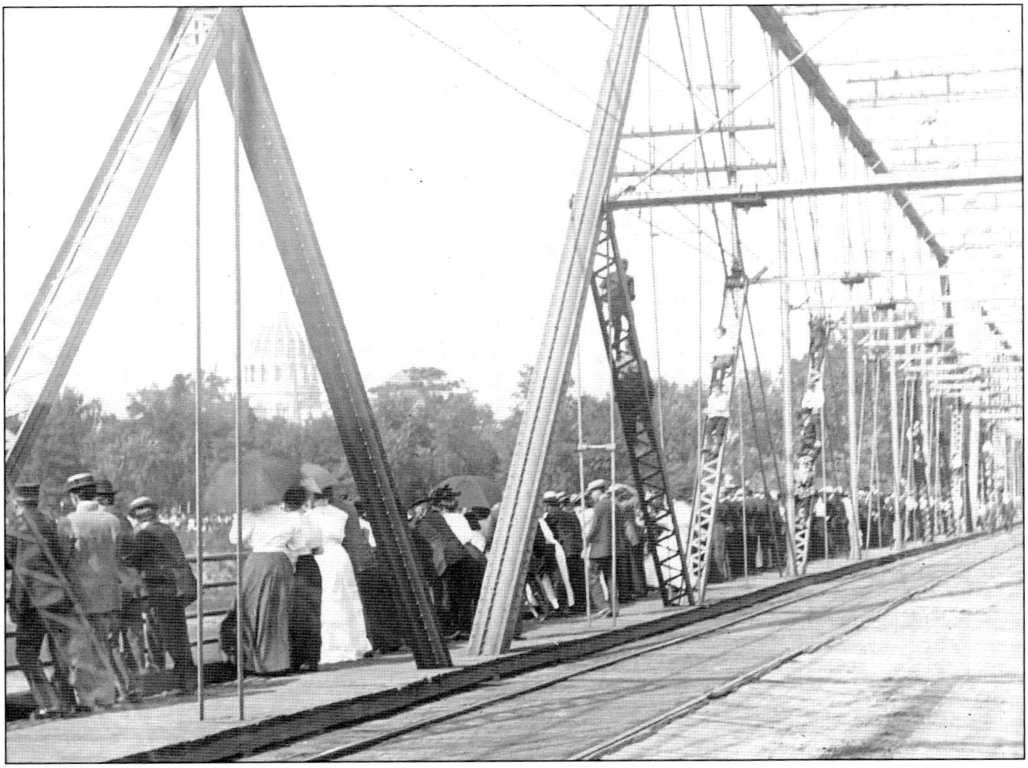

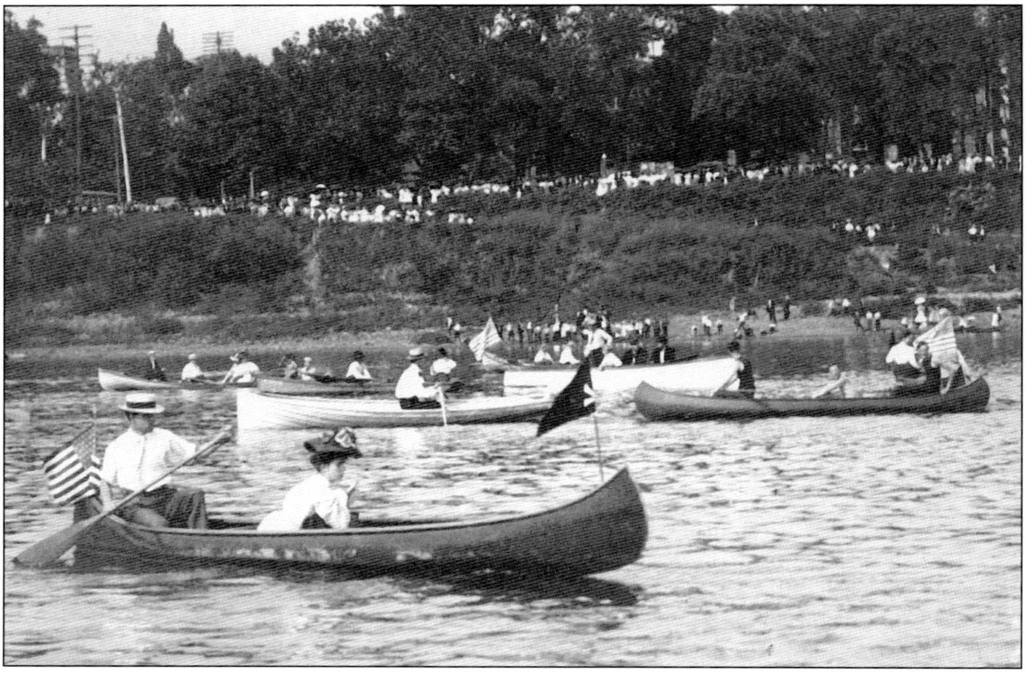

However, the Water Carnival was not always held on Labor Day. In 1909, the event moved to July 4 to observe Independence Day, with boats gliding across the river above the Market Street Bridge flying the 45-star flag of the United States of America. After the early success of the Water Carnival from 1907 to 1909, it was not held again until Independence Day of 1912. Low river levels in 1913 cancelled that year's events and the program in 1914 was cancelled for the anticipation of the completion of the river steps and dam by the following year.

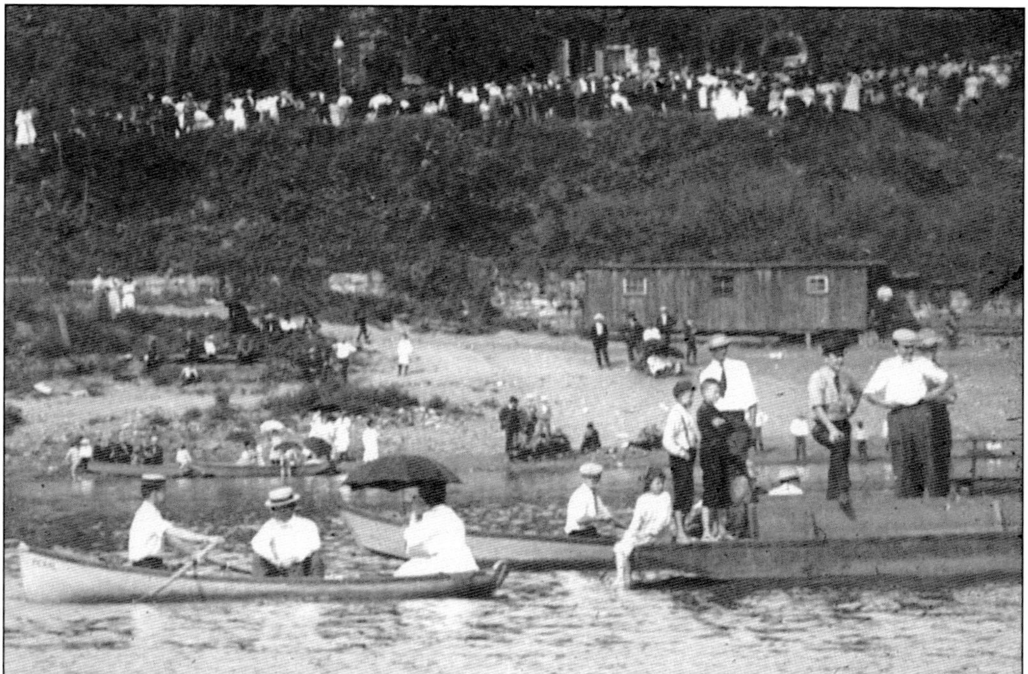

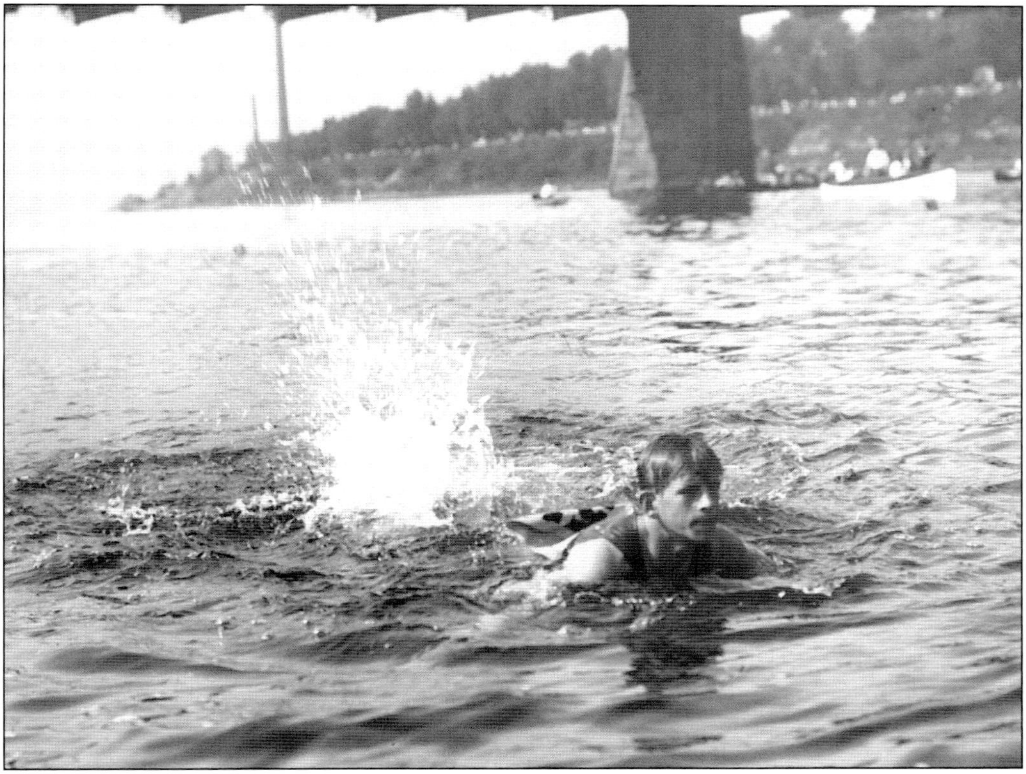

The two images shown on this page were taken around 1909 during a Water Carnival. In the photograph above, contestant no. 51 competes in a swimming event just south of the Walnut Street Bridge. The swimming events for that day were the half-mile and quarter-mile events along with the shorter 50- and 100-yard sprints. The marshal of the swimming events, Harry J. Berrier, oversaw the activities from a motorboat to keep all other boats from interfering with the swimmers and act as a lifeguard for any swimmer suffering from exhaustion from the river currents. The image at right shows the *Alcyon* plying the waterway in the event someone was in need of help. That being said, it is uncertain why the city policeman in the photograph is holding his billy club at the ready.

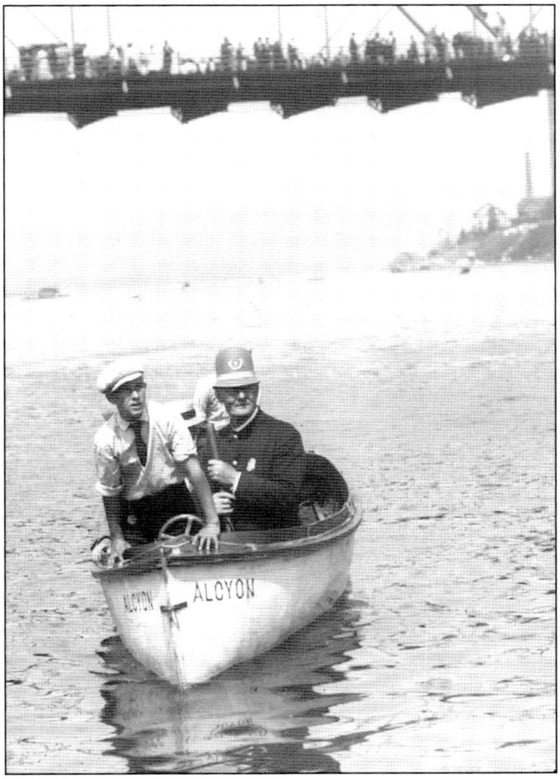

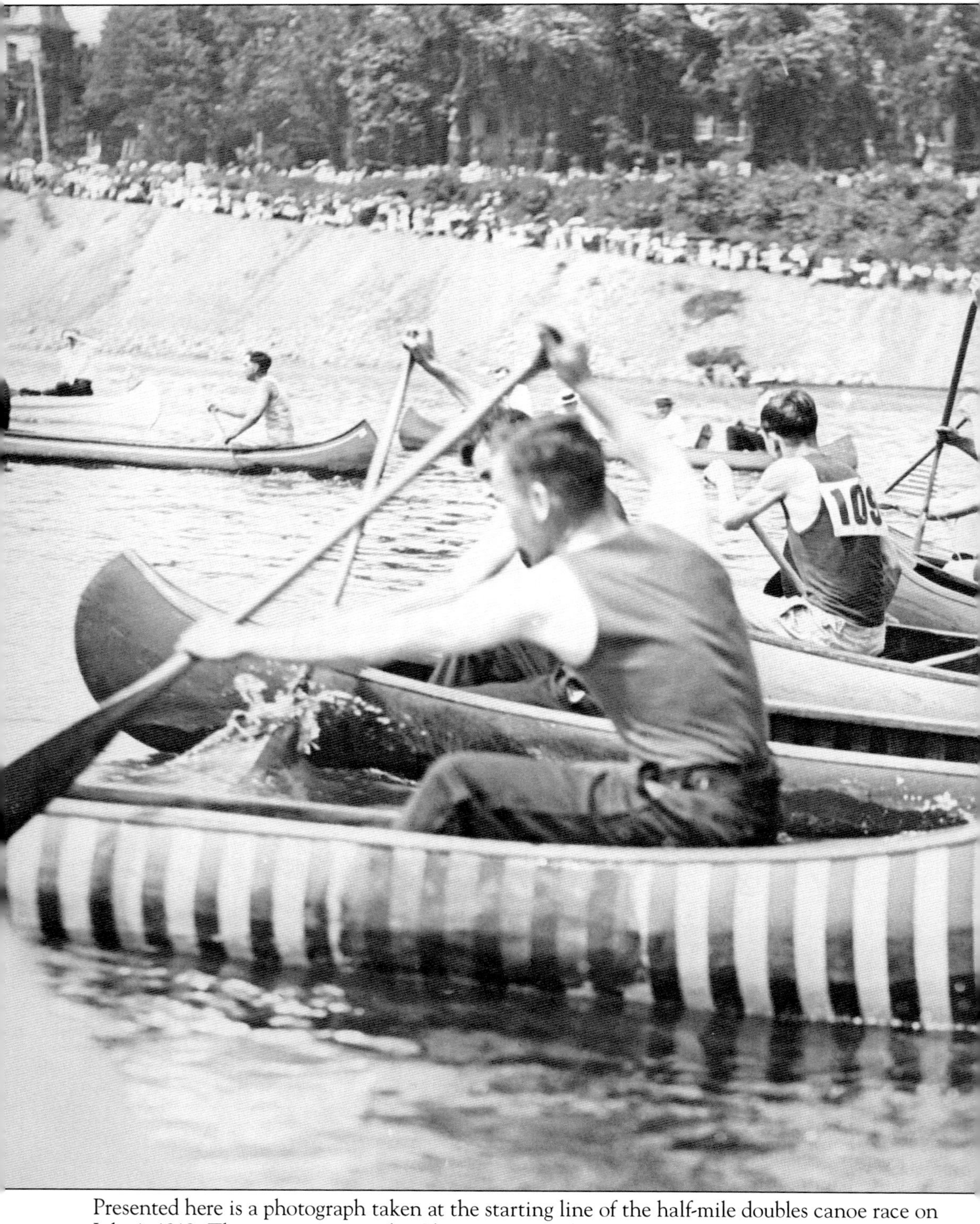


Presented here is a photograph taken at the starting line of the half-mile doubles canoe race on July 4, 1912. The event was won by Clayton Keys and Harry Lindsey with a time of 7 minutes and 38 seconds. For their effort, they took home a first prize of two swimsuits valued at $3 each. Other events from that day included a 100-yard swim for boys less than 14 years of age, 100-yard

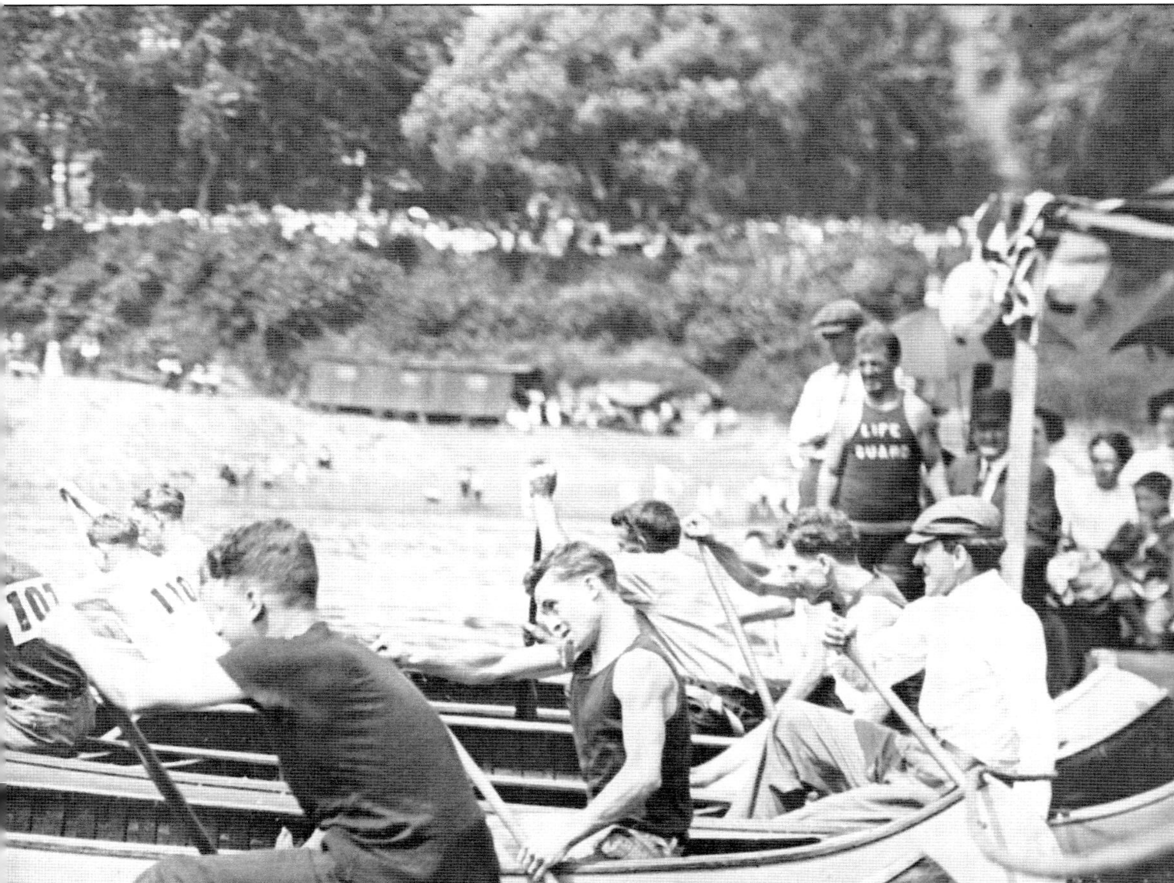

swim with open umbrella, 100-yard tub race, a half-mile single rowboat race, and a canoe-tilting contest. Nighttime festivities for the day's events included a fireworks display taken in by crowds lining the river's banks and bridges. This was followed by a boat parade decorated in red lights and accompanied by a band that set out from the shore playing "Auld Lang Syne."

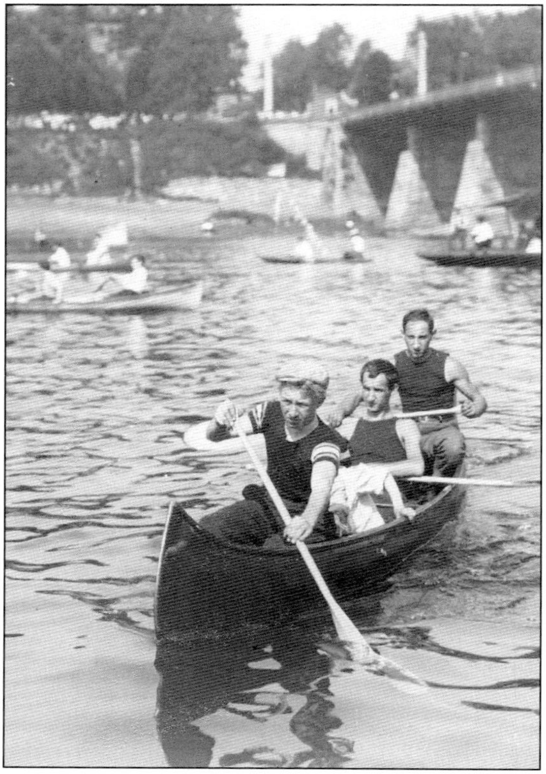

During the Water Carnival, the river was alive with a myriad of boating activity in addition to the competitions and exhibitions that were part of the day's program. Spectators could gain an up-close view of the action in and on the water, and thus needed to be policed if that got a bit too close for safety concerns.

After an absence of two years, the Water Carnival returned in late September 1915 as a means to showcase the results of the City Beautiful movement that began with Mira Lloyd Dock's speech in December 1900. Around 50,000 spectators gathered by the river to view the culminating spectacle that was the result of 15 years of planning and hard work to beautify and modernize the riverfront landscape.

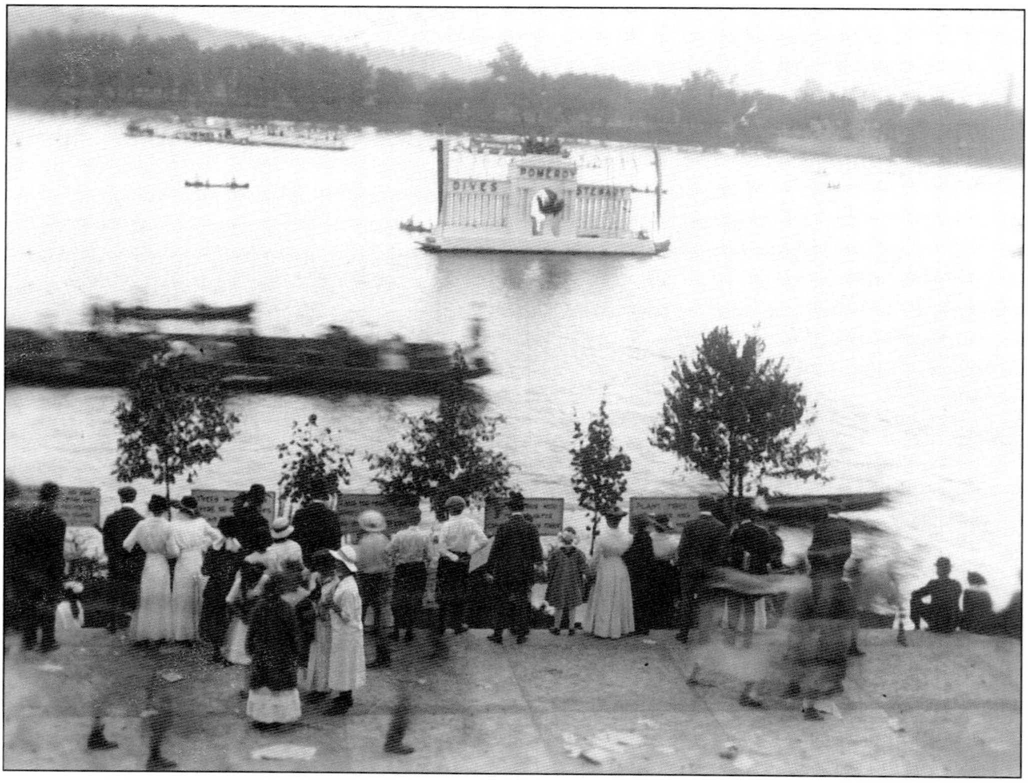

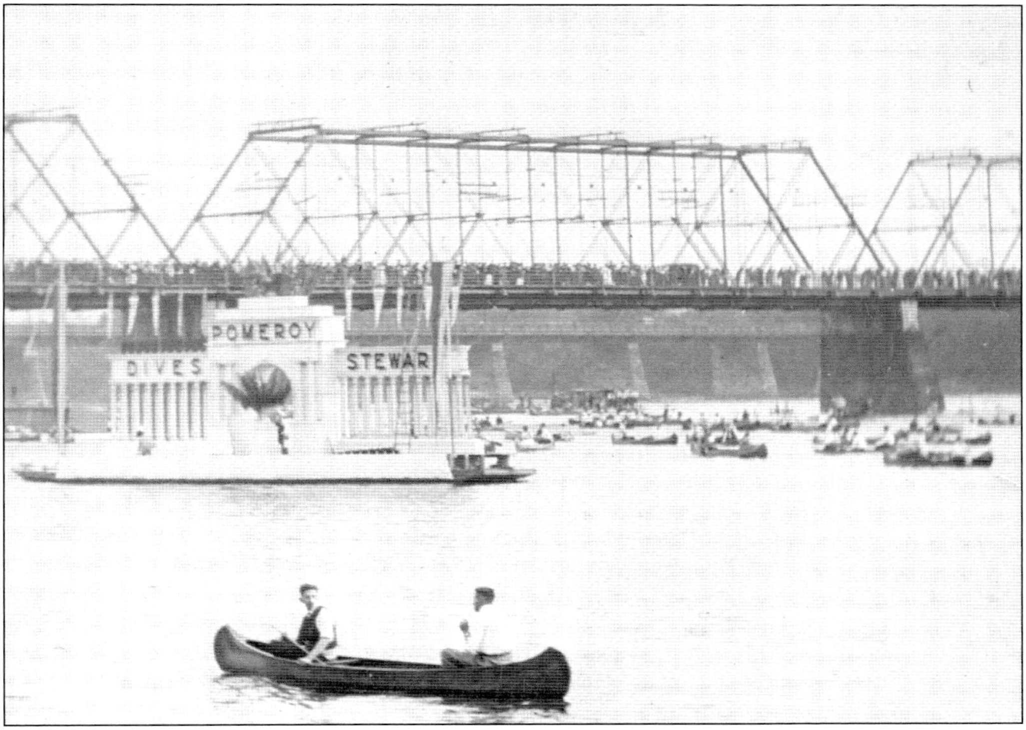


By September 1915, the riverfront steps and park, sewage interceptor, Dock Street dam, and the new Market Street Bridge had all but been completed to bring the large crowds to the river to witness the renaissance of the capital city. In the images seen here, commercial floats from the three large Harrisburg department stores—Dives, Pomeroy and Stewart, Kauffman's, and Bowman's—are anchored in the Susquehanna just north of the Walnut Street Bridge. Beginning in 1916, the Water Carnival was renamed, or rebranded, as the Kipona Festival. *Kipona* is believed to be a Lenni-Lenape term meaning "sparkling waters" and was a reflection of the improvement measures taken along the riverfront.

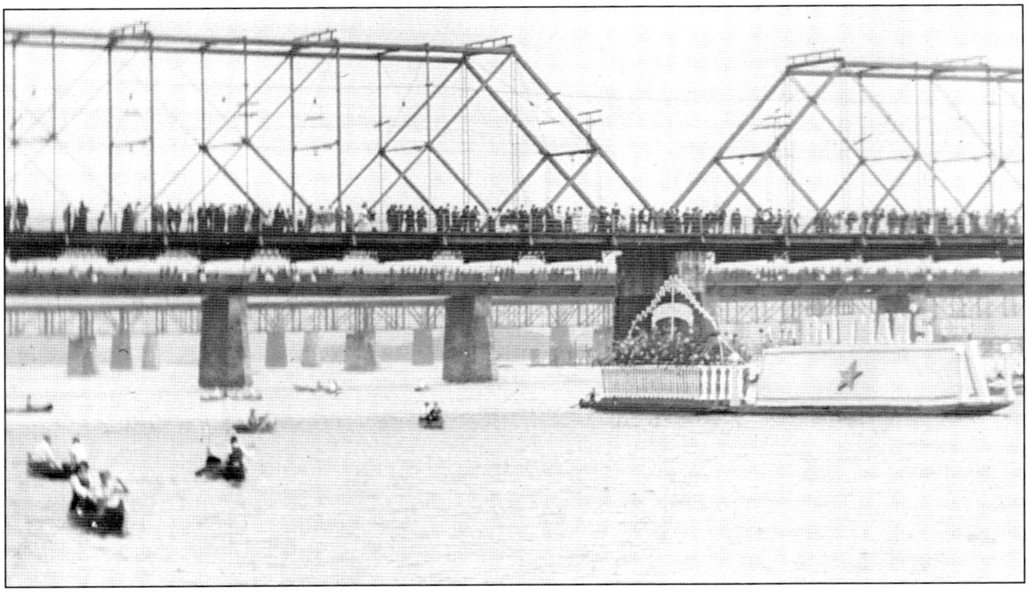

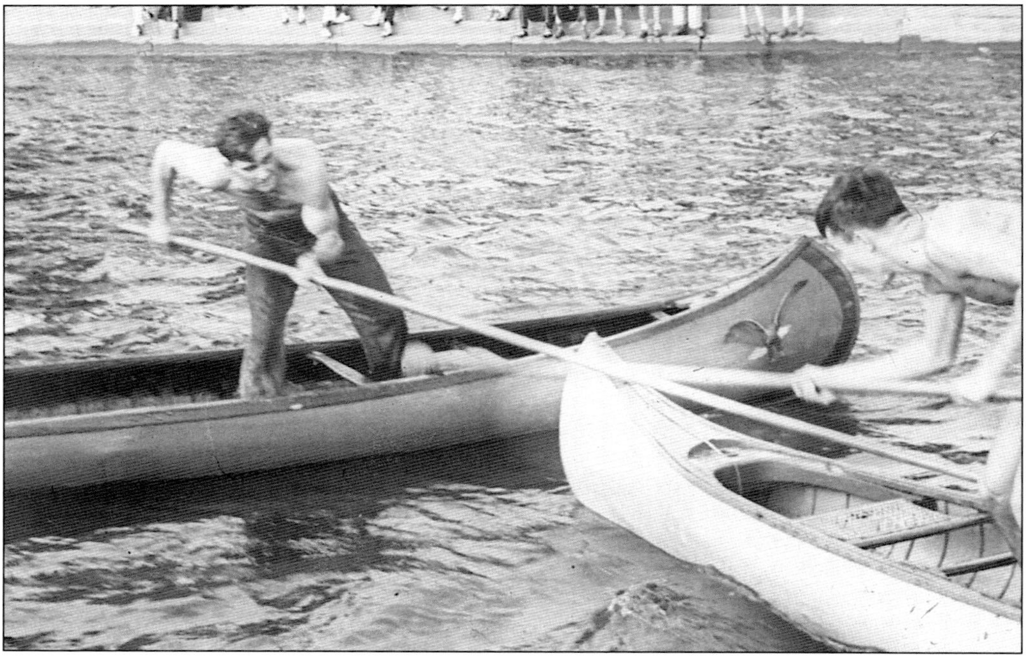

A staple at the Kipona Festival was an event seen here, around 1919 and 1936 respectively, called canoe-tilting. The object of the event was to tip the opposing team's canoe in order to dump the men into the river. This was performed as a two-man team; one member would remain seated in the canoe to paddle and steer the vessel, while the other member would stand and joust with his opponent using a long pole with a padded end until one or both teams ended up in the water.

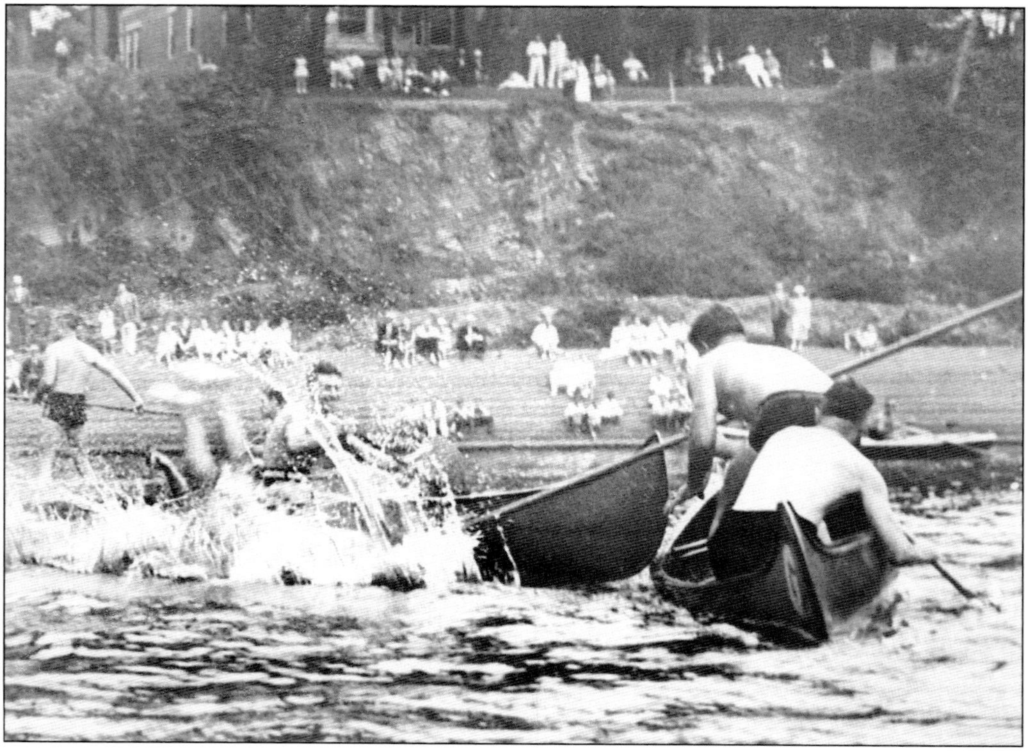

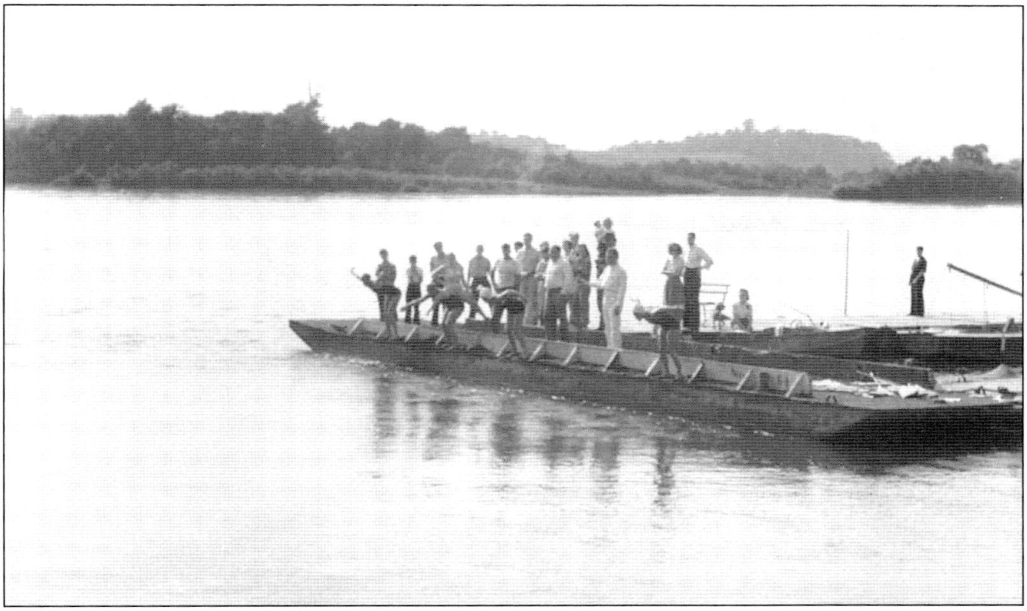

Renaming the festival was not the only major change to the Water Carnival in 1916; that year, women and girls were included in the swimming and boating events. Up to that point, the events were deemed to be too physically demanding for the fairer sex, and they were relegated to spectators at the events. Seen here are swimming events for girls at the Kipona Festival around 1940. The swimming events started from a floating dock, or flatboat, that was positioned just south of North Street and the Pumping Station. After resurgence in interest and a renaming in 1916, the event was cancelled in 1917 and 1918 due to World War I. Interest was renewed after the war, and Kipona was revived in 1919 and enjoyed success through 1922. (Above, courtesy of Keith Ward.)

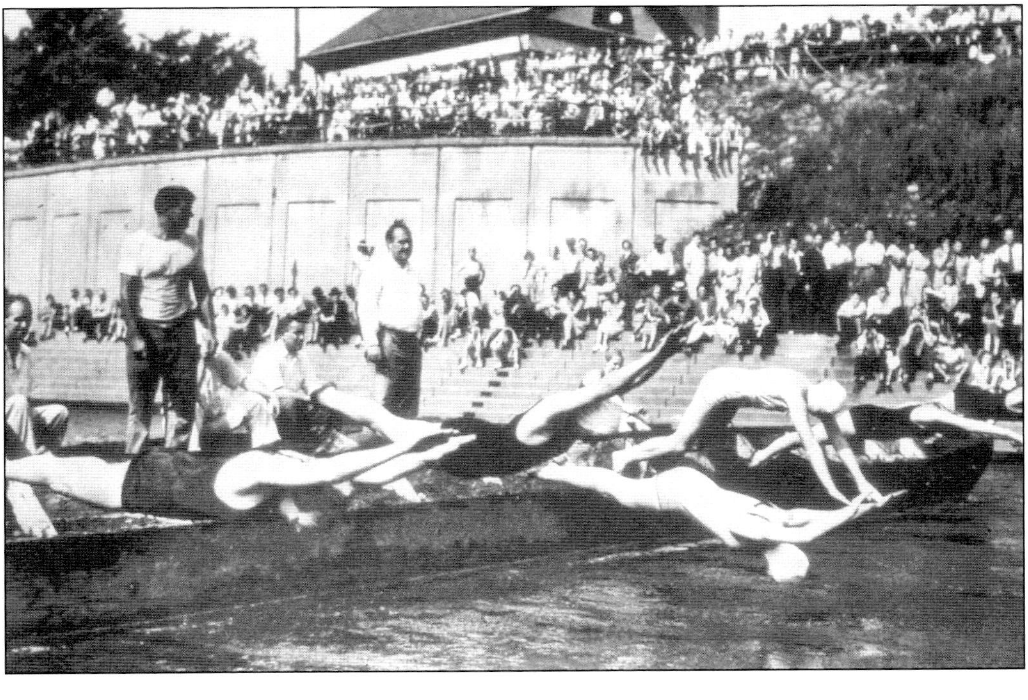

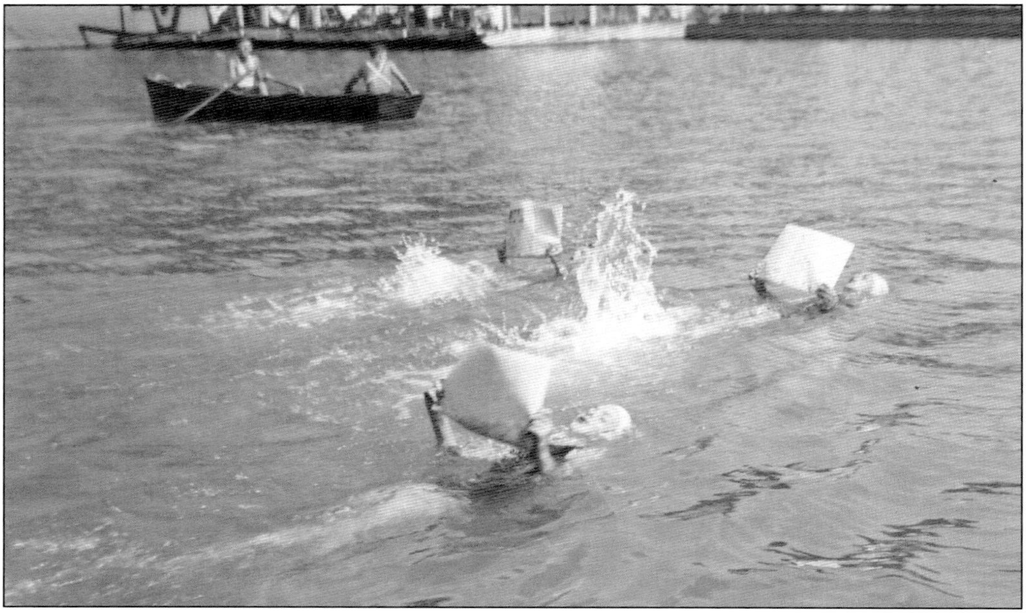

In 1940, a novelty race called the "Newspaper Race" was added to the slate of Kipona events. The simple objective of the competition was to swim while reading a newspaper without getting it wet. The competition was open only to men in the first year and then only to women the second year it was held, in 1942. The race was not held in 1941, as the entire Kipona festival was cancelled due to the perceived threat of the spread of infantile paralysis, or polio. By the early 1940s, the Kipona festival was no longer drawing large crowds. In the photograph below, a canoe race is held about 1942, with no crowds to be seen on the river steps or on the Walnut Street Bridge. (Both, courtesy of Carol Schleig.)

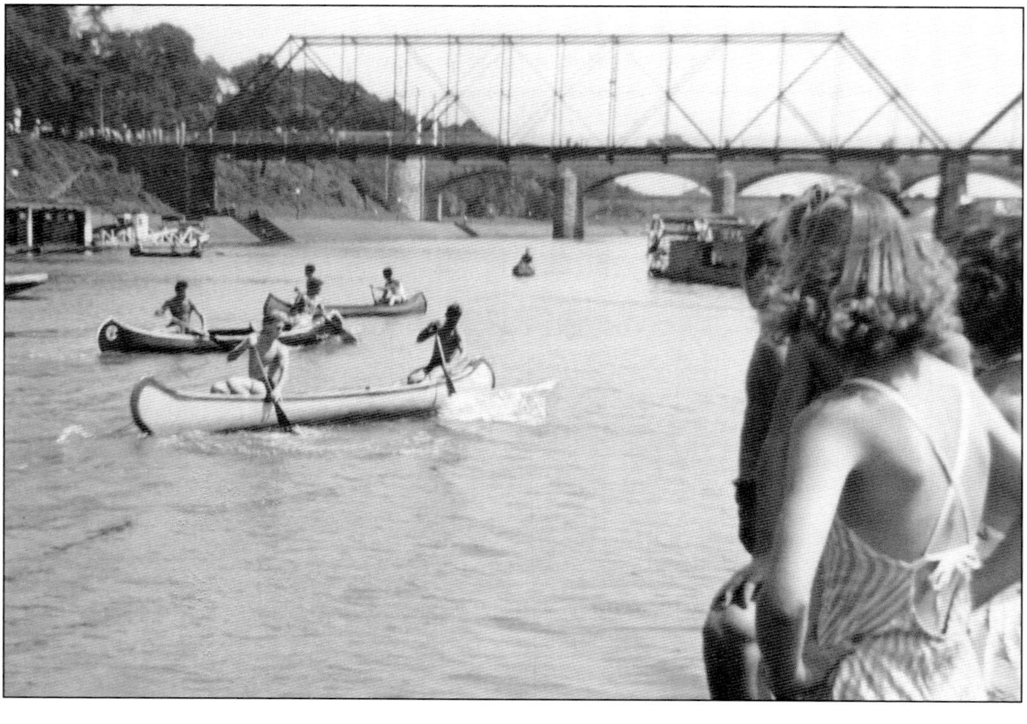

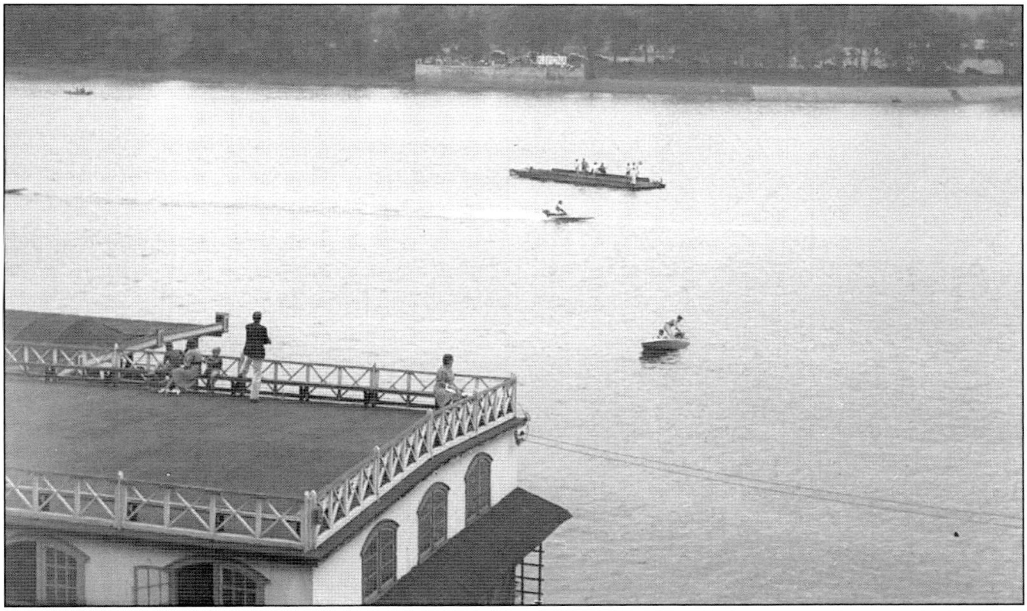

The 1923 Kipona festival was cancelled due to a lack of funds and waning volunteer help. The following year, a semiprivate regatta sponsored by the Keystone Aquatic Club replaced the event. In 1925, Kipona was replaced by the county fair. It would not be until 1936 that Kipona was finally revived after a long hiatus. Kipona enjoyed success again until a threat of polio cancelled the events in 1941, then World War II intervened, and Kipona was again put on hold in 1944 and 1945. The image above shows a view of the sparse Kipona events taking place on the river in the 1940s. The image below shows an unnamed Kipona queen and her court from the mid-1950s. (Above, courtesy of Keith Ward; below, courtesy of Annalisa Young.)

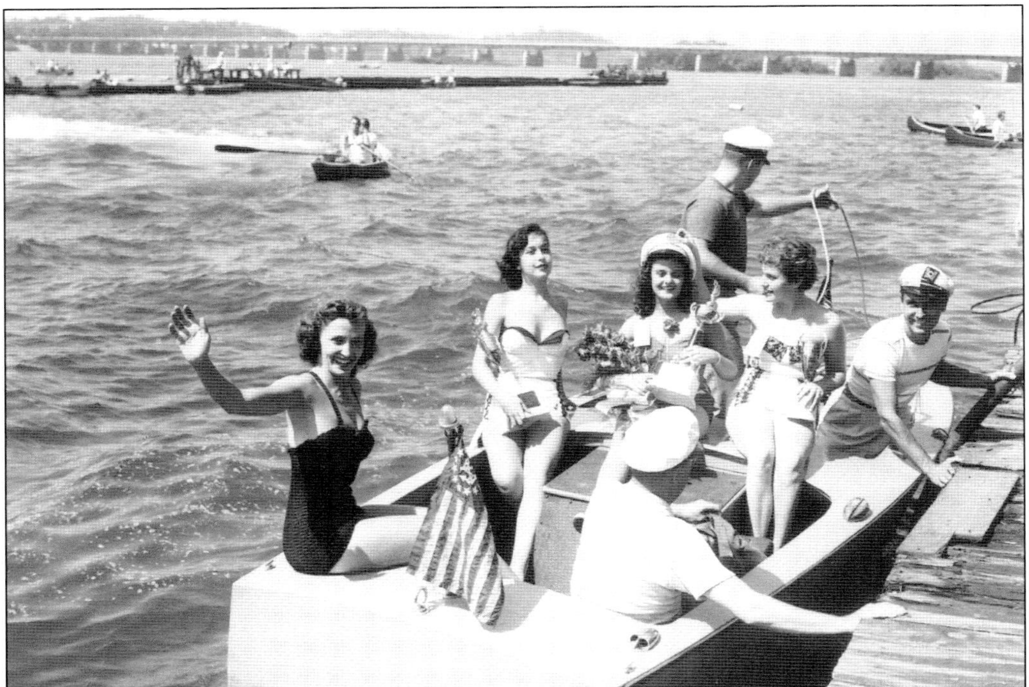

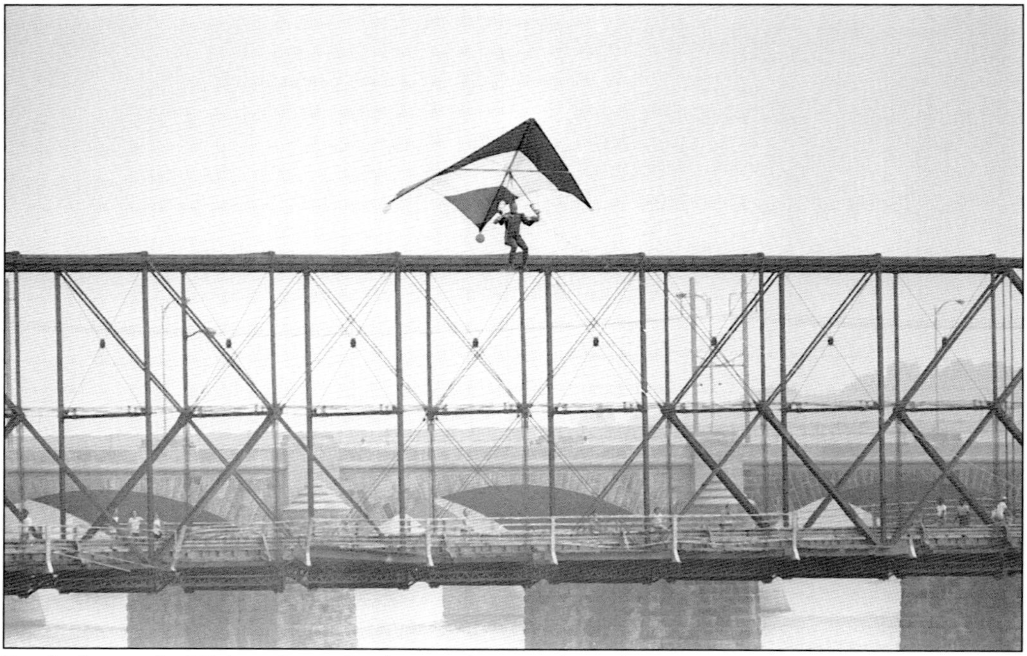

Perched atop the Walnut Street Bridge, Dick Myers from the Conestoga Marine takes flight as a speedboat pulls him aloft in his delta wing hang glider during the Kipona festivities over Labor Day weekend of 1972. Still recovering from Tropical Storm Agnes from the previous June, the appropriate theme of "Beat Those Agnes Blues" was adopted for the event.

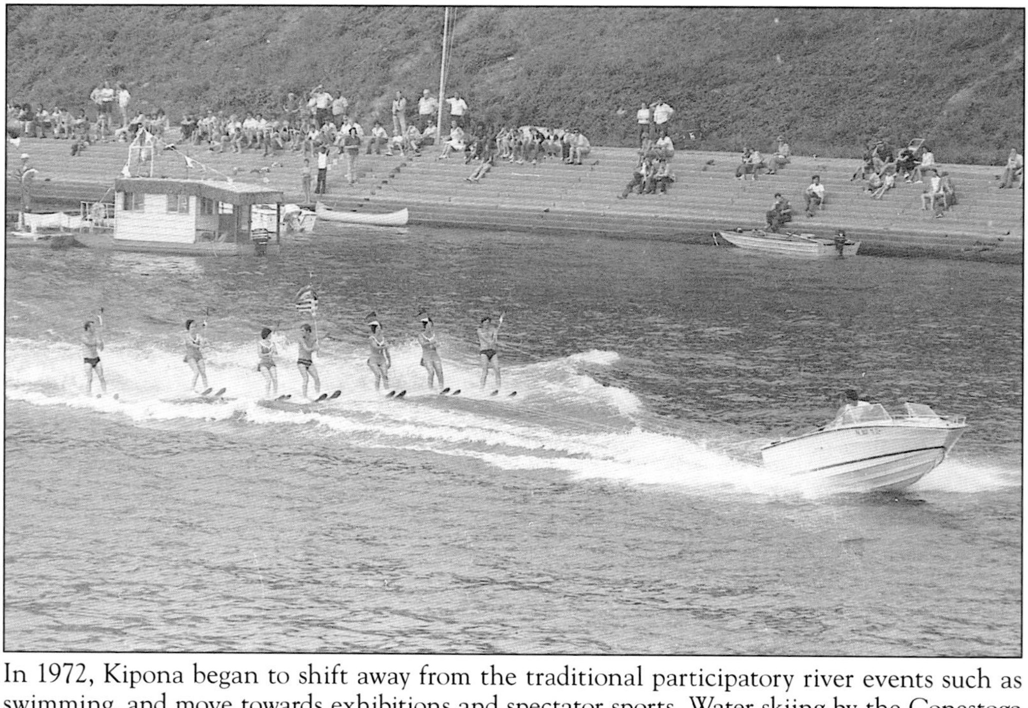

In 1972, Kipona began to shift away from the traditional participatory river events such as swimming, and move towards exhibitions and spectator sports. Water skiing by the Conestoga Marine, as seen here, and speedboat races were well received, but they often included talent that was brought in from outside the Harrisburg area.

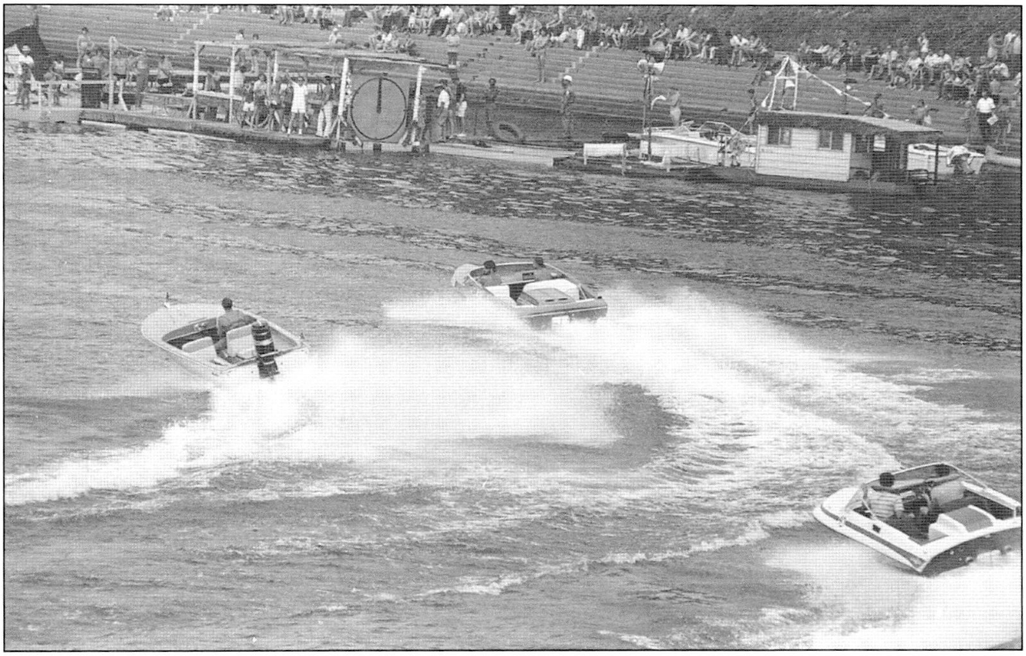

The outboard motorboat races, as seen here during Kipona in 1972, provided a dangerous element to the weekend proceedings, as the boats whipped wildly around the river course with entrance into the races open to anyone with a boat and the nerve to let it all hang out.

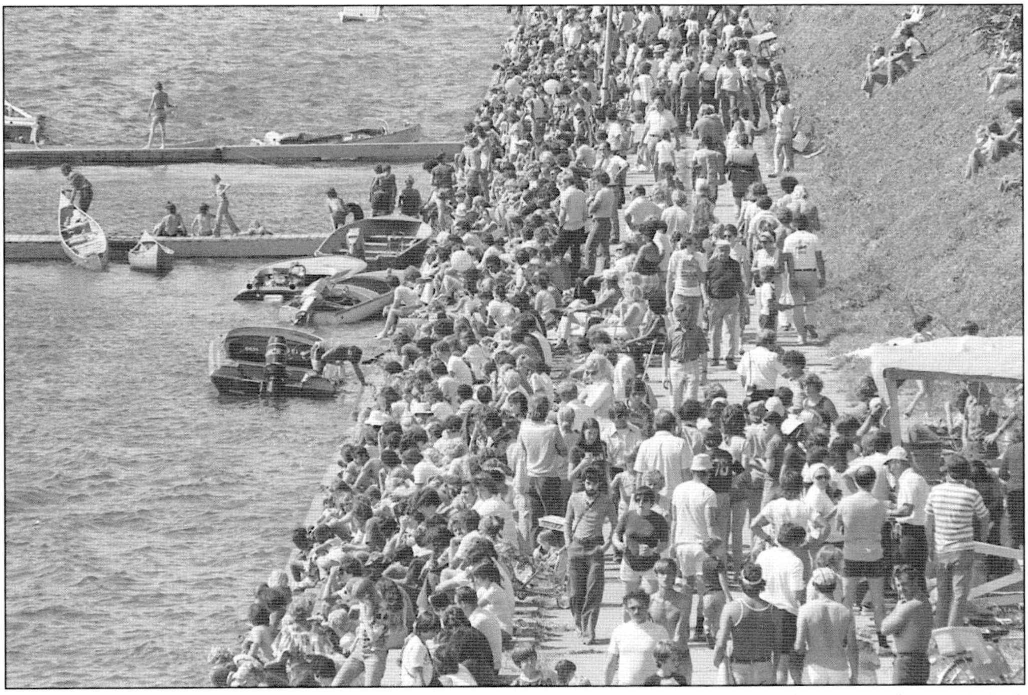

The 1976 Kipona was billed as "A Really Big Show," with Labor Day crowds approaching 20,000 expected along the banks of the Susquehanna to take in the Kipona events. Above the riverfront steps, in Riverfront Park, Harrisburg River Rescue held its annual carnival featuring food, games, and children's rides.

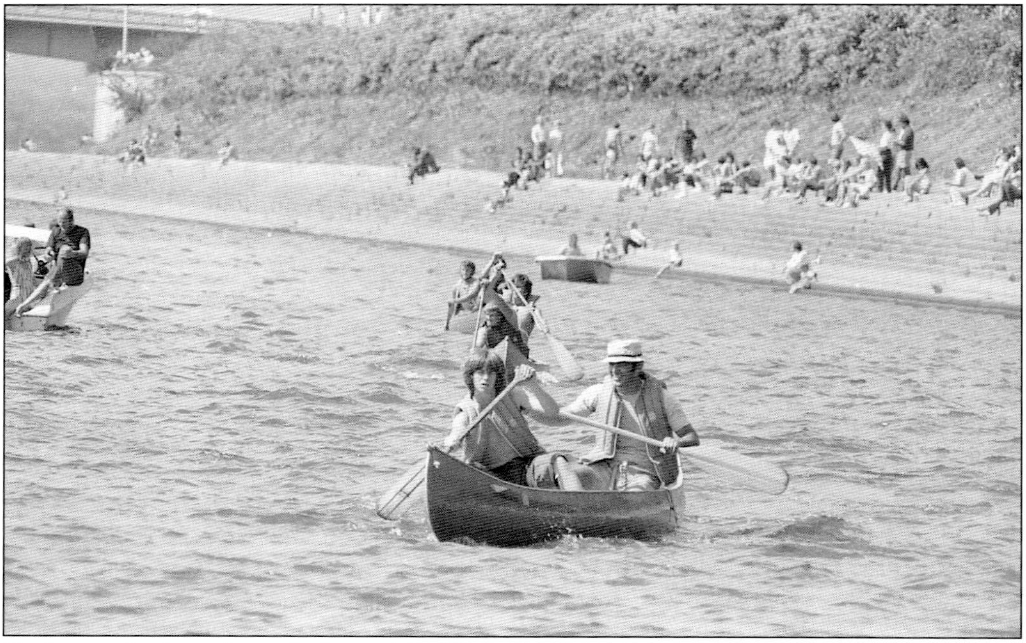

Harkening back to the early days of the Water Carnival, a canoe race is held during the 1976 Kipona festival. There was a choice of two different canoe races for entrants to compete in that day. A one-mile course traveled around City Island, while a longer four-mile course, for the more adventurous, started north of the city and floated southward to the heart of the festivities.

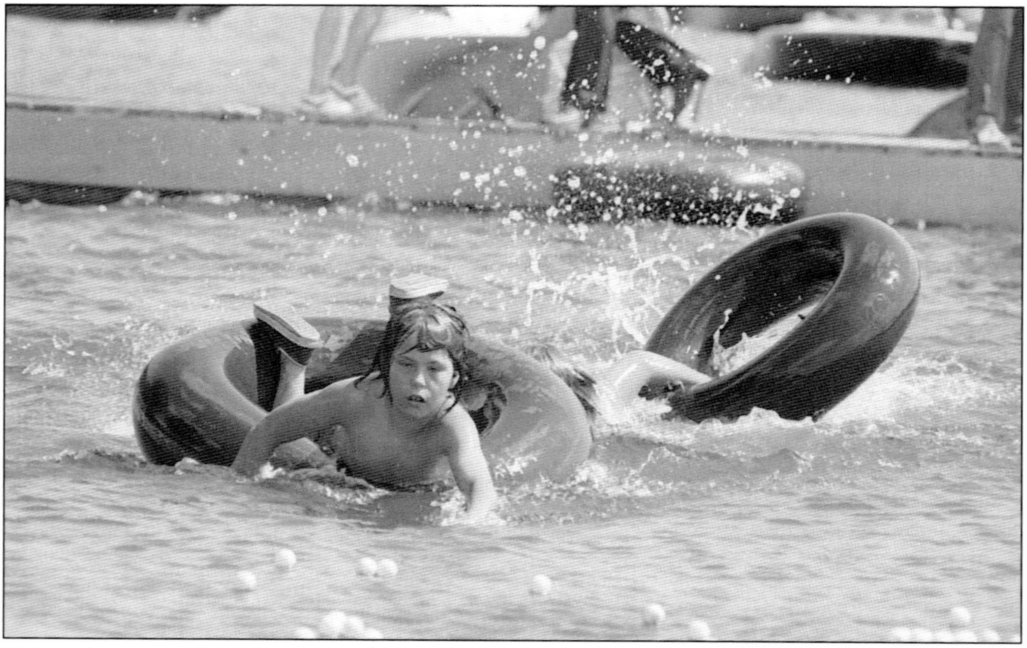

Swimming events had disappeared from Kipona by the 1970s, as the focus drifted more towards boating events and races. One event that remained during the 1976 Kipona was a variant of the Peanut Battle Royal game from the 1940s, where peanuts were thrown into the water and children dived after them. The new version of the game involved children chasing after table tennis balls while swimming in an inner tube.

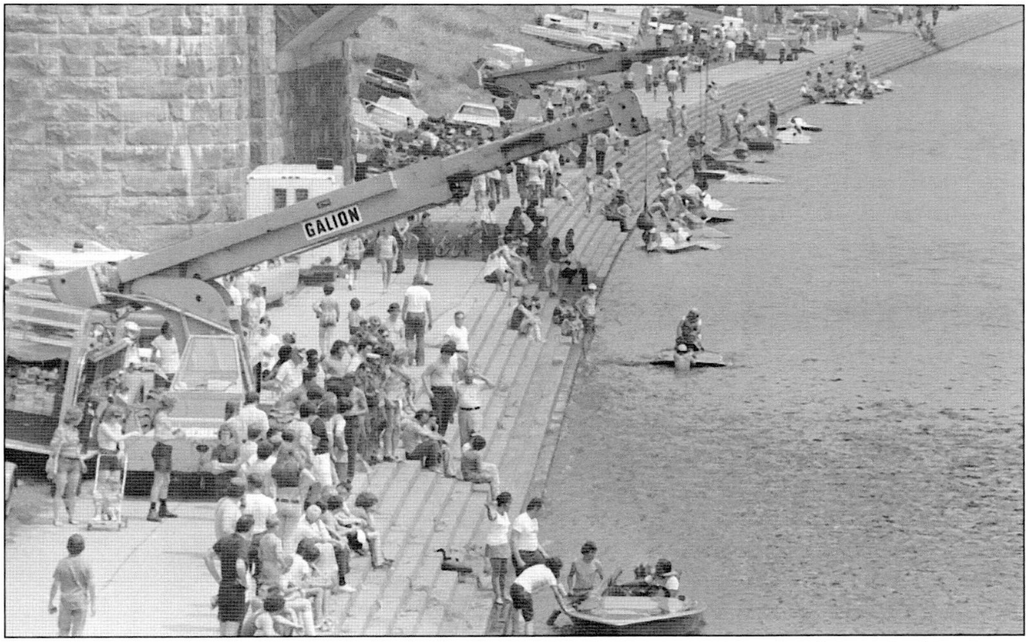


In the image above, cranes are positioned along the riverfront steps to lower and raise the boats into and out of the water during the Independence Day boat races of 1973. In the image below, a boat races across the stretch of water between the Market and Walnut Street Bridges. By comparison, the two-mile motorboat race held at the 1907 Water Carnival was won by Gilbert Oves with a time of 15 minutes and 30 seconds. The race was handicapped, giving some of the entrants a 1 minute and 15 second head start ahead of Oves, but he still managed to win the contest.

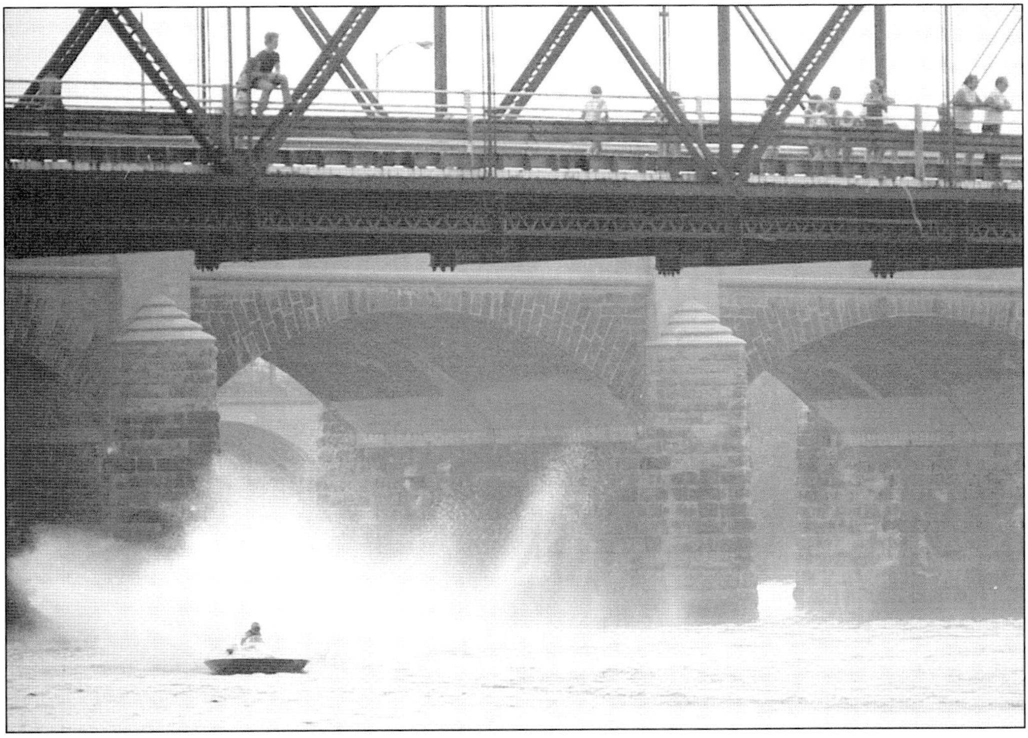

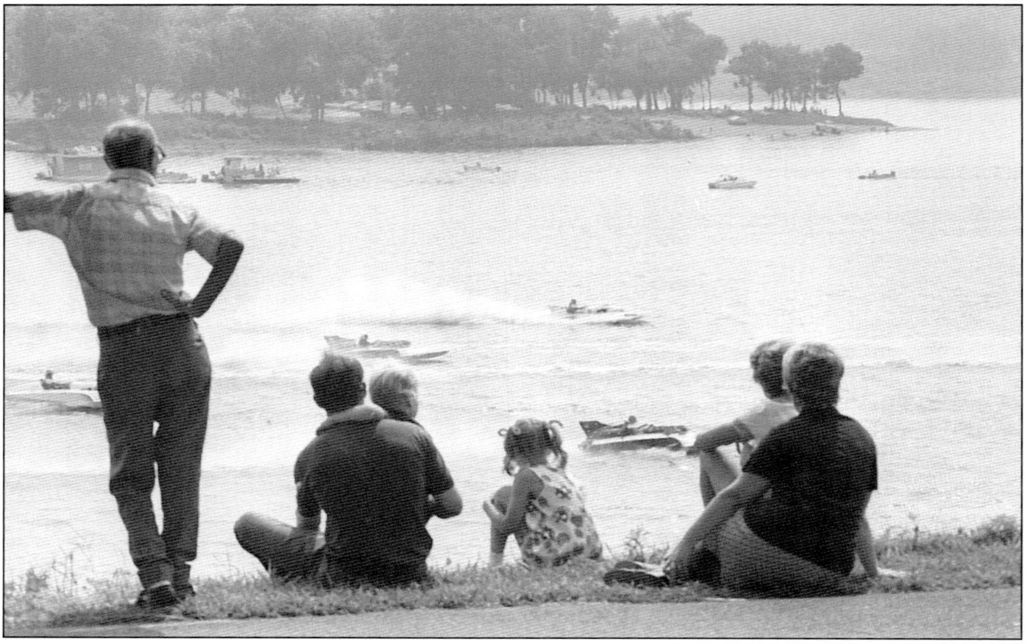

By the mid-1940s, the motorboat races at the Kipona and Independence Day events had begun to move away from local participatory events and towards spectator exhibitions where talent was brought in from up and down the eastern seaboard to compete. According to the August 31, 1946, *Harrisburg Telegraph*, the boat races at the 1946 Kipona featured "world-famous drivers . . . with the co-operation of the National Outboard Association of Philadelphia." The image above show spectators in Riverfront Park taking in the races during the Independence Day events of 1973. However, it was not always a matter of speed and competition. In the image below, crowds on the riverfront and afloat on the water stop to relax and listen to a performance of the Harrisburg Symphony performing at its annual barge concert on the Susquehanna River.

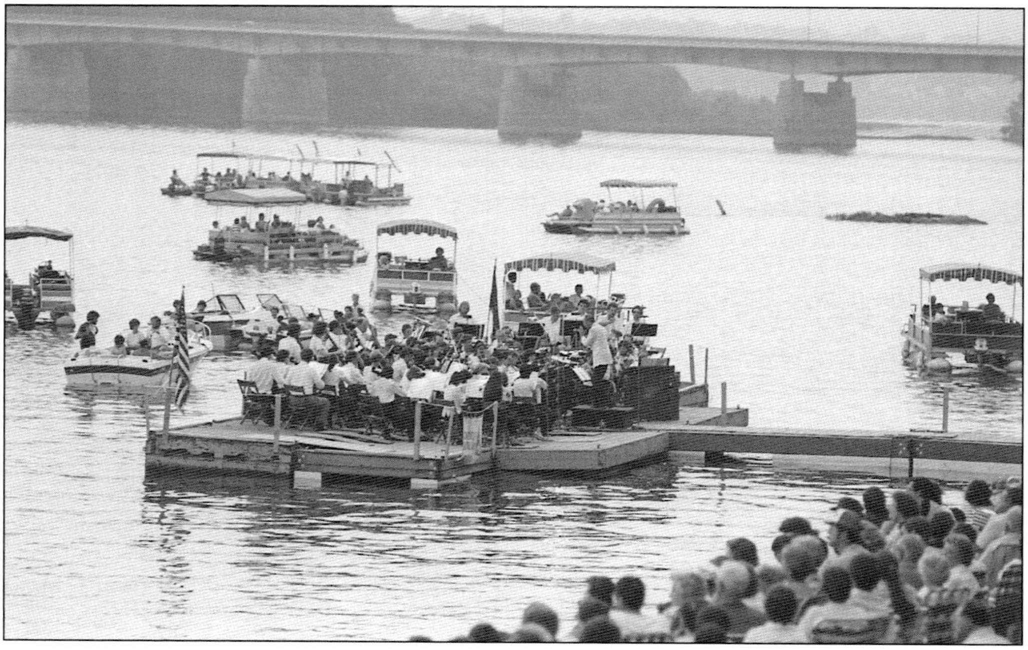

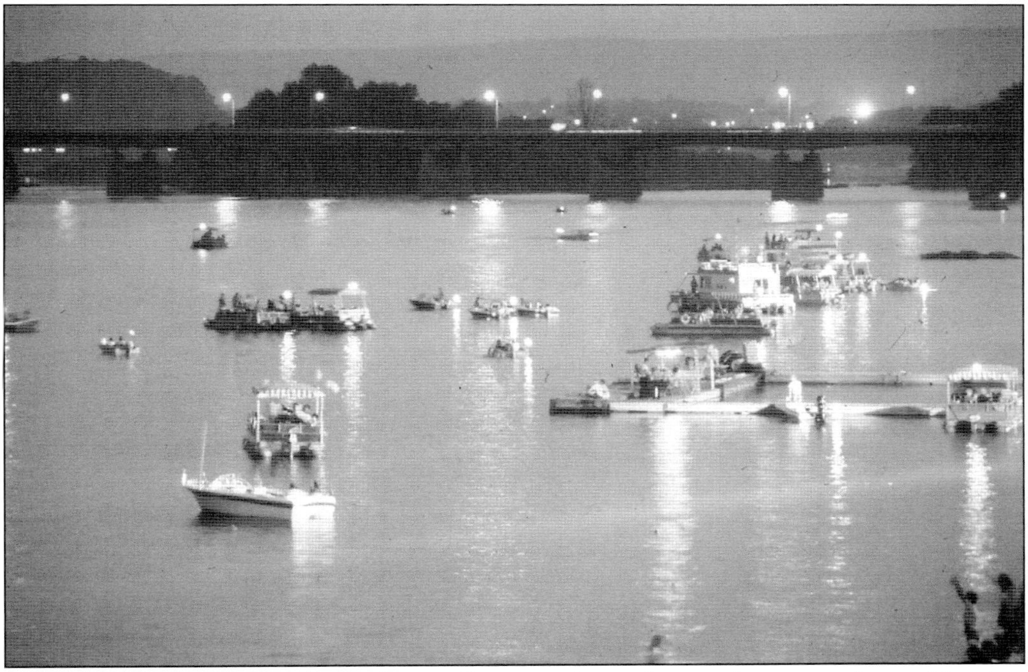

In this image, pontoon boats and other small watercraft mingle near the eastern shore of the river during the nighttime Kipona festivities about 1982. Situated out on the water, the view provides a central vantage point to listen to the barge concerts along the shoreline and view the fireworks sent up from City Island.

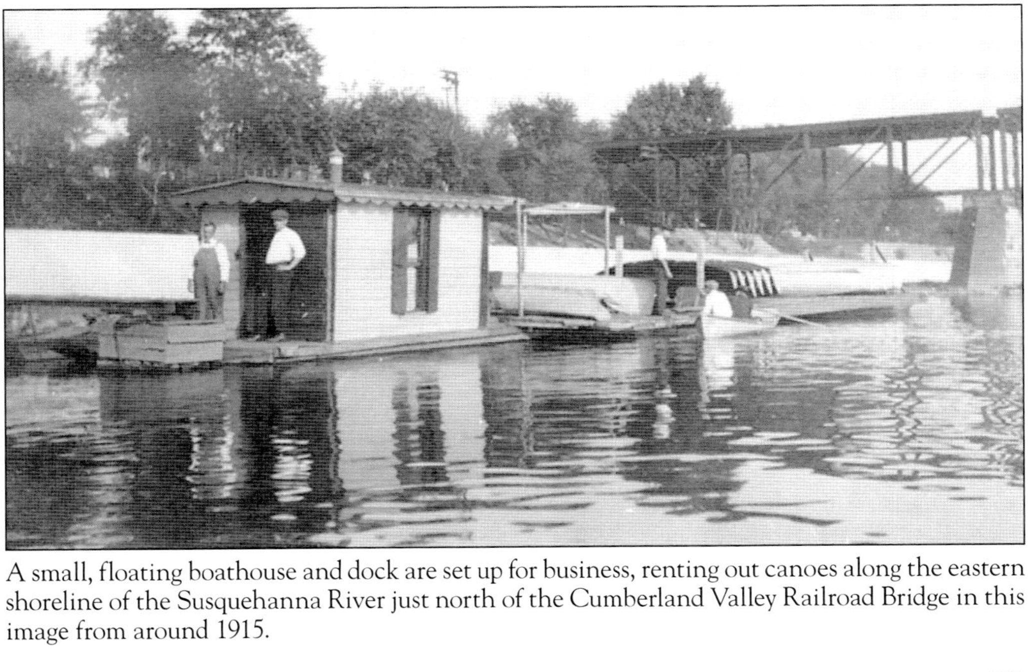

A small, floating boathouse and dock are set up for business, renting out canoes along the eastern shoreline of the Susquehanna River just north of the Cumberland Valley Railroad Bridge in this image from around 1915.

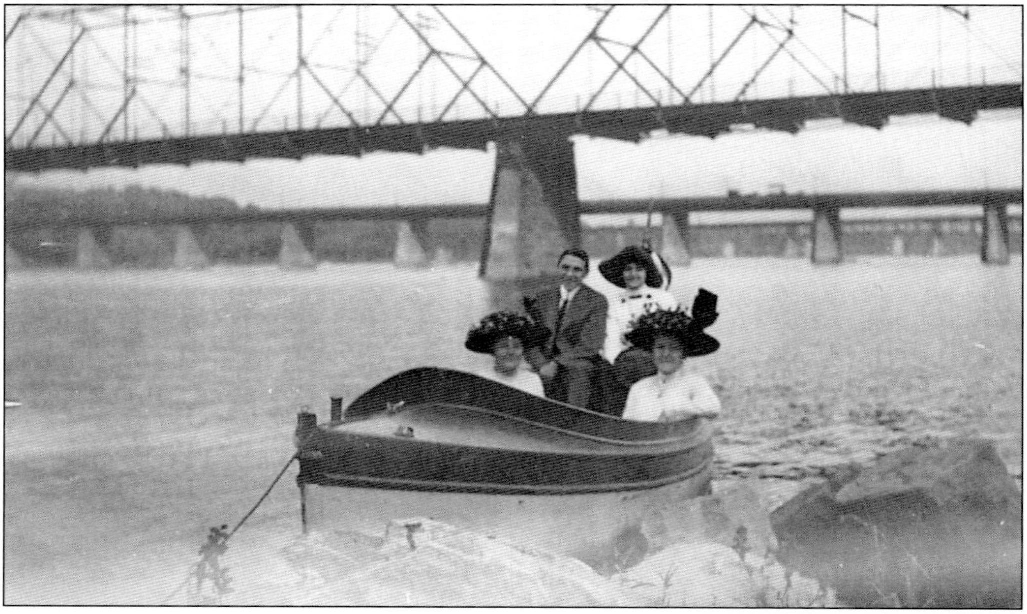

In this c. 1914 photograph, Clarence Deller and his family enjoy a day out in their motorboat along the western shore of the Susquehanna River just north of the Walnut Street Bridge. Deller was a competitor and committee member in the early motorboat races at the Water Carnivals, including an entry in the four-mile motorboat race at the 1909 Independence Day Water Carnival.

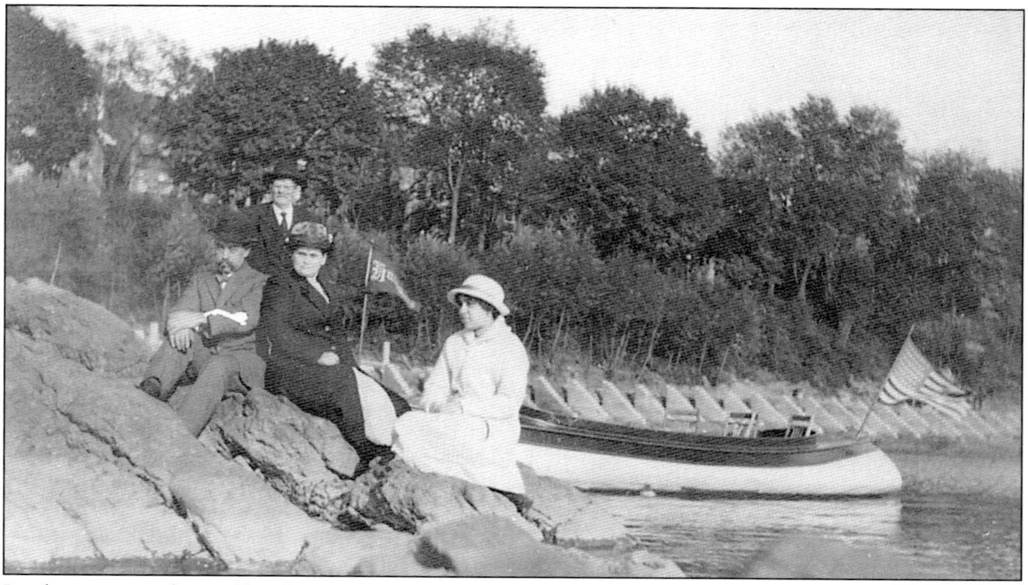

In this image, the Deller family rests on a rocky outcropping near the river shoreline with the concrete stringers of the Riverfront Steps in the background.

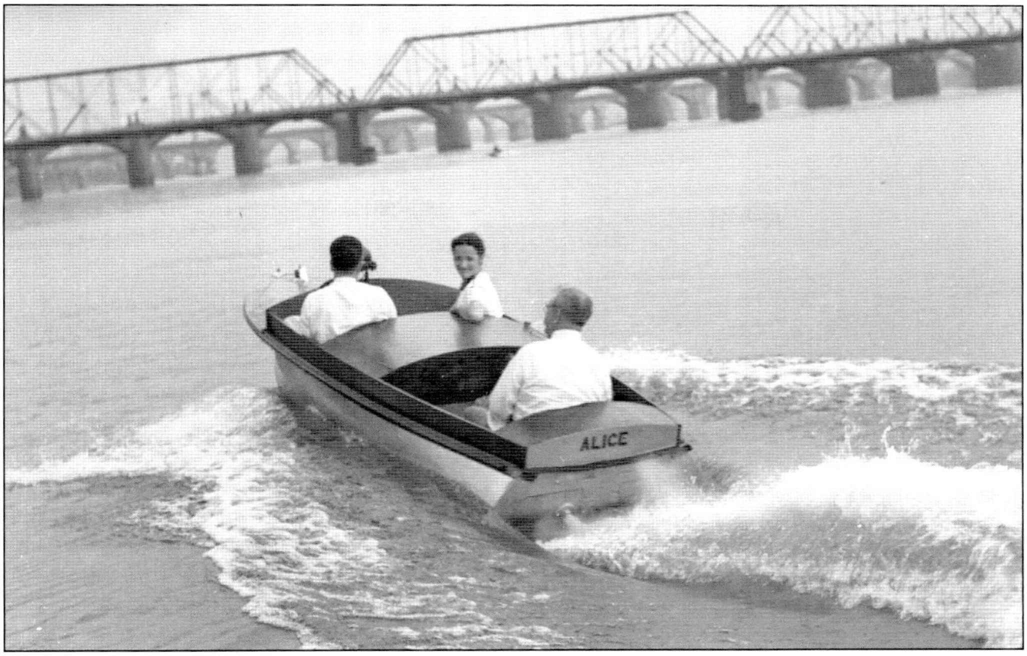



Gasoline-powered motorboats began to make an appearance on the river near Harrisburg around 1905. Purely for pleasure rides, some of these vessels were powered by nothing more than one-and-one-quarter-horsepower engines. In this image, taken around 1940, the *Alice* shows how far gasoline motorboats had come since 1905. (Courtesy of Keith Ward.)

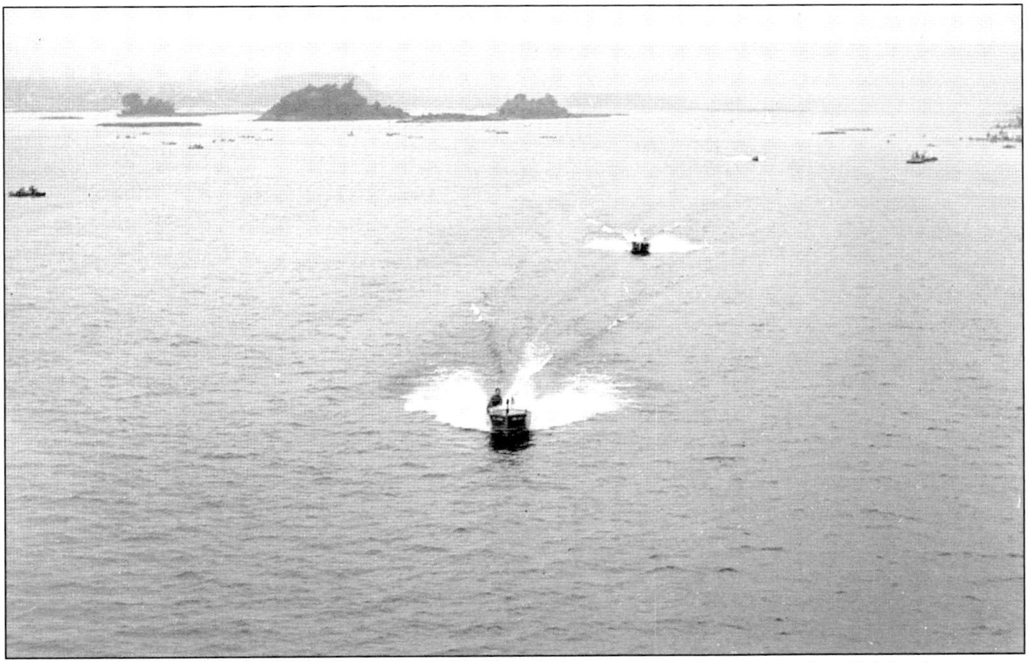

Taken from the Walnut Street Bridge during a motorboat race at Kipona in the 1940s, this image shows the expanse of open water that existed prior to the construction of the M. Harvey Taylor Bridge in 1950. Independence and Bailey Islands can be seen in the background, with smaller watercraft lining the race route. (Courtesy of Keith Ward.)

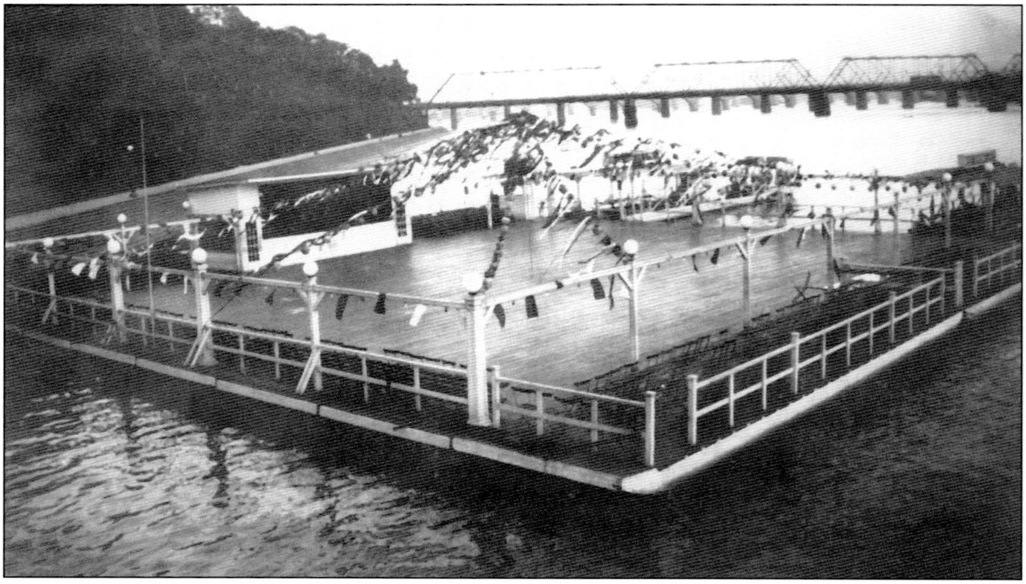

In July 1916, George K. Reist opened the Municipal Port, anchored off of the riverfront steps at South Street. The first boat of the Reist fleet was a small houseboat with an open deck on the roof. The Reist fleet would grow to include a number of larger houseboats and dance barges, as seen in the images above and below from around 1930. In 1942, one of the barges was utilized by the USO for dances for servicemen during World War II. The dance barges were also aimed at events for children, including excursions to the island beaches, kiddie hour dances, and special events for children and their mothers in the Child Welfare Association.

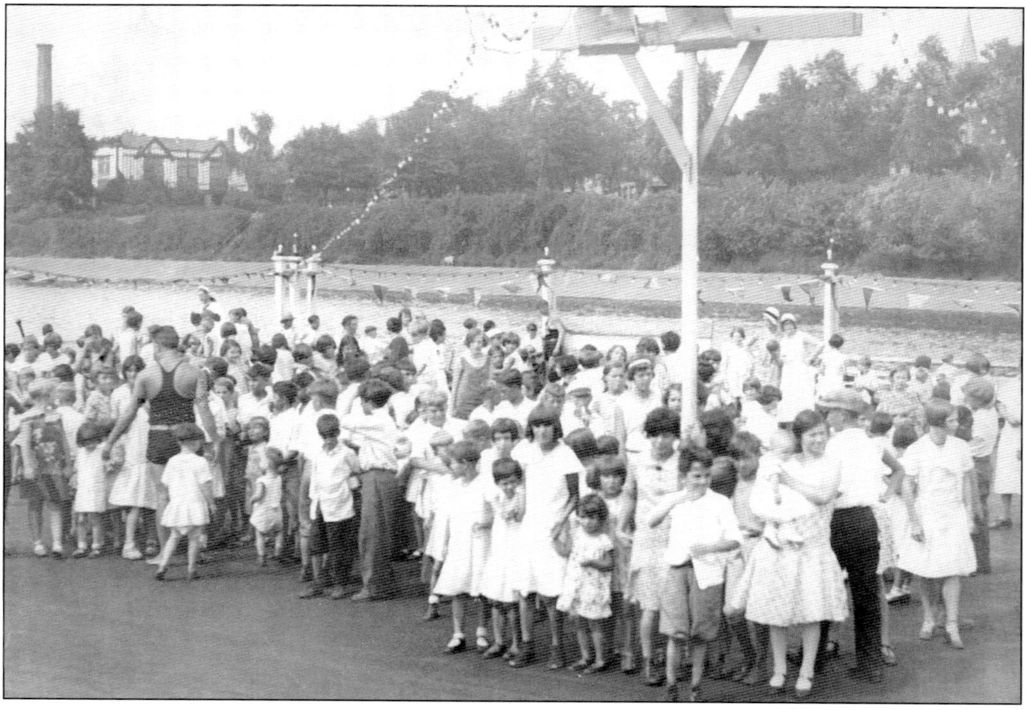

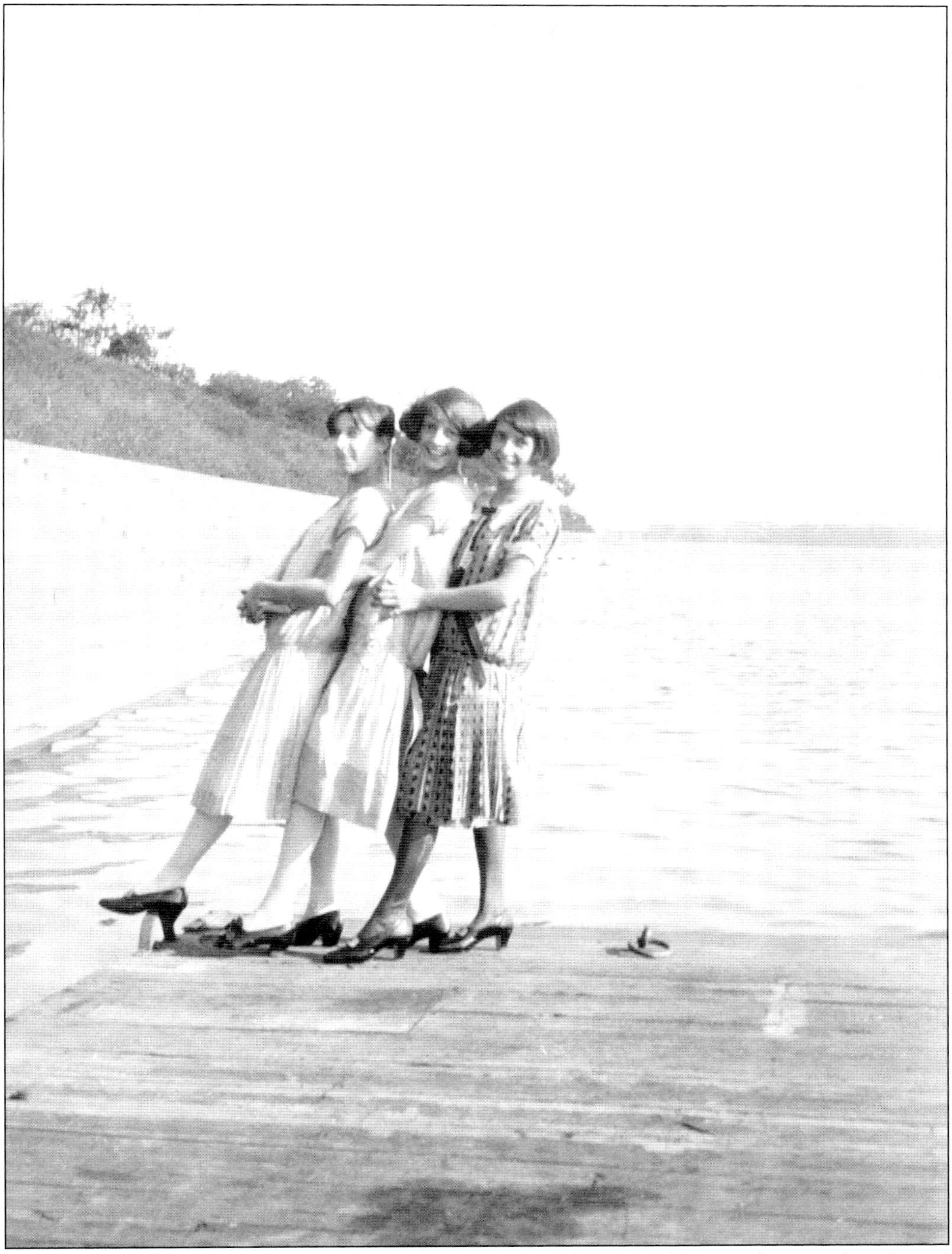

The dance barges would become a hot spot for nightlife along the river, hosting bands and orchestras well into the 1940s. The May 28, 1924, *Harrisburg Telegraph* reports that some of the barges were outfitted with an orchestra shell "designed to give the music the utmost harmony and volume." In the image seen here, taken about 1925, Ethel Janes (center) poses with her sisters on a barge along the river front. Ethel's future husband, Kenny Frew, who was playing trumpet for the Dan Gregory Orchestra, caught his first glimpse of his future wife on a Reist dance barge. (Courtesy of Ken Frew.)

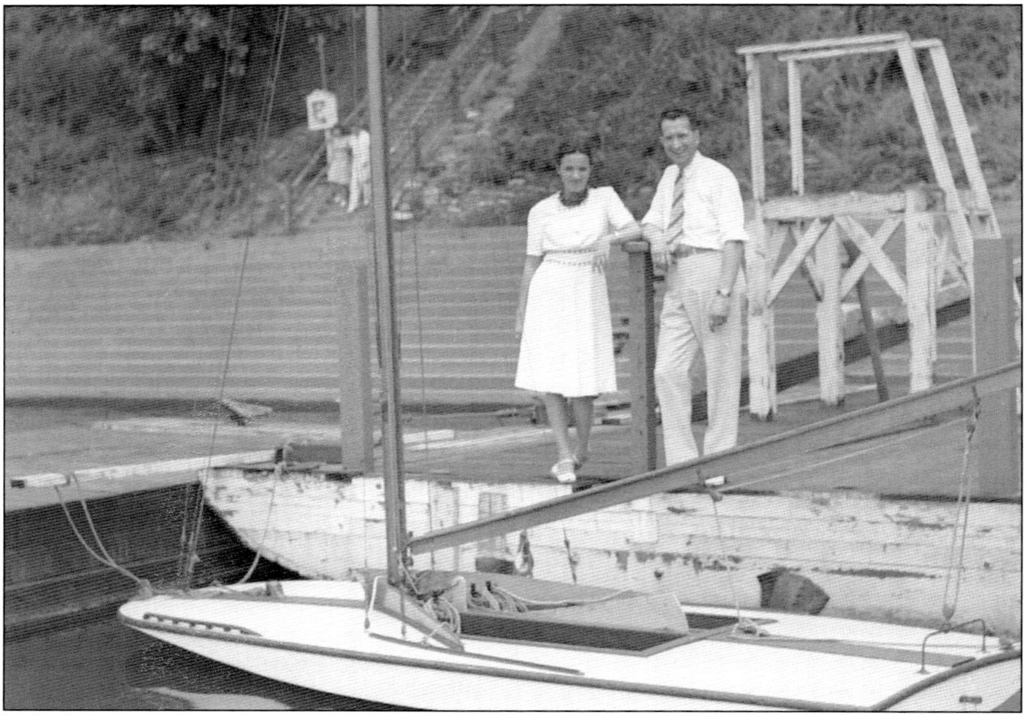

The large Reist boathouse (below) capsized and was submerged in the river along the east side of City Island due to flooding in the spring of 1945. The boathouse was ultimately purchased as is by Dale Zeiders and resurrected from the river. The boathouse and the accompanying docks also served as a storage area for boats and canoes in addition to a dance hall and social gathering place. (Above, courtesy of Keith Ward.)

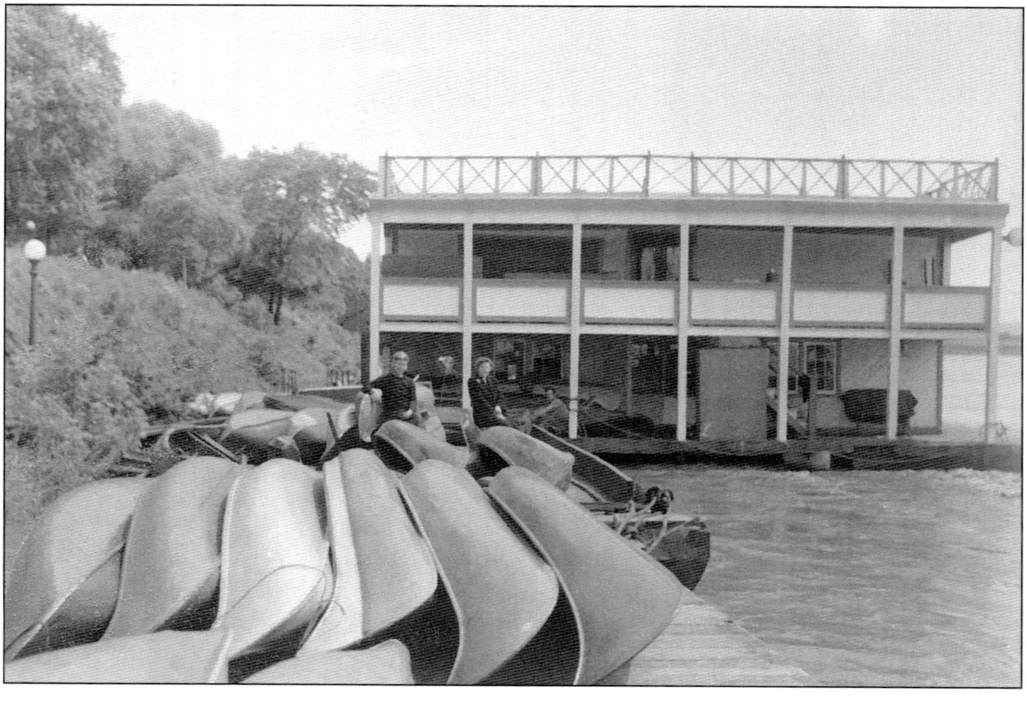

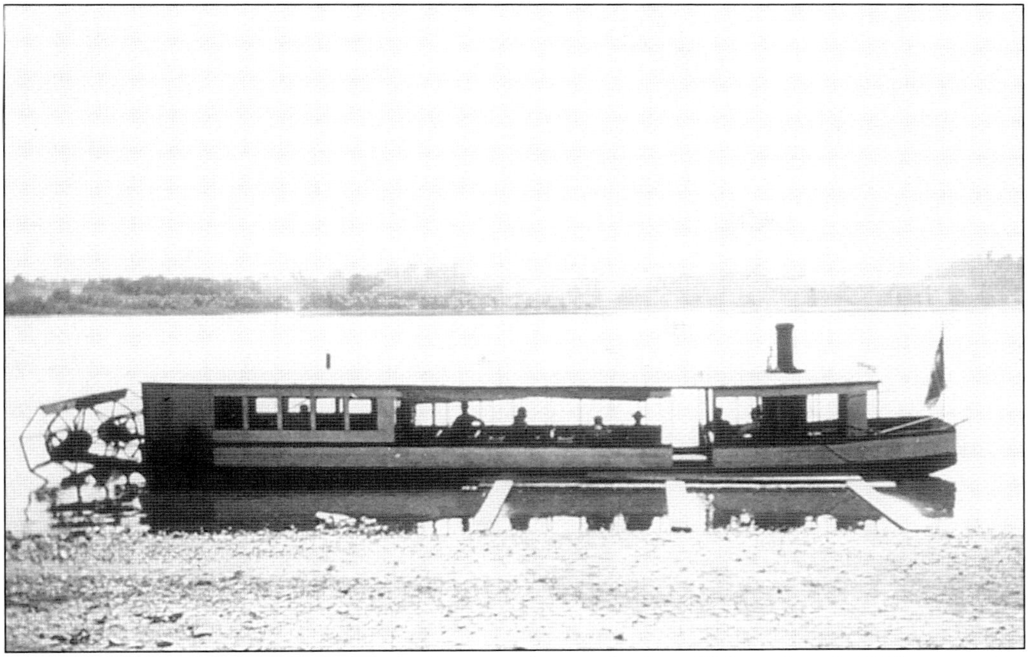

Paddleboats were a common sight on the river during the late 19th and early 20th centuries, seeing a multitude of uses, including ferrying beachgoers to Independence Island. Revisiting this tradition is the *Pride of the Susquehanna*, a stern-driven paddlewheel riverboat, seen below at its launch in 1988. The project to bring a paddlewheel boat back to Harrisburg was driven by local businessman Mike Trephan, along with the Harrisburg Area Riverboat Society. The *Pride of the Susquehanna* provides educational programs for schoolchildren, in addition to sightseeing and dinner cruises.

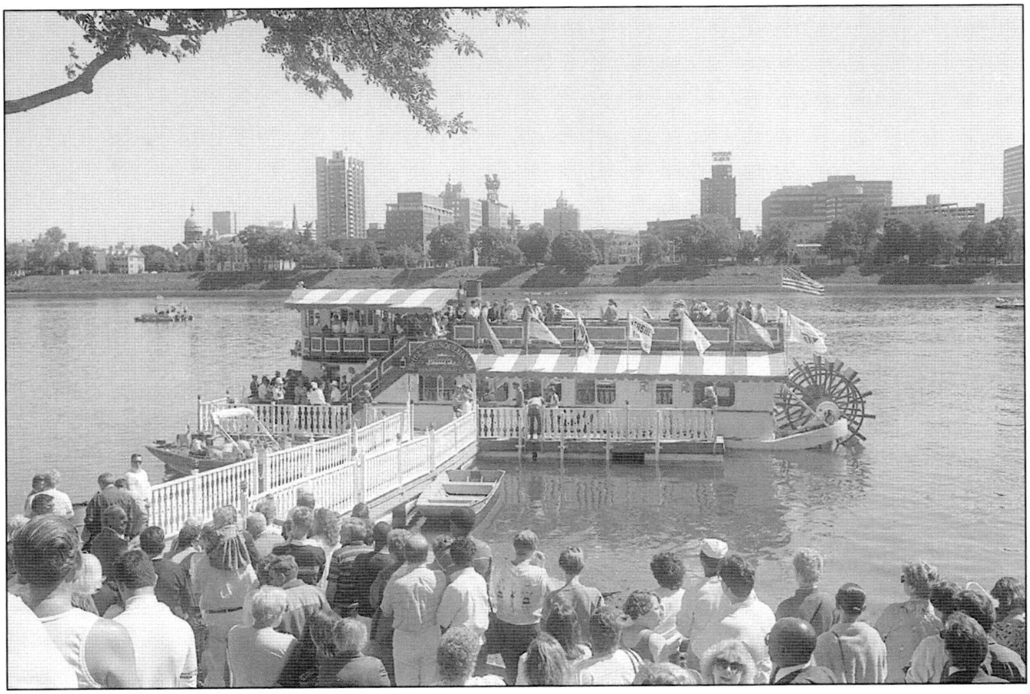

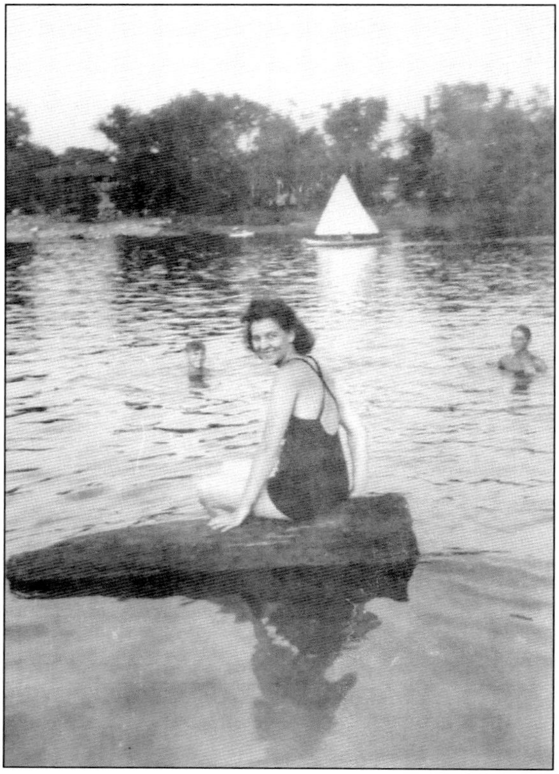

In a pose reminiscent of the famous *Little Mermaid* statue in Copenhagen, Jen Milisavic O'Brine is perched on a river rock in the western channel of the Susquehanna with City Island in the background in this 1940s image. Below, her husband, Armand O'Brine, who worked as a lifeguard at the Municipal Beach on City Island during the 1930s and 1940s, poses on one of Vanderbilt's Piers, where a makeshift diving board has been inserted between the stones around 1960. (Both, courtesy of Carol Schleig.)

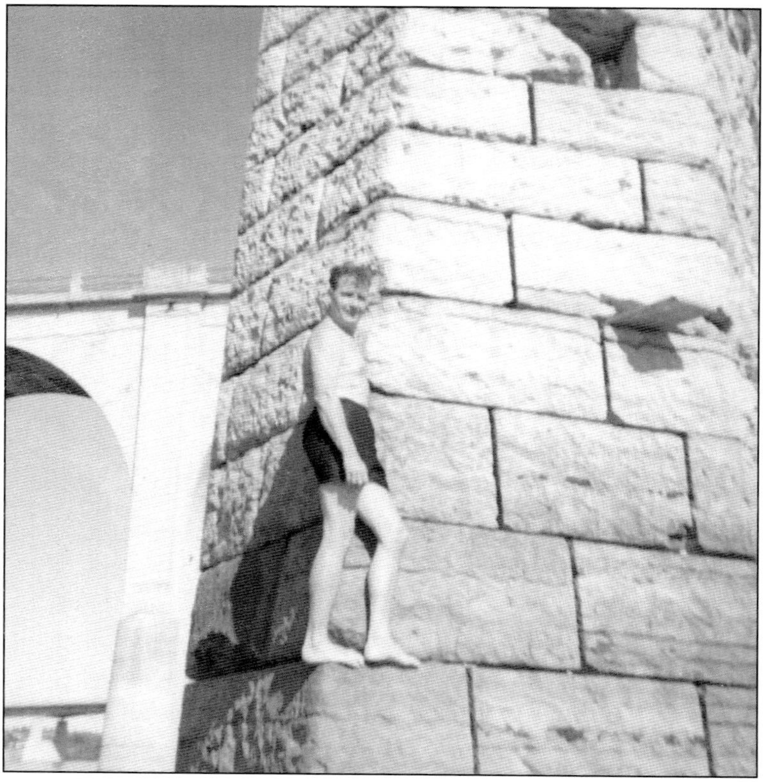

The partially obscured sign on the Reist Float advises to "use at your own risk" as a diver jumps head first into the deeper water under the piers of the Walnut Street Bridge about 1930. In 1941, the People's Bridge Company would settle a suit against Lillian Reist to have the boats and floats removed from beneath the bridge, which was deemed to be bridge property.

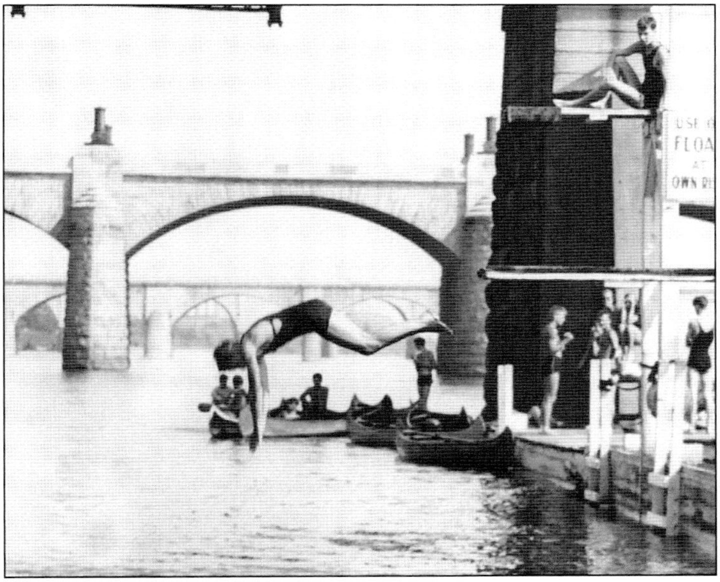

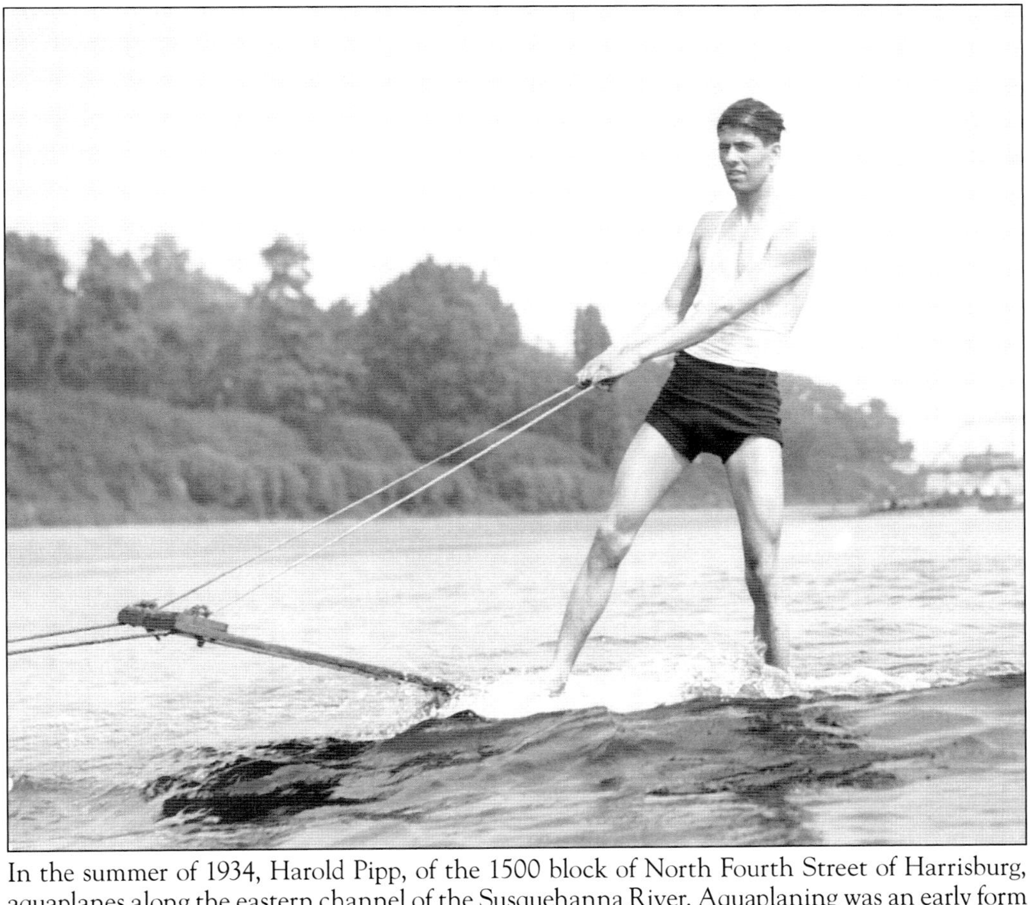

In the summer of 1934, Harold Pipp, of the 1500 block of North Fourth Street of Harrisburg, aquaplanes along the eastern channel of the Susquehanna River. Aquaplaning was an early form of wakeboarding that was a popular exhibition at the Kipona festivals of the 1920s and 1930s. Ever the daredevil, Pipp would later take the title of captain, serving as a pilot during World War II.

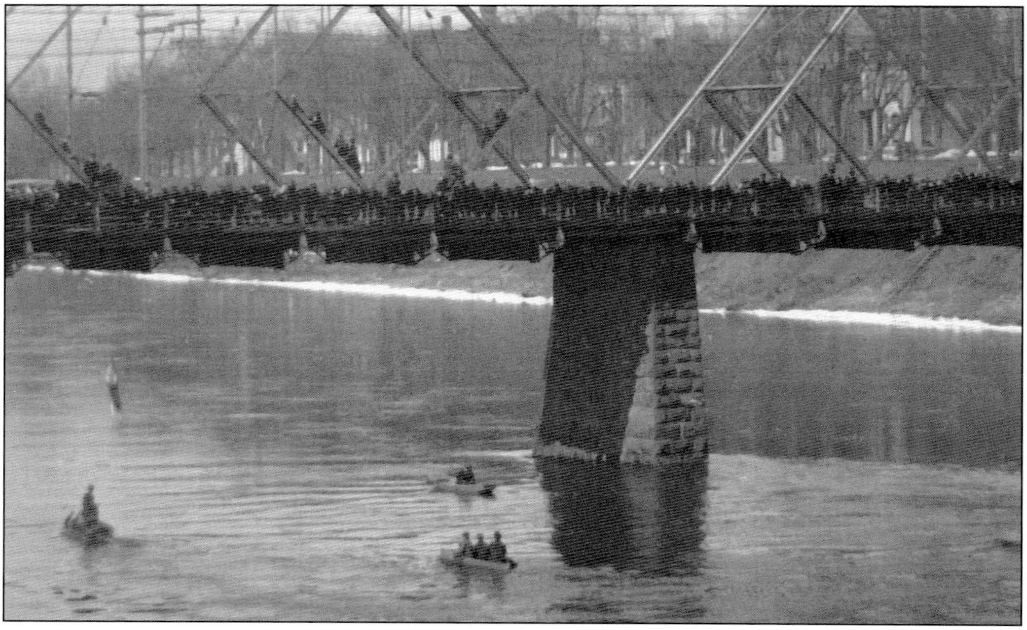

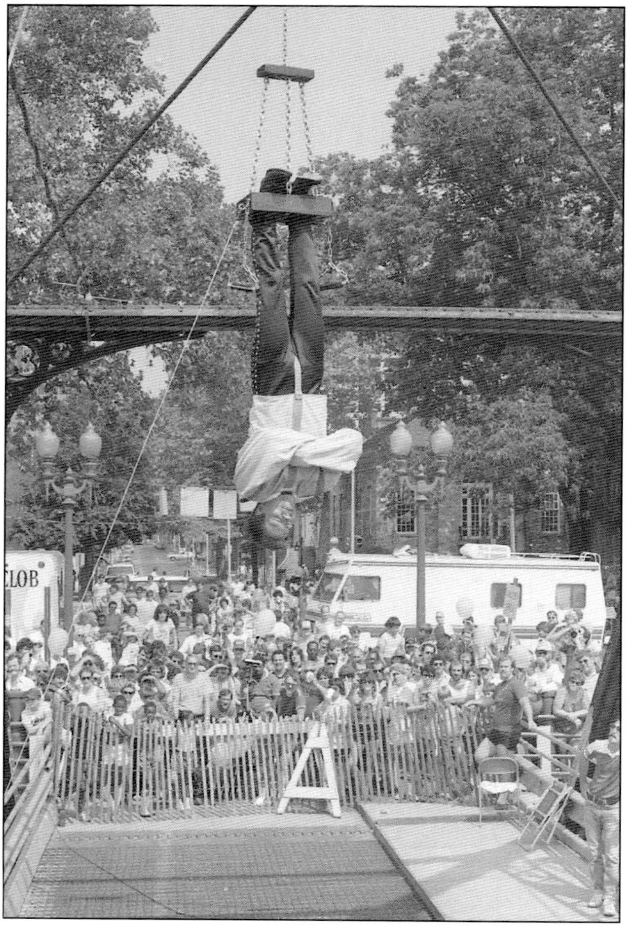

In a stunt occurring ironically on Leap Day, Brindamour, the self-proclaimed "Handcuff King," is seen above just over the water's surface after diving from the Walnut Street Bridge on February 29, 1908. A contemporary of Houdini, Brindamour was appearing that week at the Orpheum Theater performing acts of escape with handcuffs, locks, and a steel cage. At 1:00 p.m. on the cold February afternoon, he arrived at the bridge and was handcuffed by Sergeant Sullivan of the Harrisburg police. Then he plunged 30 feet, headfirst, into the icy river. He emerged above the surface six seconds later, holding the handcuffs above his head. Brindamour hurried back to the theater and gave an afternoon performance. In the image at left, Lebanon County magician and escape artist Barry Yiengst hangs upside down from the Walnut Street Bridge, before freeing himself from a straitjacket at the 1980 Kipona festival.

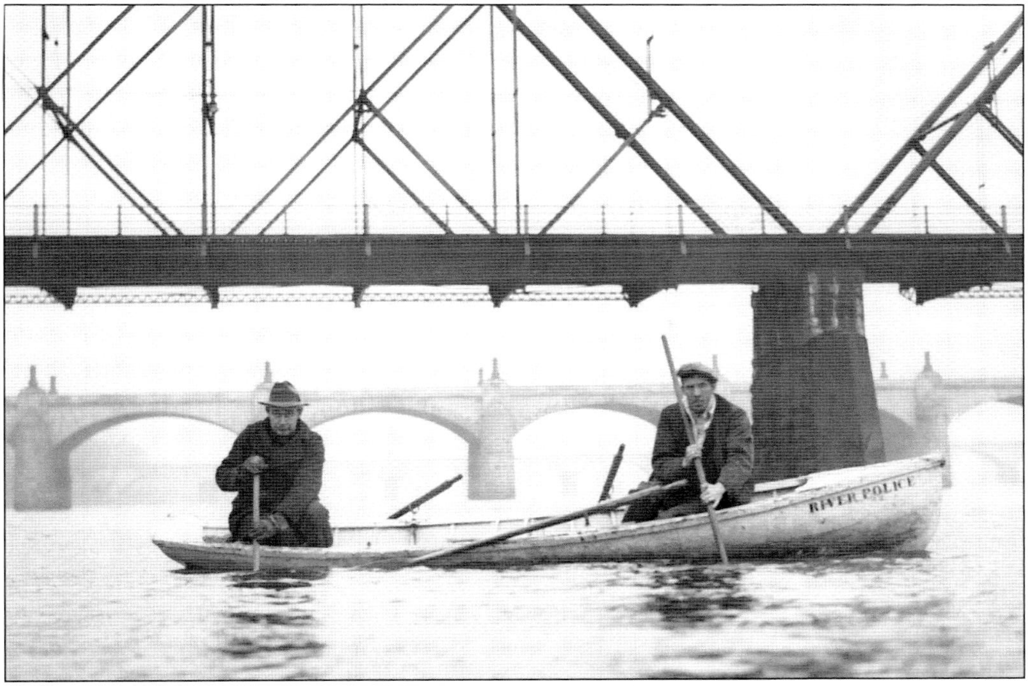


The March 31, 1933, *Harrisburg Evening News* relates that "William Emanuel (left) and Benjamin Shindler, life guards at the city bathing beach, are shown grappling for the body of a man, believed to be Robert T. Wilson, 52, of 1412 Green Street, who was seen to fall or jump into the Susquehanna River at the foot of Verbeke Street" on the afternoon of March 30, 1933. Wilson's body was found on April 25 by a fisherman three miles south of Middletown.

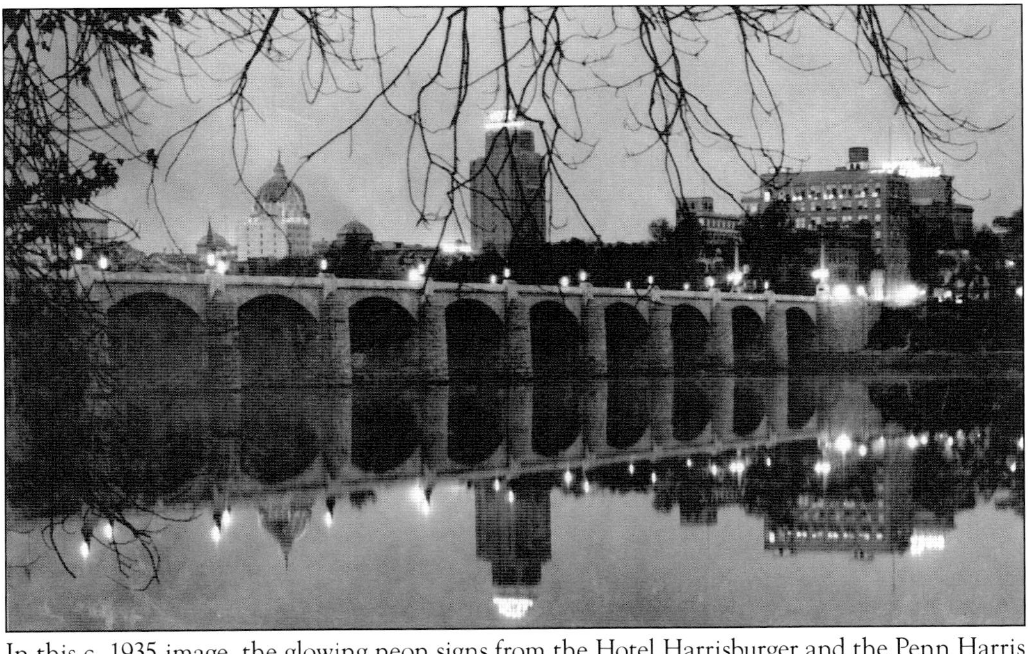

In this c. 1935 image, the glowing neon signs from the Hotel Harrisburger and the Penn Harris Hotel, along with the lights from the Market Street Bridge, reflect off of the seemingly serene surface of the Susquehanna River.

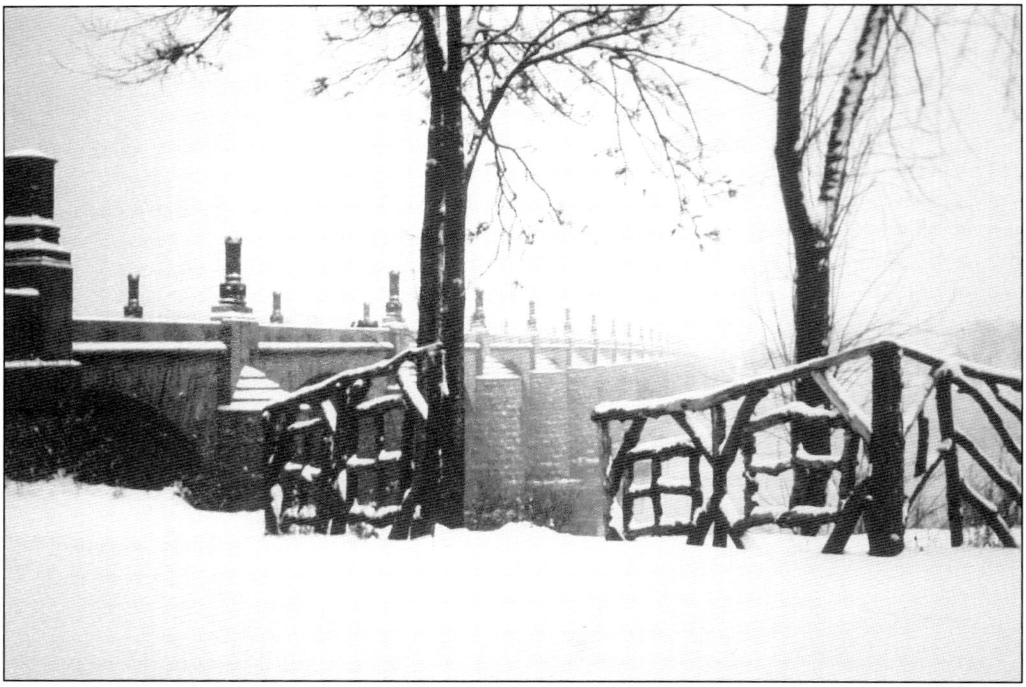

The image above provides a scenic view of the Market Street Bridge and Riverfront Park during a light snow around 1940. In the image below, taken about 1900, on the western side of City Island, two gentlemen stand confidently on the frozen river, surveying the snow-covered winter landscape. In wintertime, when the Susquehanna had frozen to a sufficient thickness, it would become a passable road, thwarting bridge tolls and providing a playground for ice-skating.

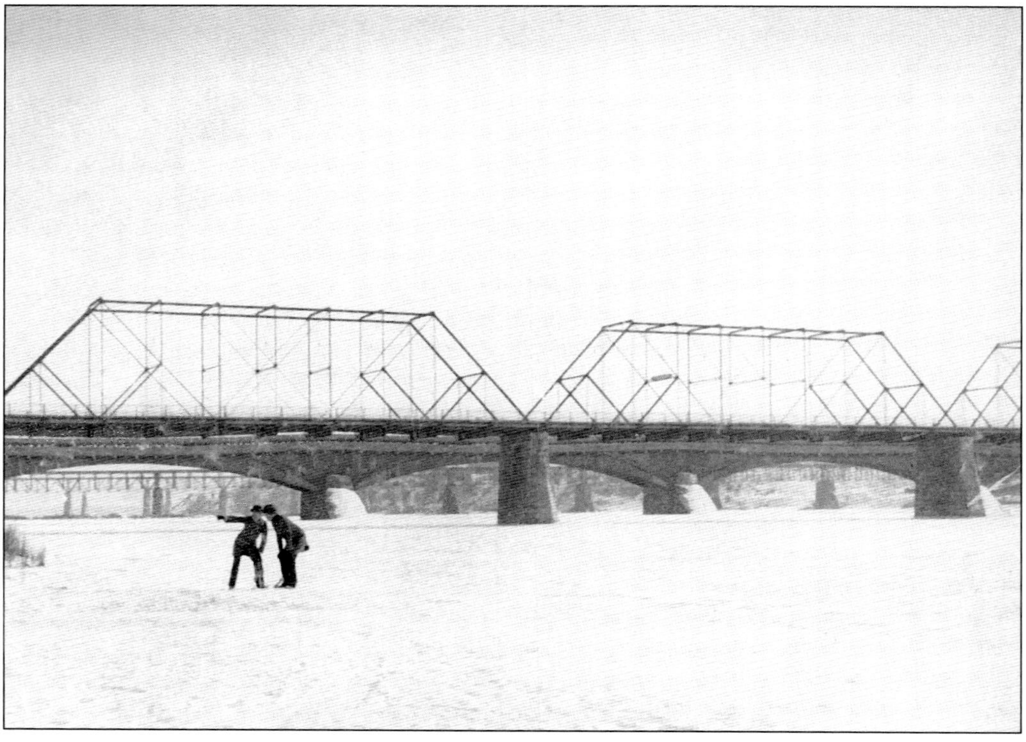

# *Five*

# The Forces of Nature

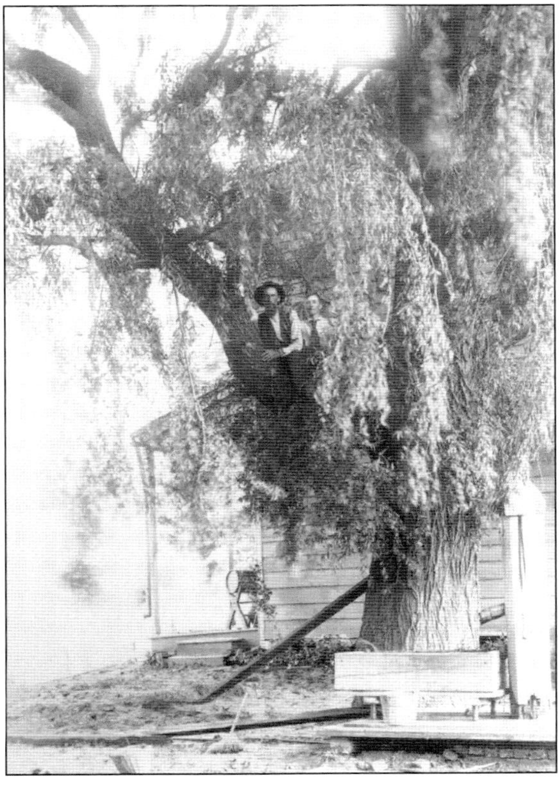

William Davis and his son pose for a photograph in a tree on McCormick's Island where they took refuge during the flood of 1889. The Susquehanna River, when subjected to extraordinary weather conditions, is highly susceptible to large changes in the water levels. Most of the river flooding occurs from two types of weather conditions. The first type occurs with extended heavy downpours, often from tropical storms lingering over the river basin. The second type occurs in winter or early spring when the river is choked with ice, and spiking temperatures cause melting and the movement of ice resulting in flooding behind the damming up of the ice.

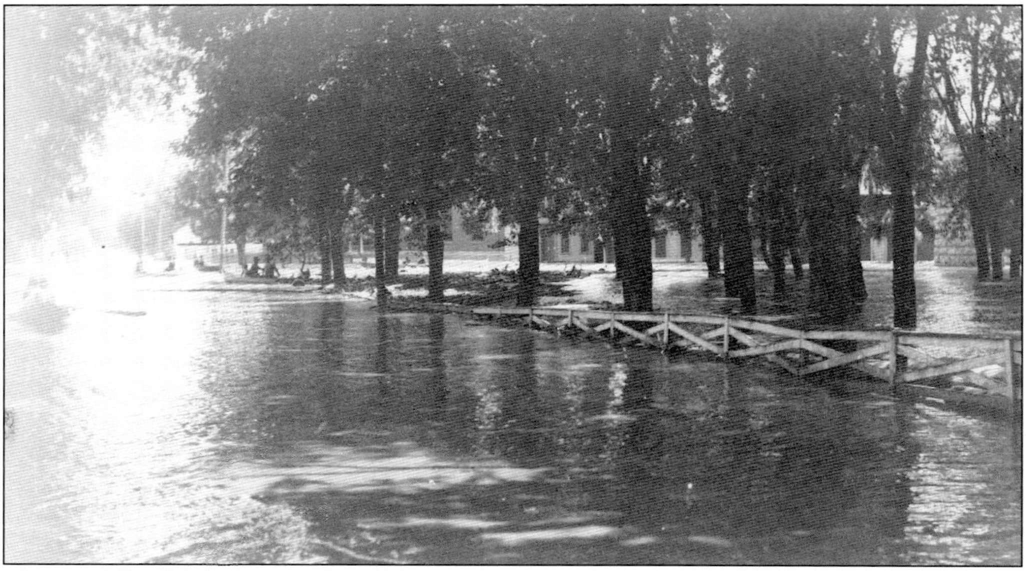

The 1889 flood is best remembered for the destruction that occurred in Johnstown, when the South Fork Dam broke and thousands of lives were lost. In Harrisburg, 35 straight hours of rain, beginning on May 30 and continuing on June 1, caused the flooding of Paxton Creek, which spilled over into the Cameron Street corridor and south Harrisburg. This was followed by the inevitable rising of the Susquehanna River, which caused widespread flooding in the city as the river stage reached a height of 27 feet. In the image above, boats take to Front Street, below Washington Street, as Harris Park is inundated by the flooding Susquehanna. In the image below, one block away at Second and Washington Streets, residents survey the flooded landscape provided by the mingled waters of the Susquehanna River and Paxton Creek.

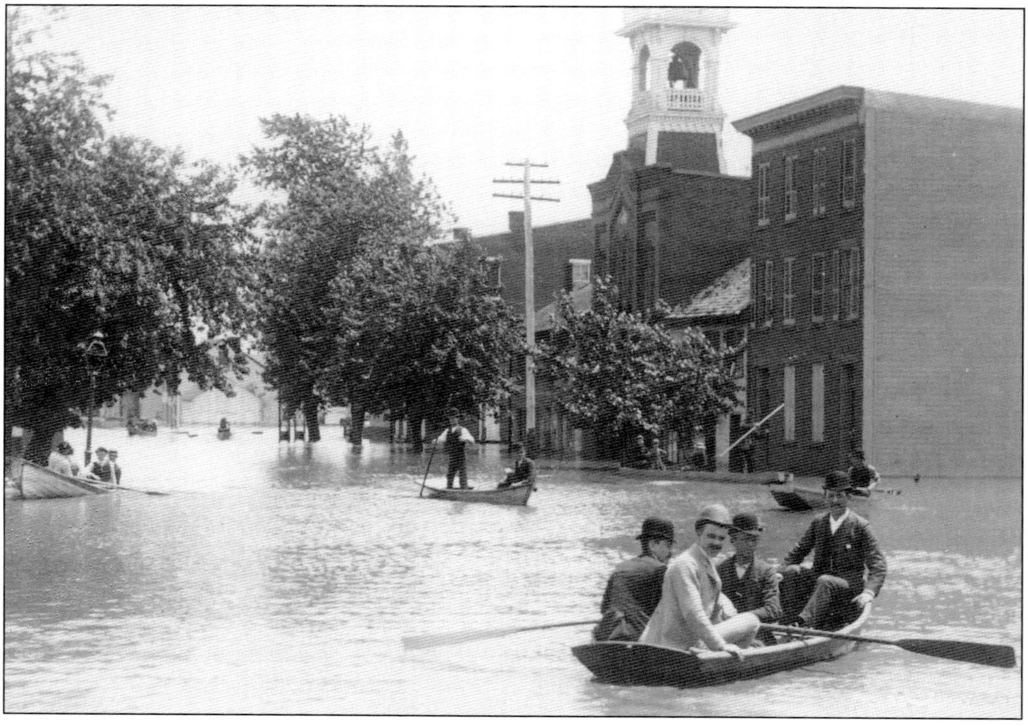

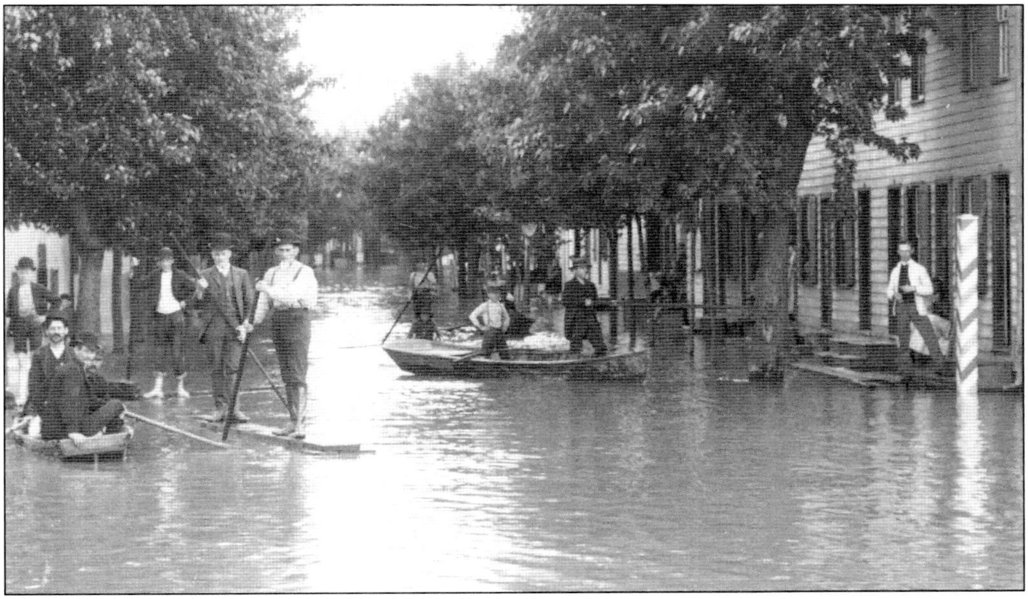

By Monday, June 3, 1889, the floodwaters, which had reached depths between five and six feet in sections of Shipoke and adjoining Sheesleytown, had receded to a mere one to two feet deep. Above, in a scene resembling something more suited to the city of Venice, the inhabitants of the South Ninth Street community of Sheesleytown navigate the flooded landscape on boats, planks, and just about anything that will float. Of note is the barber pole at 1014 South Ninth Street at right, which would also be the location of a barbershop during the Agnes flood of 1972. Below, the general population of Hanna Street pauses on doorsteps and out in the flooded street to have a photograph taken.

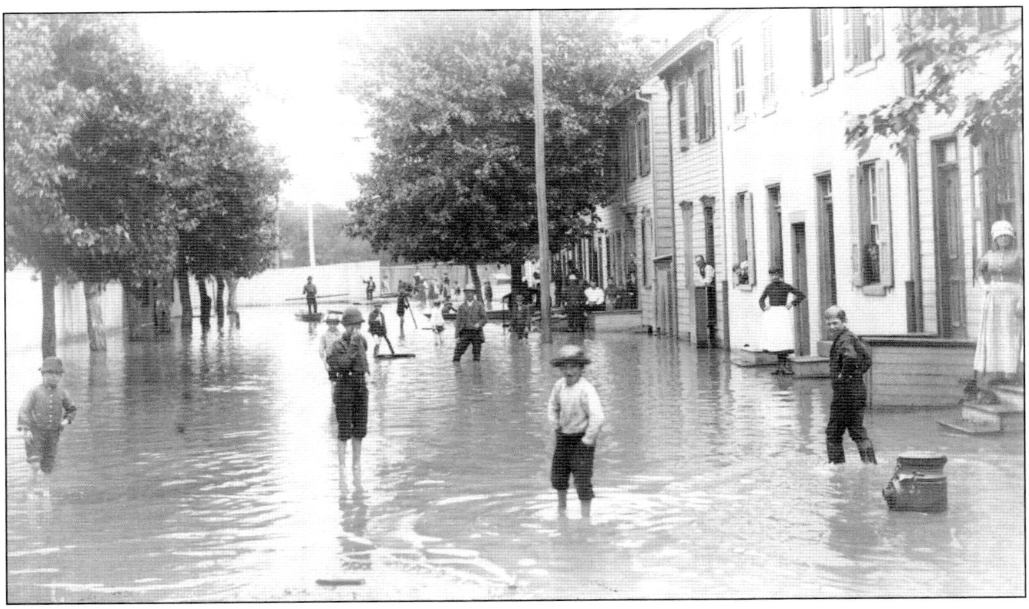

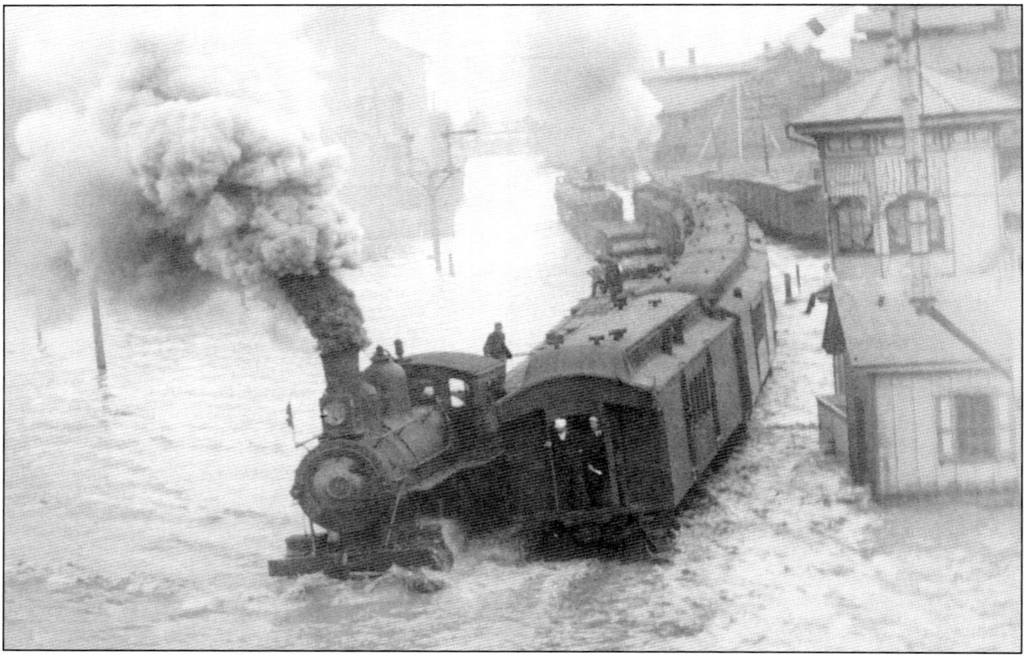

Along the Pennsylvania Railroad lines in south Harrisburg, the routes remained open during the flooding that occurred on June 1, 1889, as freight and passenger trains continued to slog through several feet of water. The trains, seen here at the Pennsylvania Railroad Station located below the Dock Street Bridge, were able to continue running as long as their fireboxes remained dry.

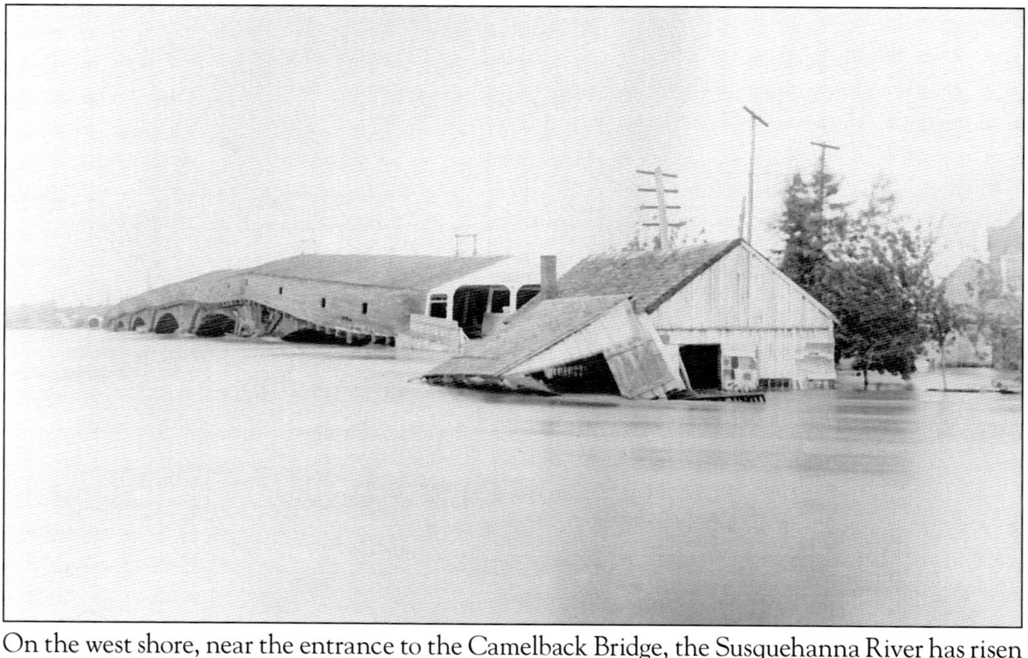

On the west shore, near the entrance to the Camelback Bridge, the Susquehanna River has risen to a level that has covered the entire landscape, giving the appearance of one broad expanse of water. The western spans of the Camelback would escape extensive damage from the flood, but the side ventilating windows would be expanded, creating an opening across the entire length of the bridge.

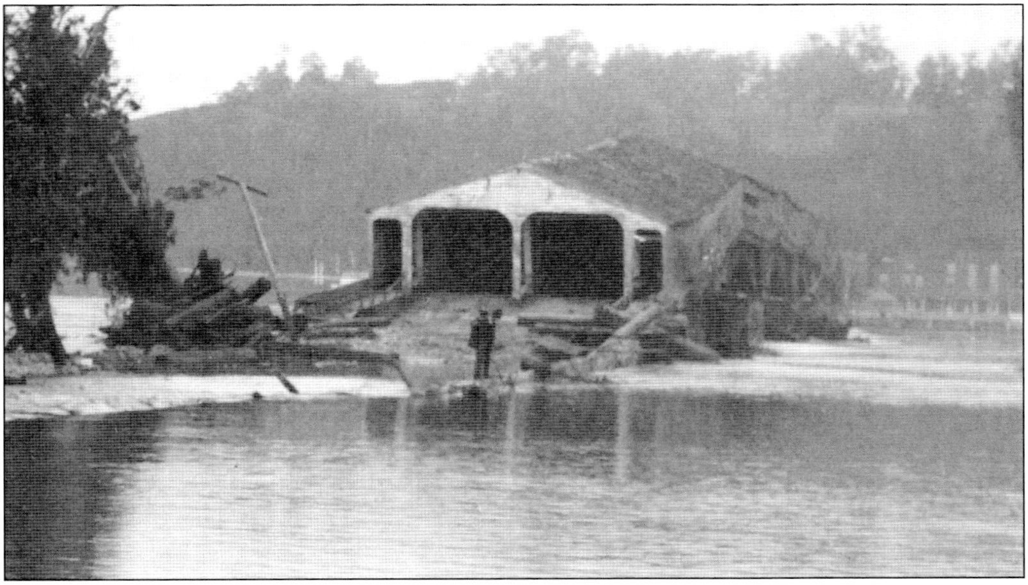

The two images on this page show the extent of the damage on Hargest's (City) Island from the 1889 flood. In the image above, two men inspect the entryway to the western section of the Camelback Bridge, as Hargest's Island remained largely submerged beneath the floodwaters, excepting the raised causeway connecting the two sections of the bridge. In the image below, Hargest (far left) and companions sit on the remains of an out shed that received extensive damage from timber and various debris carried by the high waters The main house and the summer kitchen (seen at right) also saw damage from the flood but were not beyond repair. However, the destruction of the barn was nearly complete, as it was reduced to its sandstone foundation.

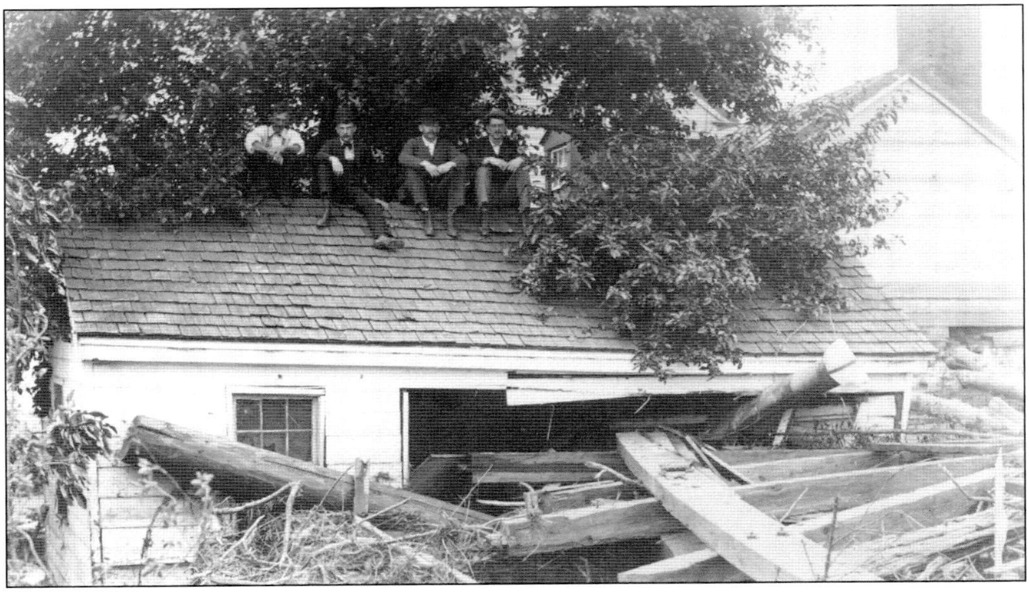

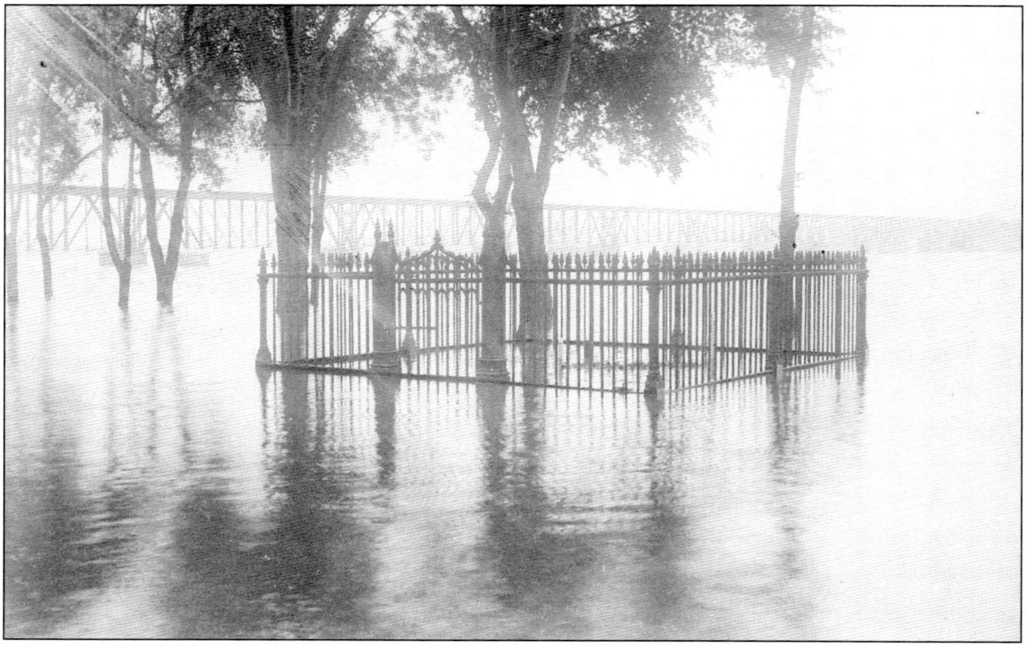

The two images presented here were taken during the flood of May 1894, which saw the river rise to a height of 25 feet. In the image above, within the gated resting place of John Harris Sr., the floodwaters reach up high enough to cover his grave. Harris passed away in 1748 and was buried beneath the famous mulberry tree at this site. Legend claims that he was tied to the tree by Native Americans who threatened to kill him when he refused to provide them with rum. The stump of the tree remained next to his grave until 1889 when it was knocked over by the flood of that year. In the image below, taken in Wormleysburg south of the Walnut Street Bridge, boom logs, debris, and spectators collect along the flooded shoreline.

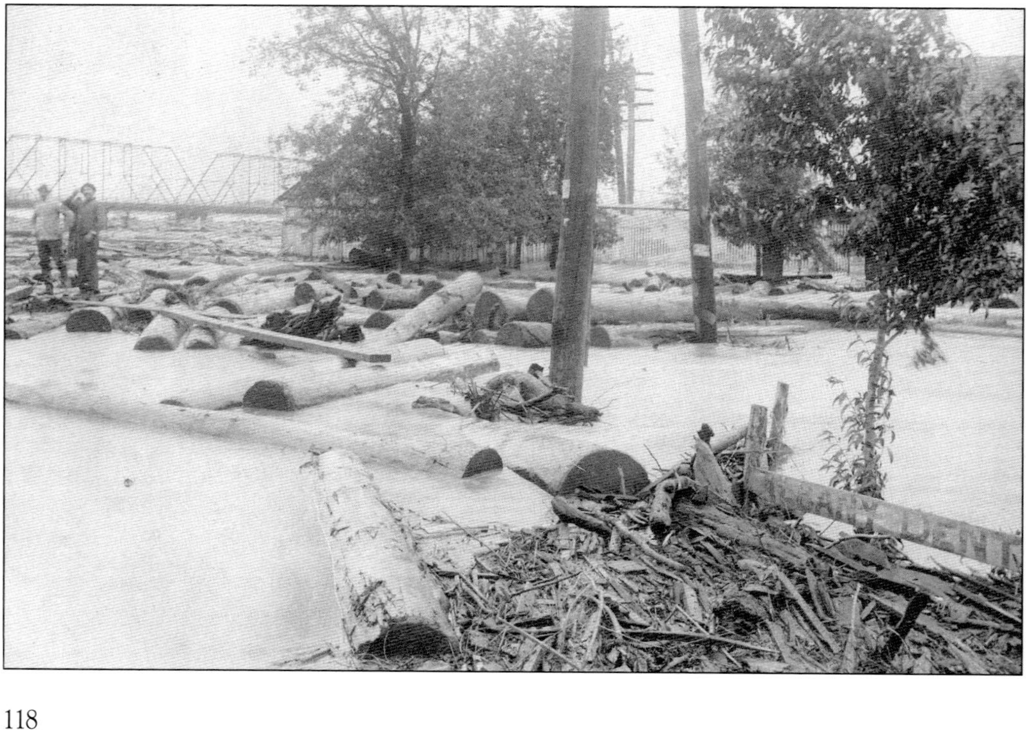

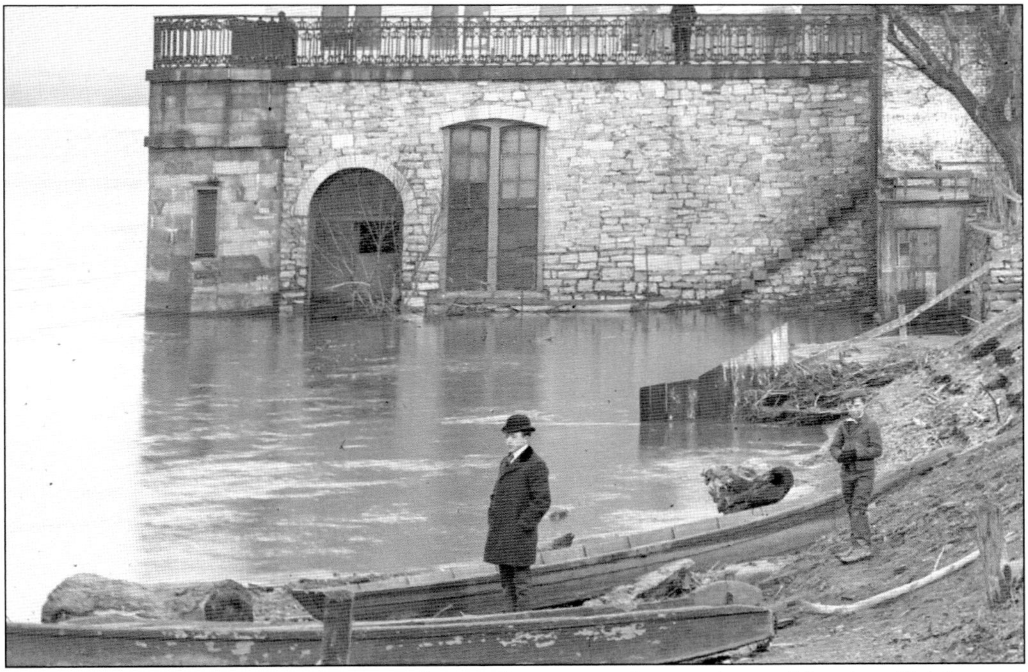

On Sunday, March 2, 1902, the Susquehanna River crested at an observed height of 23 feet and 11 inches. The above image was taken at the pumping station as the waters were receding on March 4, 1902. A close inspection of the turret at the left edge of the building reveals horizontal lines and dates marking the high water of previous floods, which although presently hidden, remain there even today.

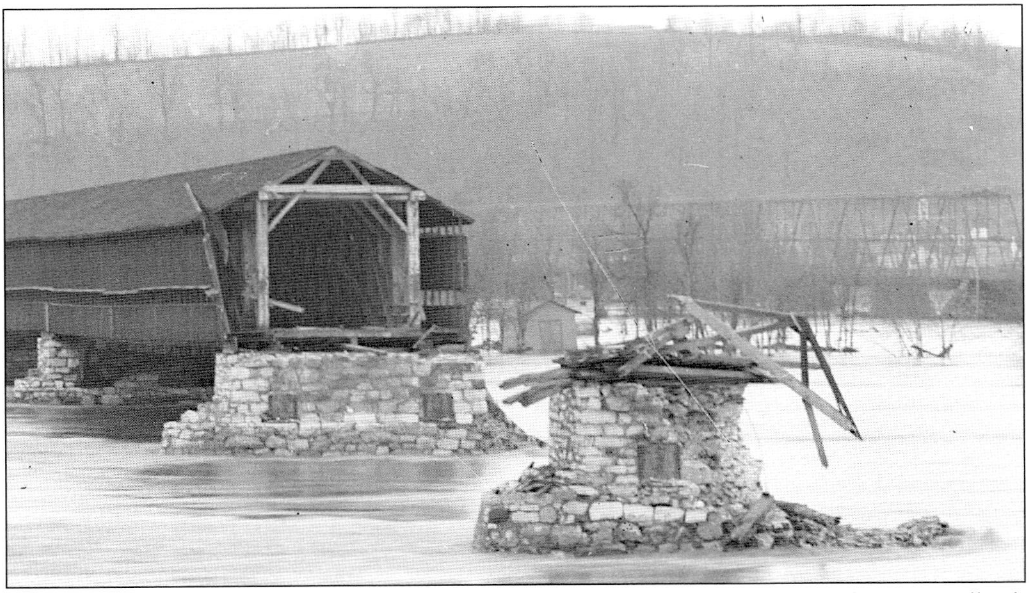

At 12:45 a.m. on March 3, 1902, the span between the first and second pier of the Camelback Bridge broke loose and was carried downstream. Within minutes, the span between the second and third piers also broke loose and was similarly lost. The second pier (seen here) sustained structural damage from ice striking against the support and could no longer bear the weight of the bridge's spans.

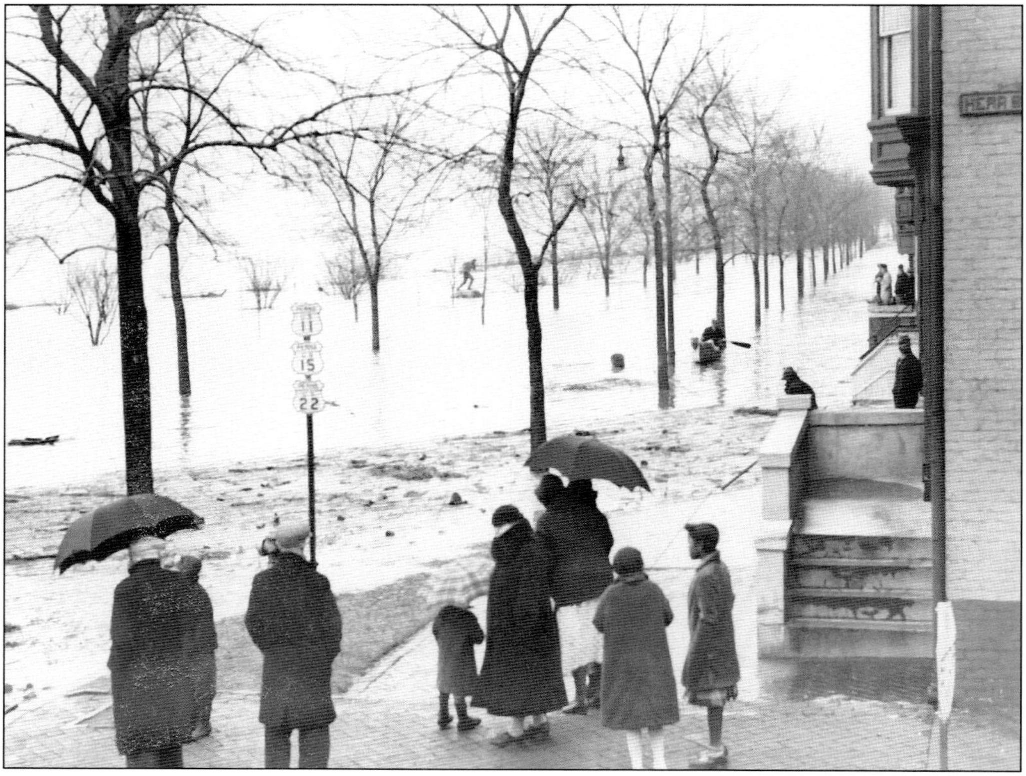


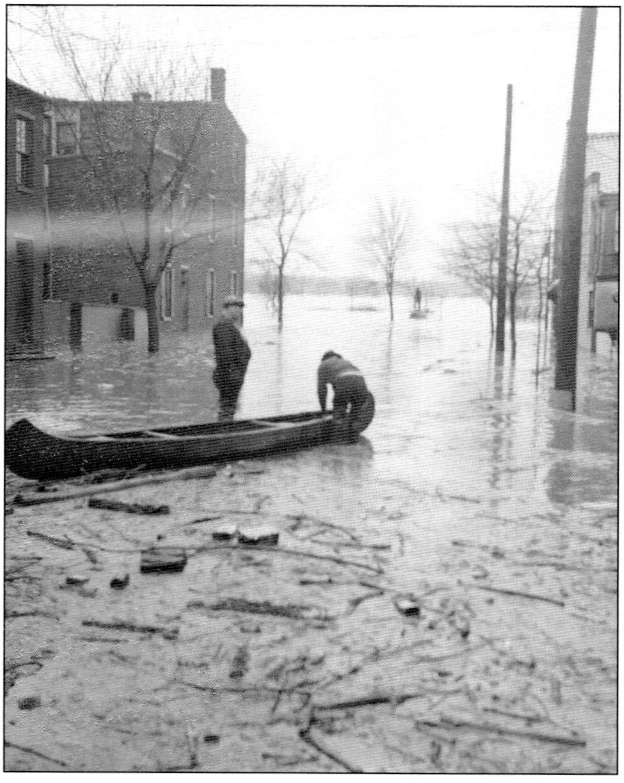

The flooding that occurred during the late winter of 1936, commonly called the St. Patrick's Day flood, was the result of heavy accumulations of ice on the Susquehanna River accompanied by a period of warmer temperatures and moderate rain. This resulted in the damming of the river water behind ice jams, which ultimately spilled out over the riverbanks. The first wave of flooding occurred on March 13, when the river level rose to a level of 21.7 feet, causing moderate flooding along the riverfront in Shipoke. By March 16, the threat of flooding was thought to have passed, and cleanup began as the waters began to recede. By March 17, the river level had dropped to just over 12 feet. Pictured here are two views along Front Street in Harrisburg at Herr Street (above) and Verbeke Street (left).

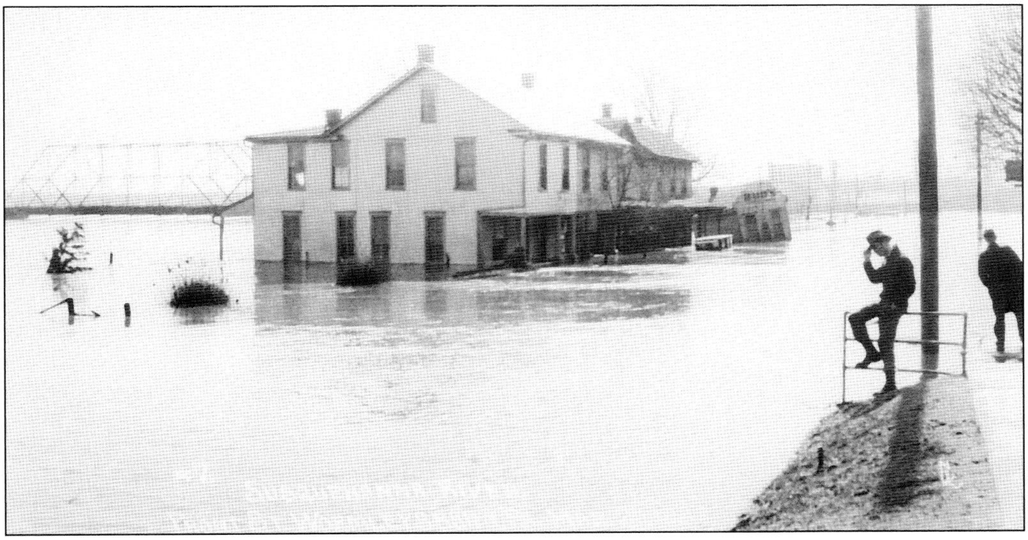

The dropping river levels would soon rebound as heavy rains and thunderstorms cut through the river basin, and by the afternoon of March 18, the river had risen back up to 21 feet, pushing once again over the banks at Front Street. The Market Street and Walnut Street Bridges were closed to all traffic, and the pumping station ceased operations, leaving the city to ration its water. The river would continue to rise until it crested at 30.33 feet at 6:00 p.m. on March 19. As with Front Street in Harrisburg, the riverfront in Wormleysburg was also inundated. At the bottleneck, the floodwaters reached depths between four to five feet deep. Floodwaters also caused a measure of damage to the piers of the Walnut Street Bridge, which would bring the trolley lines on the bridge to an end.

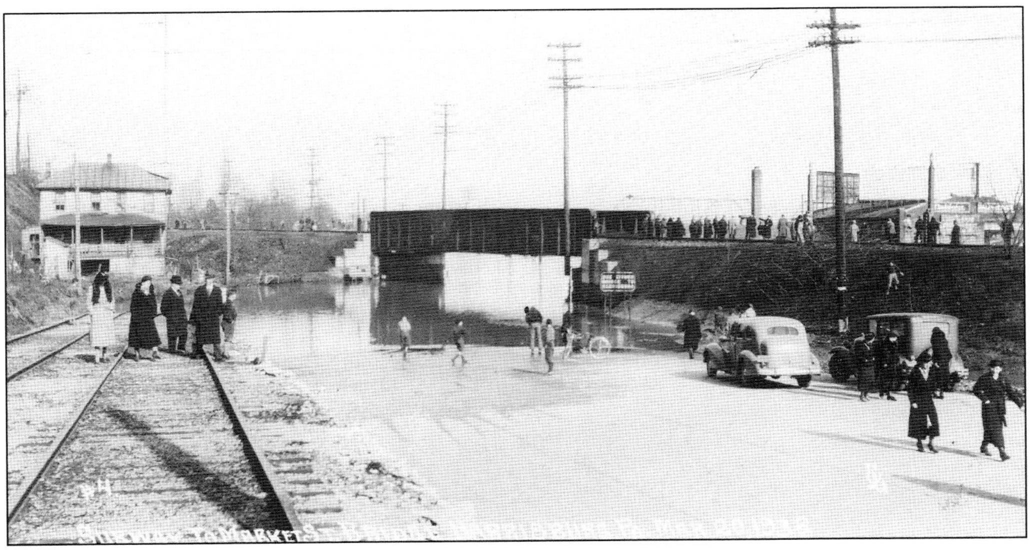

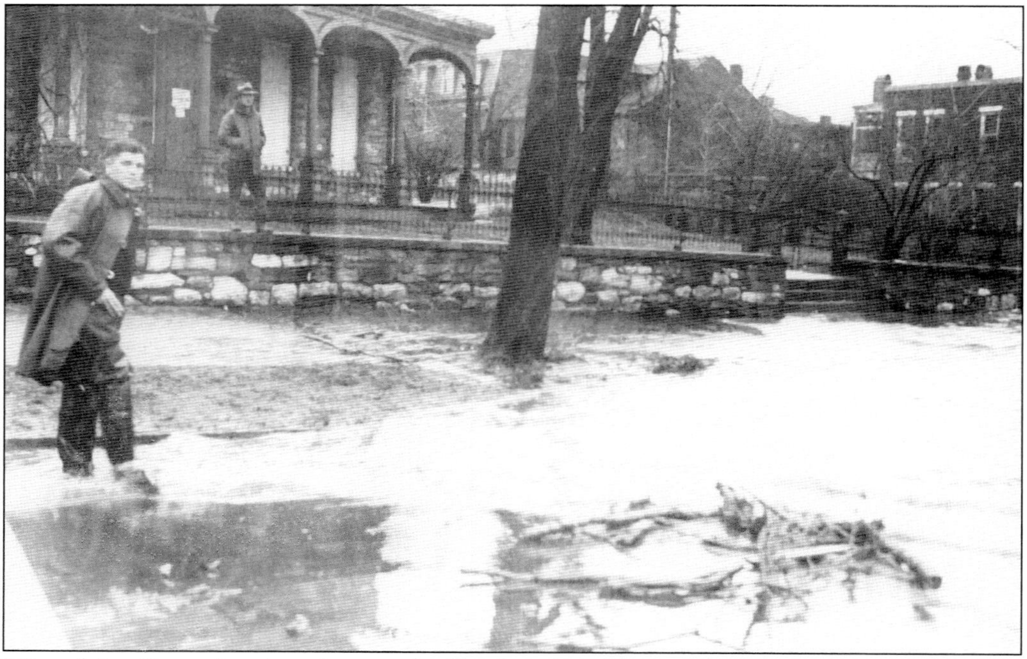

When John Harris Jr. selected a parcel of land in the 1760s on which to build his stone house near the river, he was directed by the local Native Americans to a rise of land that they claimed had always remained above the river floods. Even during the severe flooding in 1936, the water barely reaches the front wall of the grounds.

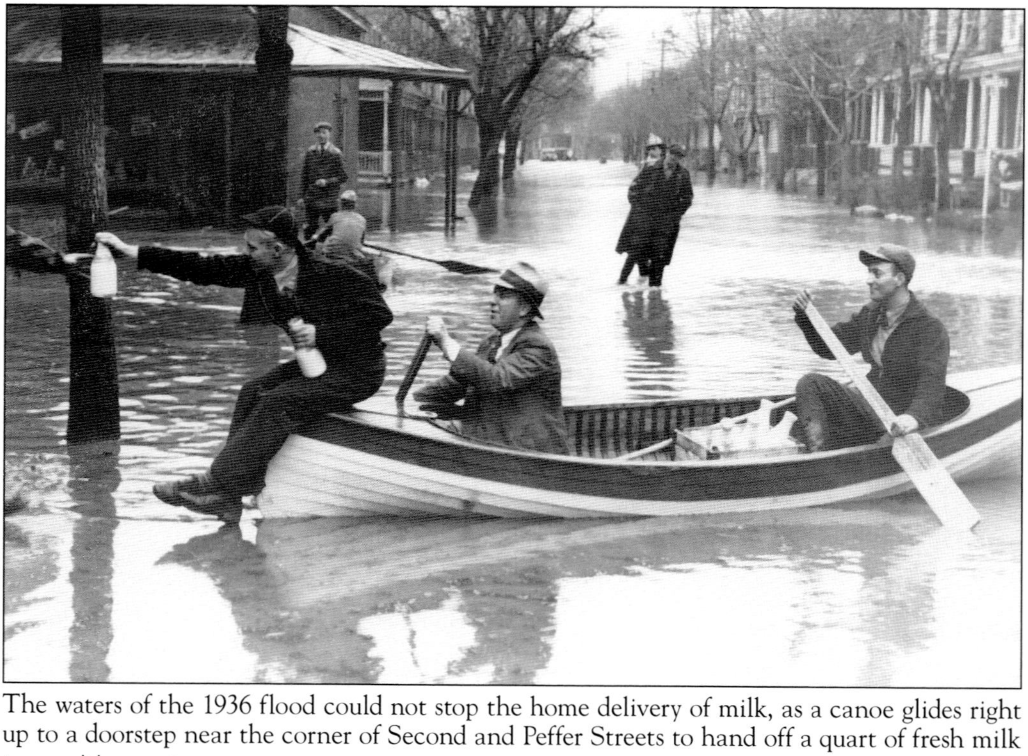

The waters of the 1936 flood could not stop the home delivery of milk, as a canoe glides right up to a doorstep near the corner of Second and Peffer Streets to hand off a quart of fresh milk to a waiting customer.

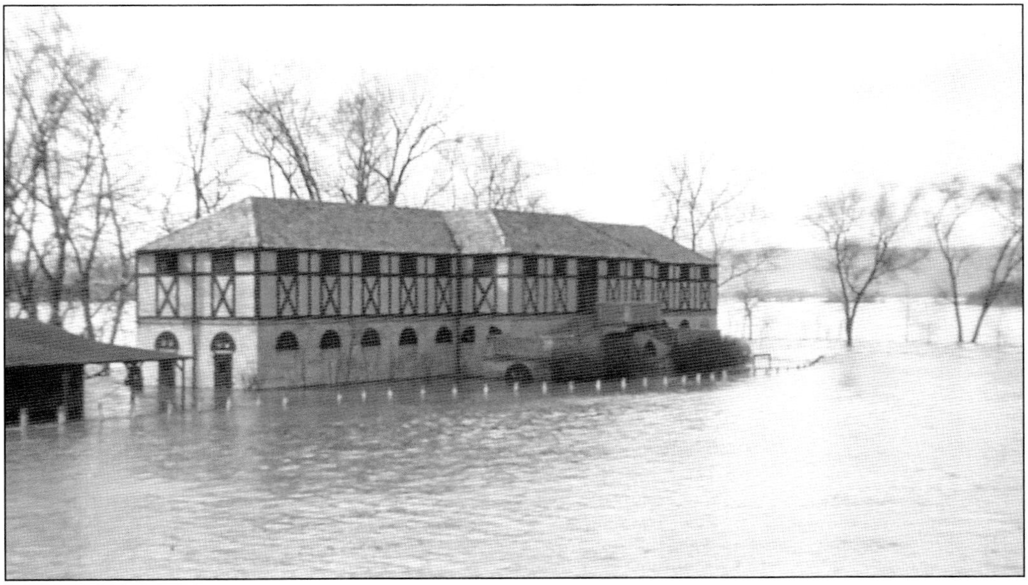

The flooding of April 1940 saw the Susquehanna at Harrisburg reach a crest of 19.85 feet. The overall impact was less than that of the flood from four years earlier, but it was still significant enough to cause moderate damage in the southern portion of the city and leave the majority of City Island submerged beneath several feet of water, as can be seen here at the City Bathhouse.

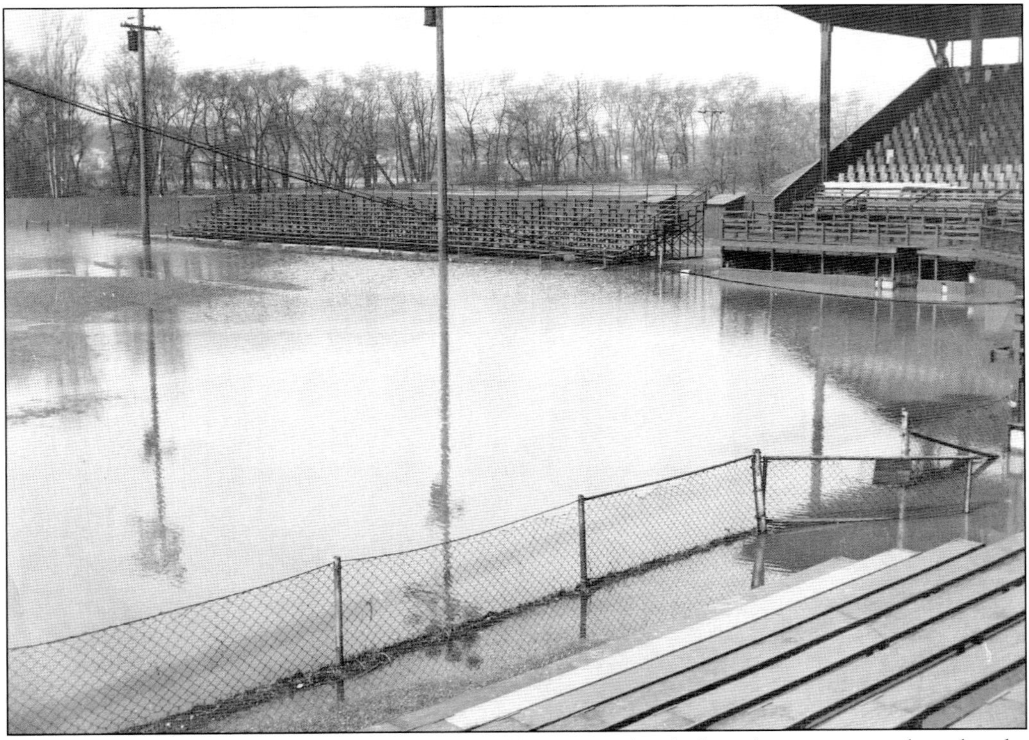

This image was taken at the flooded baseball field on City Island when the river crested at a height of over 21 feet on May 29, 1946. The floodwaters not only covered the field, but they were also forceful enough to wash away half of the outfield fence. The Senators, at the time, were forced to play on an extended road trip until the field could be repaired.

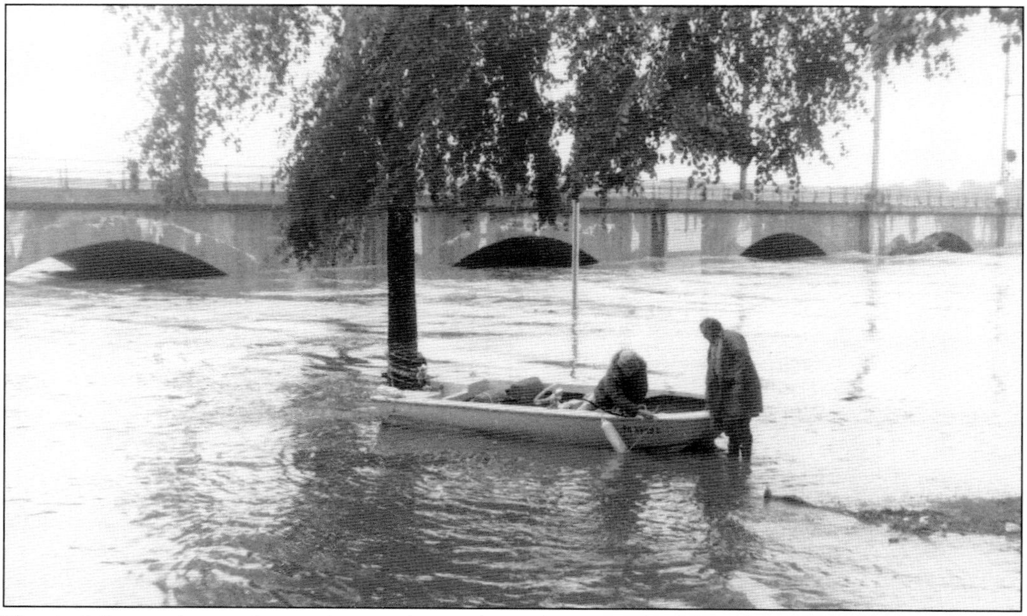

Tropical Storm Agnes dropped more than a foot of rain on the Harrisburg Area over the course of June 21 and June 22, 1972. As a result, the Susquehanna River rose to a record level of 32.8 feet and became the measuring stick for all floods in the area. (For a more in-depth look at this storm, please see *Tropical Storm Agnes in Greater Harrisburg*, also from Arcadia Publishing.)

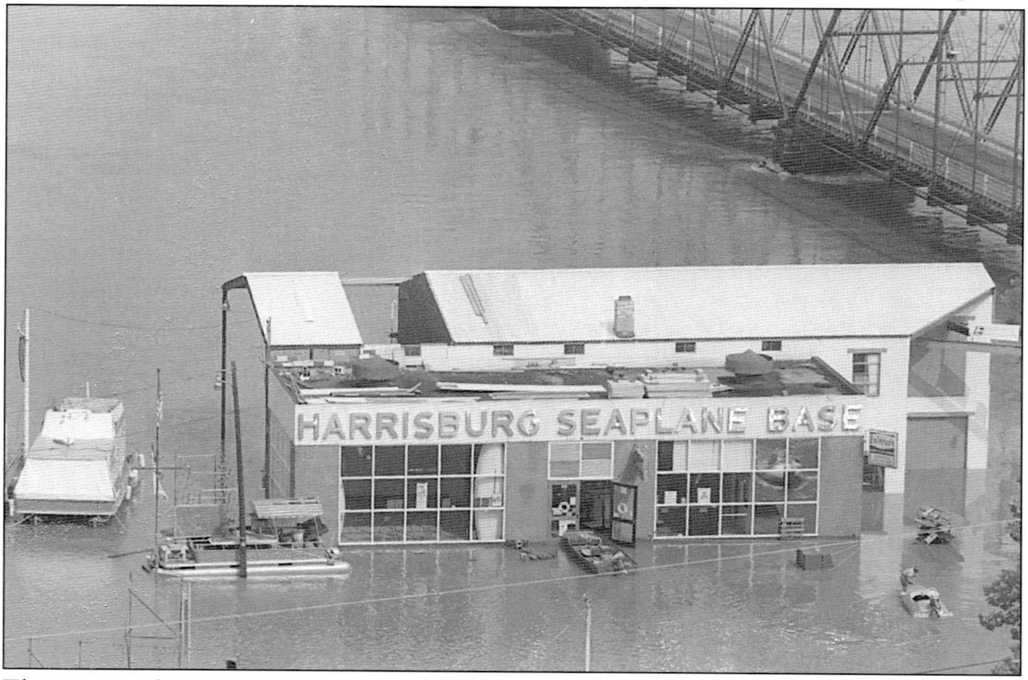


Three years after Agnes blew through the Susquehanna Valley, Tropical Storm Eloise arrived in late September 1975 and brought 10 inches of rain to Harrisburg and points north in the Susquehanna River basin. The river reached a crest of 23.75 feet and caused considerable flooding throughout the region. Here, the Harrisburg Seaplane Base along Front Street in Wormleysburg is surrounded by Eloise's floodwaters.

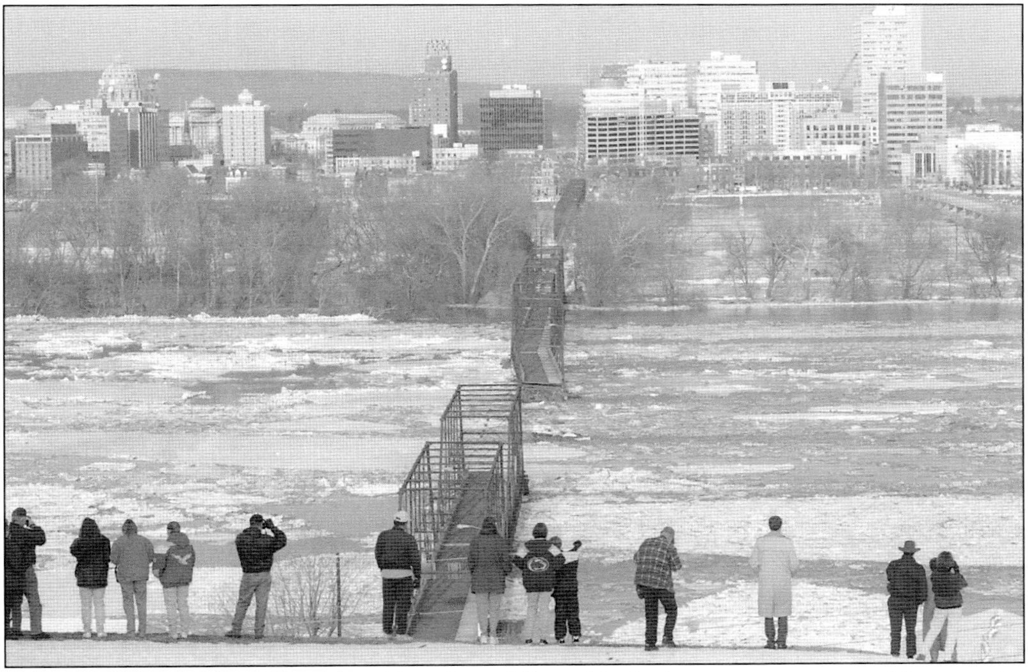

January 1996 brought a blizzard to Harrisburg followed by higher temperatures and heavy rain. This resulted in high waters that pushed ice jams against the piers of the western section of the Walnut Street Bridge, which caused piers numbered 3 and 4 to shift and spans numbered 3 and 4 to break loose and drift downstream into the Market Street Bridge. Span number 5 would also be lost.

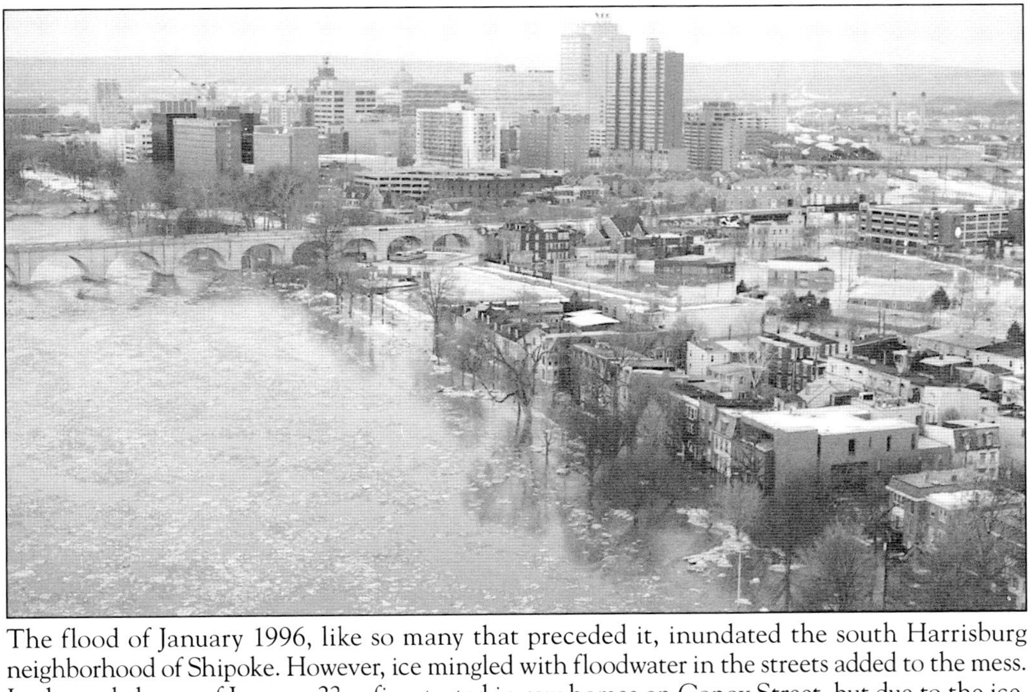

The flood of January 1996, like so many that preceded it, inundated the south Harrisburg neighborhood of Shipoke. However, ice mingled with floodwater in the streets added to the mess. In the early hours of January 22, a fire started in row homes on Conoy Street, but due to the ice, firefighters had to wait until front-end loaders cleared a path to reach the blaze.

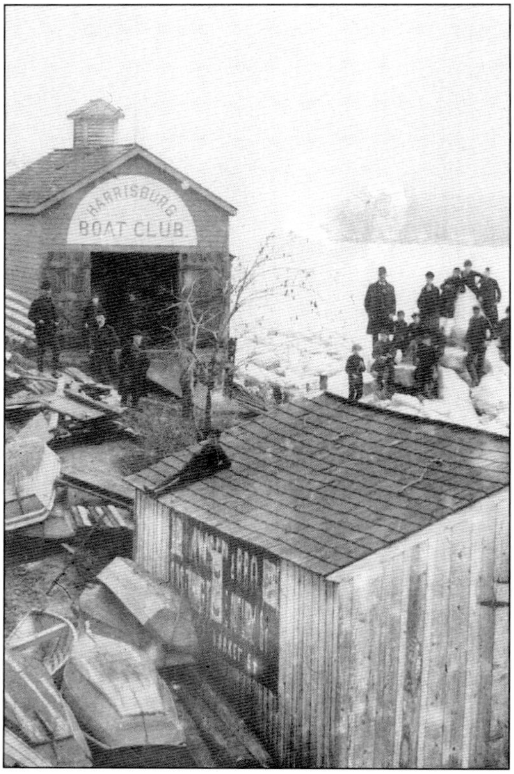


Ice and snow pile up along the riverfront near the boathouse of the Harrisburg Boat Club in this view during the winter of 1888. That particular winter, the ice reached a thickness of two feet on the Susquehanna at Harrisburg, and the residents utilized the ice bridge, crossing from the city over to West Fairview (avoiding the bridge tolls).

In this 1930s image, a break in the weather allows for the breakup of the river ice, and the flow of the Susquehanna pushes the large slabs onto the eastern shore of City Island. During the winter of 1871–1872, the river was frozen over for a period of 109 consecutive days before a spring breakup occurred on March 23, 1872.

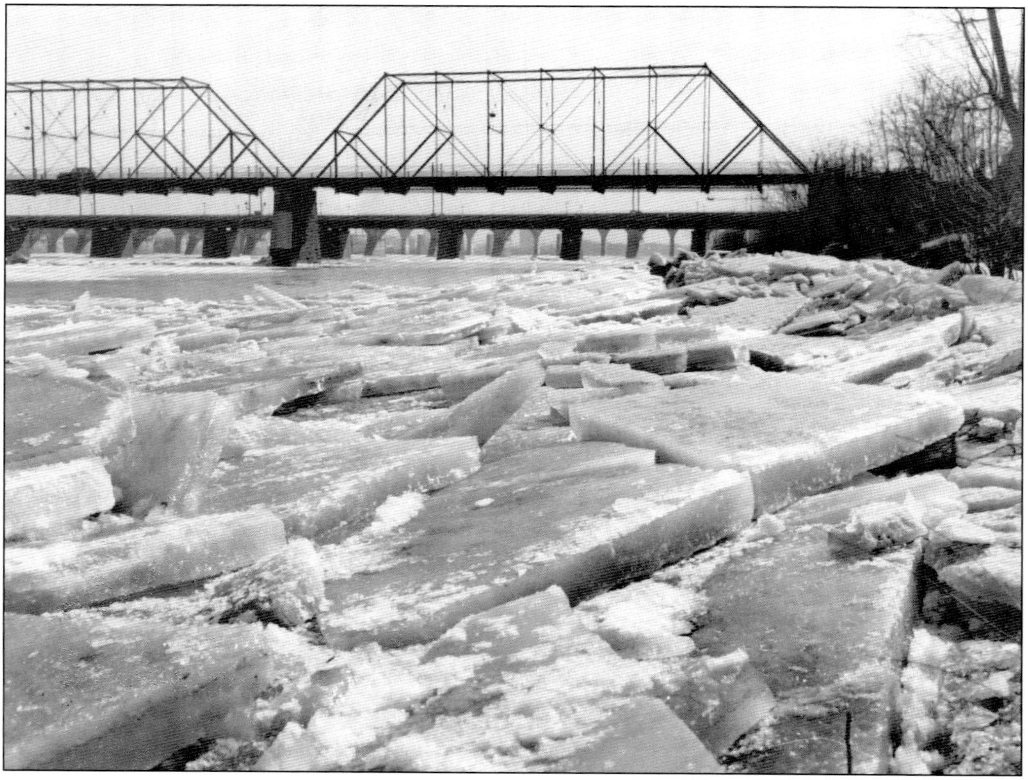

Along the riverfront in the Hardscrabble district of Harrisburg, the force of the river ice gathers up the boats, docks, canoes, and anything left abandoned along the river's edge, and either takes it for a ride or reduces it to kindling, as seen in this photograph taken about 1905.

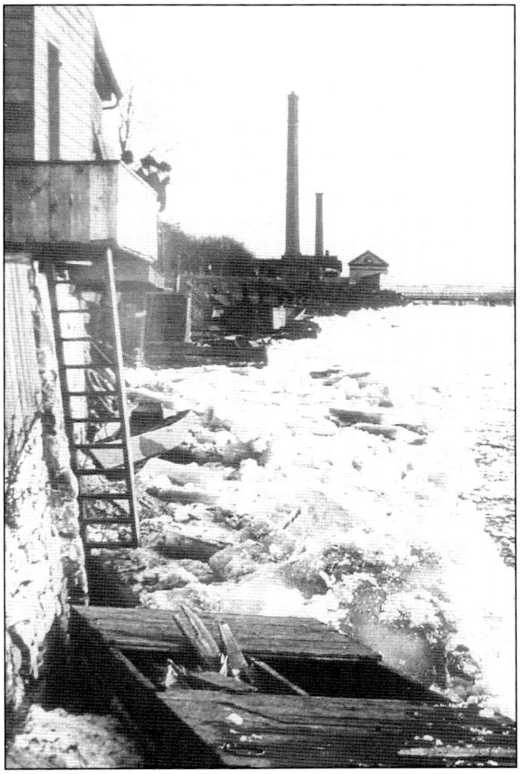

Set against a background of Harrisburg and the Susquehanna River blanketed in a layer of freshly fallen snow, a solitary figure strolls along the eastern shore of City Island around 1940.

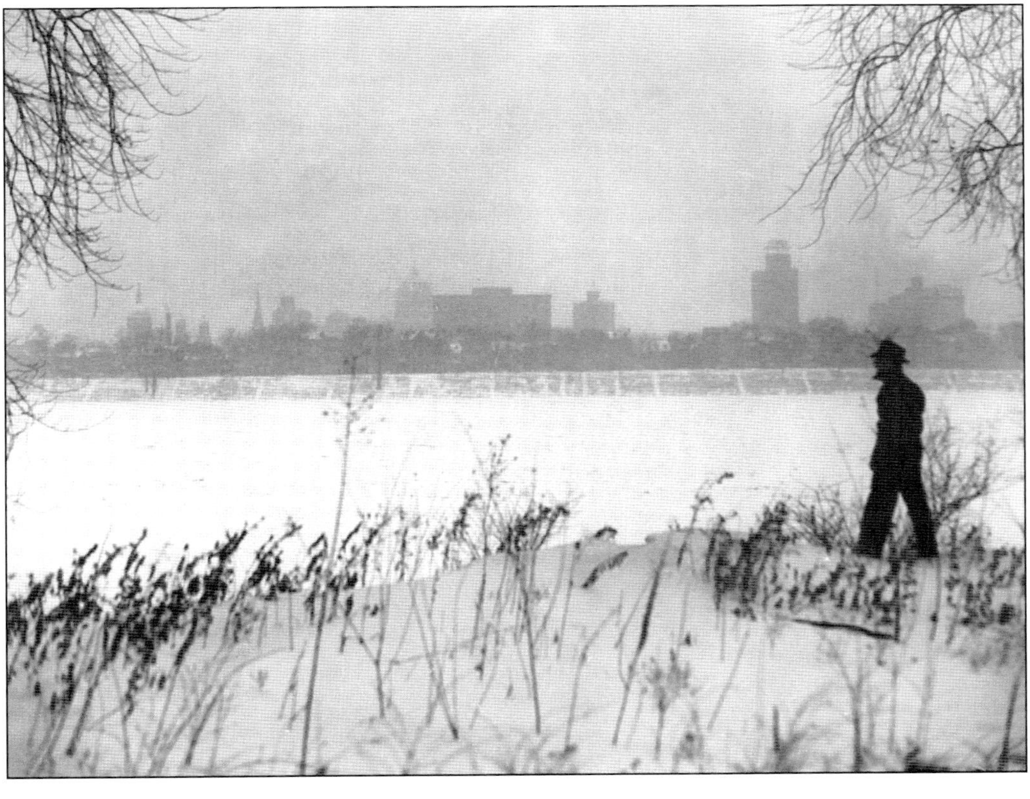